IMMANUEL
BAPTIST CHURCH

100 Years of Serving God and Serving Man

John Nichols

ISBN 978-1-64003-504-1 (Paperback)
ISBN 978-1-64003-505-8 (Digital)

Covenant Books, Inc.
11661 Hwy 707
Murrells Inlet, SC 29576
www.covenantbooks.com

This book is dedicated to the wonderful pastors and staff members who served Immanuel Baptist Church and who sacrificed deeply for God's Kingdom and for Immanuel Baptist Church. Perhaps long-time member and Sunday School teacher, Mrs. Ruby Sands, said it best in her handwritten notes concerning the fiftieth anniversary in 1967. She wrote,

> As we reach this milestone in our church's history, we pause to give thanks to Almighty God for His blessing and leadership during the 50 years of Immanuel's ministry. We would be untrue to our Lord if we should fail to pay tribute to the noble men of God who have served Immanuel Baptist Church during this period."[1]

Acknowledgments

As the editor, I would like to thank my wife, Edna Nichols, for her loving support and loyalty to me during researching and writing of this book. She cheerfully granted me the many hours that were needed to research and write this book. I am especially grateful for her sacrifice of patiently giving up a corner of our living room to house six boxes of musty and moldy minutes and issues of *The Baptist Messenger*.

I would also like to thank Ms. Rachel Hawkins, director of library collections at Oklahoma Baptist University, for the many hours she supported me in my research in the Oklahoma Baptist University Archive. She assisted me greatly in retrieving rare and fragile documents and scanning pictures from those documents for me.

I would also like to thank Bob Nigh, historical secretary of the Baptist General Convention of Oklahoma, and Grant Bivens, web developer, for the access that they granted to me to the amazingly complete Baptist General Convention of Oklahoma Archive. I was able to do much of the research for this hundred-year history across the Internet from the convenience of my home library.

Finally, I wish to thank my review team of Manoi Adair, Rowena Britt, Carl and Darla Coffman, and Pat Coker for their careful and through review of the draft manuscript and my son, Christopher Nichols, for his complete front-to-back technical review. These six individuals found many errors and inconsistencies and made wonderful suggestions for improvements.

John Nichols
Editor

CONTENTS

LIST OF FIGURES

FOREWORD

For one hundred years, Immanuel Baptist Church has been a beacon of truth and hope to the community of Shawnee and to the world. God has blessed Immanuel Baptist Church in many and indescribable ways through those years as the church earnestly sought to adhere faithfully to the Bible as the Word of God and to the Great Commission.

This book tells the story of the church for a century—its leaders, programs, accomplishments, and challenges—and how, through ups and downs, in the midst of a rapidly changing world, it never faltered in its faithfulness to God and His Word. This is the story of a people on mission who have worked tirelessly in their own community and gone literally to the farthest reaches on earth to serve humanity and share with them the life-changing message of the Gospel of Jesus Christ. For a century, Immanuel Baptist Church has shown that a church is not a physical building or a location, but a church is a people called out by God to be salt and light to the world.

More than a history about a group of people, this book tells of the faithfulness of God to provide for and use His church for His glory and Kingdom purposes. This is a history of an imperfect people seeking to follow a perfect and faithful God. In so many ways, more than can be recounted in this book, God has guided Immanuel Baptist Church and showered her with His grace. This book tells His story every bit as much as it tells the story of Immanuel Baptist Church.

I would like to thank John Nichols who spent countless hours of research, conducted interviews, and lovingly wrote to make this history a reality. Without his dedication, such a comprehensive history of the church would not have become a reality. We are in his debt for taking on such a monumental task. Thank you, John!

Finally, this book recounts our past one hundred years, but this is certainly far from the end of our story. By the grace of God, Immanuel Baptist Church has many more years ahead of faithfully proclaiming and living out the Word. May He find this church faithfully carrying out His mission until that glorious day of the appearing of His Son, Jesus Christ!

Soli Deo Gloria,
—Todd Fisher, DMin
Senior Pastor
Immanuel Baptist Church
July 24, 2017

CHAPTER 1

The Early Years

Rev. T. B. Holcomb, September 1917–October 1922
Rev. William Smith, October 1922–August 1923
Rev. O. G. Matthews, September 1923–January 1924
Rev. T. B. Holcomb, January 1924–March 1926

The Beginnings of Immanuel Baptist Church

On September 6, 1917, a group of sixty-two Baptists interested in beginning a new Baptist church in Shawnee met at the Draper Street Mission of First Baptist Church, Shawnee, to discuss starting such a church. The Draper Street Mission was located at Ninth and Draper Streets in a building that was formerly known as the Grace Methodist Church. The group determined a new church was feasible and set September 16, 1917, as the formal date to organize the church. These sixty-two people became the charter members for the newly organized Draper Street Baptist Church.

Revs. T. B. Holcomb, Bill Smith, and O. G. Matthews were the pastors who served the church in the first years of its growth. Rev. T. B. Holcomb, a professor at Oklahoma Baptist University, was called as the first pastor of the growing congregation. Reverend Holcomb assisted in organizing that small band of believers into a viable and growing Baptist church. His personality was especially well suited for the task of laying a foundation for what was to become a great Baptist church. He was a diplomat and an organizer. Many of his skills came from his years as a pastor and his years as a teacher. He was well versed in the fundamentals of Christian theology and Baptist beliefs and taught them well to the congregation.[1]

Draper Street Baptist Church assumed a debt of $1,500 and the deeds to the property from First Baptist Church, Shawnee. Reverend Holcomb started a growing, dynamic, and thriving church. The tenures of Reverend Smith and Reverend Matthews were short, but both saw growth in numbers and in spiritual strength.[2]

The world scene during the years that Reverends Holcomb, Smith, and Matthews served Immanuel was one of war, victory, and a peacetime boom called the Roaring Twenties. World War I had ravaged the countries of Europe since 1914, but the United States had remained neutral until 1917. A worldwide influenza pandemic began in 1917. By 1920, nearly twenty million were dead from the virulent disease. In United States alone, five hundred thousand perished.[3] In 1919, the signing of the Versailles Treaty by the Allies and Germany ended the devastation of World War I. The treaty levied harsh terms and heavy reparations of Germany and incorporated Woodrow Wilson's draft covenant of the League of Nations. The United States Senate subsequently rejected the treaty.[4]

The national scene during the years that Reverends Holcomb, Smith, and Matthews served Immanuel paralleled the world scene. World War I dominated 1917 and 1918, but the end of World War I brought a period of the peace and prosperity in the early 1920s known as the Roaring Twenties. In January 1919, the Eighteenth Amendment to the Constitution ushered in Prohibition. In August 1920, the Nineteenth Amendment granting full women's suffrage was ratified. The presidents during these years were Woodrow Wilson, Warren Harding, and Calvin Coolidge.[5]

Rev. T. B. Holcomb, the Years before Immanuel

Thomas Benjamin Holcomb was born in Paris, Tennessee, in 1879. He accepted Christ as his Lord and Savior at an early age, and shortly thereafter, he surrendered to preach. After graduating from high school, he matriculated at Union University in Jackson, Tennessee, and studied for a few years but did not graduate. In 1912, at the age of thirty-three, Rev. T. B. Holcomb moved to Purcell, Oklahoma, to take the pulpit of First Baptist Church, Purcell.[6]

Rev. T. B. Holcomb immediately became active in the Oklahoma Baptist General Convention of Oklahoma (BGCO), attending the 1912 BGCO Annual Meeting that was held at First Baptist Church, Shawnee, on Friday, November 8, through Monday, November 11.[7] Reverend Holcomb consistently attended BGCO annual meetings until his death in 1936. In the early years of Oklahoma's statehood, BGCO annual meetings were held at various churches throughout the state in towns such as Enid, Chickasha, Durant, Tulsa, and Blackwell. In an era with few automobiles and few reliable roads, train travel was often required to attend a BGCO annual meeting. An overnight stay of one to three nights in a local hotel was usually required for out-of-town attendees. Reverend Holcomb's consistent attendance and active participation at BGCO annual meetings demonstrated an unusual dedication to the well-being of Baptists in Oklahoma.[8]

Rev. T. B. Holcomb also attended the 1913 BGCO Annual Meeting that was held in Chickasha.[9] The 1914 BGCO Annual Meeting was again held in Shawnee, and Reverend Holcomb again attended. Reverend Holcomb's service at First Baptist Church, Purcell, and his activities with the BGCO had provided him with sufficient stature within the convention that he was asked to give the closing prayer on Wednesday evening.[10] In 1916, the BGCO annual meeting was held at First Baptist Church, Oklahoma City. Rev. T. B. Holcomb attended the annual meeting as a messenger from First Baptist Church, Purcell, and was listed as a pastor from the McLain Baptist Association. At the 1916 BGCO Annual Meeting, Reverend Holcomb was placed on the 1917 Systematic Beneficence Committee.[11]

Rev. T. B. Holcomb, the Immanuel Year

Shortly after the 1916 BGCO Annual Meeting, Rev. T. B. Holcomb resigned as pastor of First Baptist Church, Purcell, and moved to Shawnee where he enrolled as a student at Oklahoma Baptist University for the spring semester. He was thirty-six years old at the time.[12] Oklahoma Baptist University had been incorporated in 1910, and construction on the first building—known as Shawnee Hall—began in February 1911.

The first academic year for Oklahoma Baptist University started in September 1911 with Dr. J. M. Carroll—a noted pastor, leader, historian, author, and educator from Texas—as president. Oklahoma Baptist University had 150 students, 15 professors, and 2 administrators. Since Shawnee Hall was not complete, classes met at First Baptist Church, the convention hall, the Carnegie Library, and the laboratories of the Shawnee High School. However, necessary funding from the BGCO had not come forward, and the university was closed in 1912. Once Shawnee Hall was completed, the university reopened in September 1915 with 143 students. Of those students, 47 were male students studying for the pastorate, and 3 were female students studying for special Christian service.

In its first year as a reopened institution, finances were still difficult. At the close of the first academic year, total receipts for all fees, tuition, and other sources were $7,431.26. Total expenses were $14,974.99, for a net loss of $7,543.73. With the university again in a dire financial situation, additional loans and additional BGCO funding were obtained to keep the university open.

In May 1917, based on his academic work from Union University and his work experiences from First Baptist Church in Purcell and the BGCO,

Figure 1.1. Rev. T. B. Holcomb with OBU students

Reverend Holcomb was awarded a bachelor of arts degree from Oklahoma Baptist University. He was one of three students who graduated from Oklahoma Baptist University in 1917. At the time of his graduation, Oklahoma Baptist University also had a secondary school and an elementary school.

The Oklahoma Baptist University Secondary School hired Reverend Holcomb as a history instructor. He was one of three employees of the secondary school.[13] It is worth noting that several of the students at the Oklahoma Baptist University Secondary School were older men who had not finished high school but had been serving as pastors. These men would enroll first in the Oklahoma Baptist University Secondary School to complete their high school education and then in Oklahoma Baptist University to obtain some formal religious education. Reverend Holcomb was a natural fit for the Oklahoma Baptist University Secondary School.

As part of his move to Shawnee, Reverend Holcomb joined First Baptist Church, Shawnee, and remained a member there until Draper Street Baptist Church was established as the first mission effort of the First Baptist Church, Shawnee, Oklahoma. Three men were primarily responsible for the vision of establishing a mission church of First Baptist Church, Shawnee, on Draper Street. These men were Rev. T. B. Holcomb, just moved from Purcell to Shawnee to complete his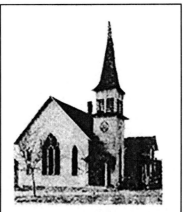

Figure 1.2. Draper Street Baptist Church

college degree at Oklahoma Baptist University; W. F. Skelton, the Sunday School superintendent of First Baptist Church, Shawnee; and Rev. E. L. Compere, the pastor of First Baptist Church, Shawnee. Also deeply involved in establishing the Draper Street Mission Church was the Student Ministerial Association from Oklahoma Baptist University. At a February 7, 1917, Student Ministerial Association meeting, the following resolution was drafted and signed by thirty-three students of the Student Ministerial Association:

> Be it resolved, We the Ministerial Student of Oklahoma Baptist University, believing that God is opening the field of East Shawnee to our Baptist cause in the establishment of a Mission in the present Grace M. E. Church property, and that the present opportunity is of such importance to our work that we must take advantage of it, even though at personal sacrifice:
>
> We Therefore, after prayerful consideration subscribe our names, with our signatures pledge our prayers and assistance of such Mission:
>
> First, – We will give our services, and under the directions of First Church, as needed:
>
> Second, – We will help financially, as we are able, each doing what he can to make possible the purchase and maintenance of the Mission:
>
> Prayerfully submitted,
> Hale V. Davis, Chairman
> B. Atteberry
> Thos. R. Gathright[14]

With the help of these enthusiastic students, in June 1917, a Sunday School was established in a little, white frame building at the corner of Ninth and Draper Streets. The building belonged to Grace Methodist Episcopalian Church and was purchased for $1,500. The facility had a total seating capacity of 300.[15] It is worth noting that Hale Davis went on to become the president of Oklahoma Baptist University. B. Atteberry went on to have a distinguished career as a pastor and a missionary to the Indians. He served at Maud and Bixby for several years. Thomas Gaithright became pastor of First Baptist Church, Wilburton.

Draper Street Baptist Church formally began on Sunday, September 16, 1917, when a special meeting was called at the facilities to constitute a new Baptist church. Approximately one hundred people gathered in the Draper Street facility. The services began with the singing of "How Firm a Foundation." The song was followed with a prayer.

Using nineteenth-century church terminology and concepts, a "presbytery" was formed to sanction the formation of the new church. The members of the presbytery were Baptist leaders of significance in Shawnee, Oklahoma Baptist University, and the state. These included Dr. J. W. Jent, Dr. W. D. Moorer, Rev. F. Erdman Smith, Rev. E. L. Compere, E. P. Downing, B. F. McBride, G. C. Halley, W. B. Taylor, W. A. Chambers, and W. F. Skelton.[16]

Dr. Jent served as a dean of Oklahoma Baptist University and was the presbytery moderator. Dr. Moorer was an OBU trustee and professor. Erdman Smith was a BGCO leader, an OBU dean, and an OBU professor. W. B. Taylor was the secretary of the OBU Board of Trustees.[17] Reverend Compere was the pastor of First Baptist Church, Shawnee, and a BGCO leader, serving on several BGCO boards. W. F. Skelton was also a BGCO leader and served on several BGCO boards.[18]

Reverend Compere and W. F. Skelton were elected as the moderator and secretary of the meeting. J. M. Pendleton's *Articles of Faith and Church Covenant* was read and accepted unanimously by the attendees. Prayer was offered by Reverend Compere. The group then voted to form a Baptist Church, and the vote was reported to Dr. Jent, who, as Presbytery moderator, called for a vote of approval by the Presbytery. Approval was granted, and Draper Street Baptist Church was duly constituted. The attendees then stood and sang "Amazing Grace." In total, seventy-seven people joined Draper Street Baptist Church at the meeting. A motto for the church was later selected from Job 31:4: "Doth not He see my ways and count all my steps?"

Figure 1.3. Rev. T. B. Holcomb, the Draper Street days

The first business meeting for Draper Street Baptist Church occurred on Wednesday, September 19, 1917. At that meeting, Rev. Thomas Benjamin Holcomb was selected as pastor and E. H. Snellings was selected as treasurer. Frank Thompson and L. B. Geren were appointed to procure one hundred *New Evangel* song books. H. C. Murphy was elected chorister, and Sister Webb was elected pianist.

At the second business meeting, the salary of Reverend Holcomb was set at twenty-five dollars per month.[19] Two things are worth noting here. First, in his 1915 report to the BGCO, Dr. F. M. Masters, President of Oklahoma Baptist University, stated, "A capable janitor was employed at the opening of school for $50.00 per month." Thus, a capable janitor was paid twice as much as the Draper Street Baptist Church pastor.[20] Second, Reverend Holcomb was a bivocational pastor, and his primary income came from the Oklahoma Baptist University Secondary School where he was a history teacher. Also, at the second business meeting, two committees were created—one to procure stoves to heat the facility in the upcoming winter months and the other to establish and manage a "poor fund." Charity work has been dear to Immanuel Baptist Church from its very beginning.

Over the next several months, Draper Street Baptist Church kept busy with the ministry of the church. Frank Thompson was elected as Sunday School secretary. At the November 7, 1917, business meeting, three stoves were approved for purchase, a revival was set for June 1918, and three messengers were selected for the BGCO Annual Meeting in McAlester.

At the May 22, 1918, business meeting, Reverend Holcomb's salary was raised to a hundred dollars per month.[21] Involvement in the Baptist movement in Oklahoma continued to be important to Reverend

Figure 1.4. Rev. T. B. Holcomb, Draper Street Baptist Church

Holcomb. At the 1918 BGCO Annual Meeting held in Enid, Reverend Holcomb was selected to be on the Committee on Nominations.

Draper Street Baptist Church was listed among the churches, making its annual contribution to the BGCO as $233.27 to the State Fund, $84.96 to the Home and Foreign Fund, $15.15 to the Christian Education Fund, and $68.59 to the Orphans' Home Fund. These offerings were very generous compared to other churches of similar size. At the Woman's Baptist Missionary Society of Oklahoma Meeting that was held in conjunction with the 1918 BGCO Annual Meeting, Draper Street Baptist Church was listed in the Standard of Excellence Honor Roll for its support of the Woman's Baptist Missionary Society as a class-A church, the second level of support. Thus, Immanuel Baptist Church has a long history, even from its second year of existence, of strong support for Baptist Woman's Ministry efforts.[22] (Although commonly referred to in modern times as the "Women's Missionary Union," the ministry was originally chartered as the "Woman's Missionary Union.")

The First World War caused a period of concern among Baptist and other Christian denominations. Not only were young men sent into the war in Europe, but in 1918, Frederick Paul Keppel, the third assistant secretary of war, issued a proclamation that all denominational chaplains would be "retired" from army camps. The BGCO, Draper Street Baptist Church, and many Baptist and other denominational churches sent resolutions of concern to their representatives and senators and to the Department of War expressing their loyalty to the nation but also their concern at the expulsion of chaplains from army camps. The Draper Street Baptist Church resolution opposing the expulsion of denominational chaplains was passed in its October 9, 1918, business meeting and was signed by all members present.[23]

Figure 1.5. Auguie Henry, the Draper Street days

The church survived the bleak period of World War I and the temporary closing of all public meetings in October and early November by the Shawnee mayor due to the Spanish influenza epidemic of 1918.[24] When public meetings were again allowed, the church membership voted in the November 13, 1918, business meeting to purchase four lots east of the church to build a parsonage.[25]

During the first years of its existence, Draper Street Baptist Church was supported by and provided support to many Oklahoma Baptist University students. Some of those students eventually became pastors and leaders within the Baptist General Convention of Oklahoma. One such example was Auguie Henry who not only helped Draper Street Baptist Church in its early days but also helped Oklahoma Baptists throughout his life.

Auguie Henry was born in 1900 in Howe, Oklahoma. When he was one year old, his family moved to Mountain View, and he accepted Christ as his Lord and Savior at Mountain View Baptist Church as a child. At the age of fifteen, he attended a revival at Forest Hill where he surrendered to preach. He was licensed to preach at age eighteen at First Baptist Church, Wister.

In September 1918, he enrolled at Oklahoma Baptist University, and in September 1919, he became assistant pastor at Draper Street Baptist Church, reporting to Rev. T. B. Holcomb. Draper Street Baptist Church ordained Auguie Henry on December 15, 1920. After completing his studies at Oklahoma Baptist University in 1925, he became pastor of First Baptist Church, Pryor.[26] One of his first actions at First Baptist Church, Pryor, was to hold a revival. Evangelist Rev. R. L. Estes and his wife conducted the revival.[27] Reverend Henry was active throughout northeastern Oklahoma and was one of the organizers of the Northeastern Assembly that met July 13–23, 1926, near Grove, Oklahoma, on Cowskin Creek.[28] Eventually, he became the director of missions for the Mayes County Association and kept a complete itinerary of inspirational meetings and engagements for the pastors of the association and distributed handbills announcing those meetings.[29]

In 1926, at the age of twenty-six, he became an Oklahoma Baptist University trustee and served beside his friend and mentor

Rev. T. B. Holcomb, who had just become pastor of First Baptist Church, Lawton, and served as a fellow trustee.[30] In 1934, Dr. John Wesley Raley left the pulpit of First Baptist Church, Bartlesville, to become president of Oklahoma Baptist University, and Rev. Auguie Henry succeeded him in that pulpit. In 1941, Auguie Henry was awarded an honorary doctor of divinity degree by Oklahoma Baptist University.[31] After successfully leading several other Baptist churches around the state, Reverend Henry became the first full-time executive secretary-treasurer of the Baptist Foundation. Dr. Auguie Henry served in that role for almost twenty years.[32]

In the first years after the founding of Draper Street Baptist Church, the leadership of Rev. T. B. Holcomb and students such as Auguie Henry brought growing numbers to the church. With the growing numbers came the need for more space and extended classrooms. In less than two years after its founding, the Draper Street Baptist Church voted to purchase four lots just west of the church for further expansion and to build Tabernacle One. A year after the construction of Tabernacle One, the church voted to construct Tabernacle Two. That construction was complete on 1921, but the fast-growing congregation was still looking for more space.[33]

Draper Street Baptist Church continued to grow and to be active in both Pottawatomie Baptist Association Annual Meetings and in BGCO Annual Meetings under Reverend Holcomb's leadership. His salary grew to $150.00 per month. Reverend Holcomb continued to serve Draper Street Baptist Church as pastor until August 27, 1922, when he submitted his letter of resignation. It is worth noting that his resignation coincided with an increase in his obligations at Oklahoma Baptist University.

Figure 1.6. Rev. Bill Smith, the OBU days

Reverend Holcomb had just completed his master of arts degree from the University of Oklahoma and had become a professor within Oklahoma Baptist University itself, a promotion from his secondary school principal and teacher positions.[34] At the September 23, 1922, business meeting, the church voted to call Rev. J. E. Kirk of Holdenville as pastor with a salary of two hundred dollars per month and use of the parsonage. Reverend Kirk subsequently declined the offer, and at the October 8, 1922, business meeting, Rev. Bill Smith was called as pastor with a salary of two hundred dollars per month and use of the parsonage.[35] Reverend Smith came as pastor immediately after graduating from Oklahoma Baptist University.

Reverend Smith was very successful in organizing and motivating the young members of Immanuel Baptist Church. The Sunday School and Training Union teaching activities were greatly enlarged under his leadership. Reverend Holcomb continued to be a member of Draper Street Baptist Church under Reverend Smith's leadership.[36] However, on August 1, 1923, Rev. Bill Smith submitted his resignation.

On August 19, 1923, Rev. O. G. Matthews from Chandler, Oklahoma, was called as pastor with a salary of $150.00 per month, moving expenses from Chandler, and use of the parsonage. Reverend Holcomb continued to be a member of Draper Street Baptist Church under Reverend Matthews' leadership. In September 1923, just one month after taking the pulpit, Rev. O. G. Matthews led a revival at Draper Street Baptist Church. Auguie Henry led the music. There were eleven additions to the church. Speaking of Rev. O. G. Matthews, Reverend Henry wrote in *The Baptist Messenger*,

> The church [was] greatly revived. These good people are learning to love this good man and because of the attitude expressed by them to co-operate with him in the work of the Master. We expect to hear great things of them in the future.[37]

However, just three months later, in December 19, 1923, Rev. O. G. Matthews submitted his resignation. His resignation was rejected unanimously by the church, with a hearty promise of cooperation. However, at the January 9, 1924, business meeting, the church voted forty-eight to twenty-one to call Rev. T. B. Holcomb as pastor.[38]

Rev. William Smith was born in 1899 and died in 1974. In the 1915 minutes of the Baptist General Convention of Oklahoma, under a section entitled "Preachers (Including Indian) Who May or May Not Be Pastors," William Smith of Shawnee was listed. In the 1920 minutes of the Baptist General Convention of Oklahoma, Bill Smith is listed as one of the members of the Oklahoma Baptist University Men's Quartette who sang on the afternoon of the second day. Also at that annual

Figure 1.7. Rev. Bill Smith in retirement

meeting, during the motion to adopt the report on Christian education that had been read by Rev. Sam D. Taylor of Chickasha, William Smith spoke in behalf of Oklahoma Baptist University.[39]

Bill Smith was a graduate of Oklahoma Baptist University and served as student body president during the 1921 to 1922 academic year.[40] He was a very active student at Oklahoma Baptist University. He was president of the Emethean academic and social club. He was part of the Glee club quartet, a member of the varsity debate team, the drama club, and the volunteer band. He was also active in the Ministerial Alliance.[41]

After leaving Draper Street Baptist Church, he became the pastor of First Baptist Church, New Lima, Oklahoma, in Seminole County, between Seminole and Wewoka.[42] He later served churches in Haileyville and McAlester. His work in these churches was sufficiently strong that he was selected by the Baptist General Convention of Oklahoma to be the southeast district missionary in 1934. He attended the 1934 BGCO Annual Meeting as a messenger from Haileyville and as the southeast district missionary. He led a devotional in one of the sessions and read the report on Christian education, moving for its adoption.[43]

In 1935, Oklahoma Baptist University celebrated its silver anniversary. President John Wesley Raley began an enthusiastic campaign to hold a significant celebration event and to raise funds for the university's debt, endowment, and operations. As an Oklahoma Baptist University alumnus and BGCO leader, Rev. Bill Smith was very active in speaking to Baptist groups about the silver anniversary and the need for donations.

Figure 1.8. Rev. O. G. Matthews, Draper Street Baptist Church

The February 21, 1935, issue of *The Baptist Messenger* reported that over a two-month period, Reverend Smith spoke in nine associational meetings. During the same period, Rev. T. B. Holcomb who was now the state missionary spoke in eight associational meetings, and OBU graduate and former Immanuel member Auguie Henry spoke in five. The same issue of *The Baptist Messenger* reported,

> [State] Missionary T. B. Holcomb, who spent a few days recently in the Frisco [Baptist] Association, is greatly impressed with the fine constructive work that District Missionary Bill Smith is doing in Southeast Oklahoma. Brother Bill Smith is well acquainted with that field, and has the love and confidence of the workers in that section.[44]

The headquarters of the Frisco Baptist Association is in Hugo, Oklahoma, in southeast Oklahoma along the Red River. Hugo is the county seat of Choctaw County.

On September 17, 1967, Rev. Bill Smith returned to Immanuel Baptist Church to participate in the fiftieth anniversary celebration of Immanuel that was hosted by the current pastor, Rev. Lawrence Stewart. Reverend Smith was living in Tulsa at the time and was sixty-seven years old.[45] Rev. William L. Smith died in 1974 at the age of seventy-five. He is buried in the Shawnee Fairview Cemetery.[46]

Rev. O. G. Matthews likewise loyally served Oklahoma Baptists for many years. In the 1916 minutes of the Baptist General Convention of Oklahoma, under a section entitled "Personal Gifts—Orphans' Home," Oney Matthews was listed for a gift of one dollar (a day's salary for a working man at the time).[47] In September 1921, Rev. O. G. Matthews served as the pastor in Chandler and led a revival in Prague for Rev. H. Tom Wiles. Reverend Wiles would eventually go on to be the pastor of Immanuel Baptist Church in the 1930s.[48] The 1923 minutes of the Baptist General Convention of Oklahoma, listed Rev. O. G. Matthews as a member of the Temperance Committee.[49]

In the August 1–2, 1923, Lincoln County Baptist Association Meeting in Stroud, Reverend Matthews was elected moderator of the association.[50] Rev. O. G. Matthews went on to become an associational missionary in northern Oklahoma. In the 1929 minutes of the Baptist General Convention of Oklahoma, Rev. O. G. Matthews was listed as supporting the Baptists in Pond Creek under the Salt Fork Association with a payment of $275.00.[51] Pond Creek is a city in Grant County, Oklahoma, along the Salt Fork Arkansas River near the northern border of Oklahoma. The city was settled as a town during the Cherokee Strip Land Run in 1893. Pond Creek currently has a population of 850 but had a population of 1,000 when Rev. Matthews served there.[52]

Figure 1.9. Rural Pastors' Conference, 1937

Later, Rev. Matthews served as the Pottawatomie-Lincoln Baptist Association director of missions from 1936 to 1938.[53] As part of his duties as director of missions, Reverend Matthews helped to host and was on the program for a rural pastors' conference held at Fairview Baptist Church in early June 1937. The program for the event included many prominent Baptists from the Shawnee area and across the state of Oklahoma. The conference leader was Dr. J. W. Jent of Oklahoma Baptist University whom the June 10, 1937, issue of *The Baptist Messenger* described as the man who "knows more about Baptist rural churches throughout the South than any other man."

Other men on the program were Dr. Andrew Potter, president and corresponding secretary of the Baptist General Convention of Oklahoma, and Rev. S. M. Scantlan of Fairview Baptist Church, who conducted a class each day on "Building a Standard Sunday School in the Country Church." Also included were T. B. Lackey, Oklahoma Baptist University president Dr. John Wesley Raley, and Rev. T. J. Doss of Immanuel Baptist Church. In addition, Rev. Chesterfield Turner of First Baptist Church, Shawnee; Rev. W. O. Miller of University Church, Shawnee; Rev. Clyde J. Foster, Chandler; Rev. Bura Stephens of Blackburn Chapel; Rev. J. B. Rounds, Crestwood Church, Oklahoma City; Rev. A. L. Lowther of First Baptist Church, Seminole; T. P. Haskins; and R. S. Bazzell were on the agenda. The music was led by John Roy Harris of First Baptist Church, Seminole. The next month, in early July 1937, Reverend Matthews led a revival with Rev. W. O. Miller at University Baptist Church in Shawnee.[54]

In the July 28, 1938, issue of *The Baptist Messenger*, Rev. James A. Hogg of Allen Baptist Church said,

> Missionary O. G. Matthews closed a two weeks revival with the Allen Baptist Church [on] July 15. There were sixteen professions of faith. Brother Matthews is the pastor's friend, and a tireless worker who bends his efforts toward the winning of the lost and the binding together of pastor and people. The meeting was immediately preceded by a Bible school in which 154 were enrolled and ten professions of faith [were

made]. This church expects to make the best associational report in its history this year.

The issue went on to say that the spirit of the church was at
high tide. Brother Matthews said that two finer young people cannot
be found in the state than Pastor and Mrs. James A. Hogg. Brother
Matthews's next revival meeting was at the Pecan Grove Church, north
of Holdenville. Meetings were scheduled held at Asher, Ray City,
Wallace Avenue Baptist Church in Shawnee, and Holdenville, as well
as in several mission meetings in the North Canadian Association.[55]
In 1940, O. G. Matthews attended the BGCO Annual Meeting
as a messenger from Tonkawa and led the opening prayer for the
Thursday afternoon session. That year, he served on the Credential
Committee and on the State Missions Committee.[56] He did not
attend the new two annual meetings, but in the 1944 minutes of
the Baptist General Convention of Oklahoma, Rev. O. G. Matthews
was listed as one of ninety-four members of the convention who were
serving as chaplains in the armed forces during World War II.[57]
After the service of Reverend Smith and Reverend Matthews,
Rev. T. B. Holcomb returned to the pulpit of Immanuel Baptist
Church on January 9, 1924. He continued as pastor until March
17, 1926. At that time, he resigned to take the pulpit of First Baptist
Church, Lawton.[58]

Rev. T. B. Holcomb, the Years after Immanuel

In 1927, Rev. Thomas Holcomb moved to Lawton to become the
pastor of First Baptist Church, Lawton.[59] He continued to serve as
pastor of First Baptist Church, Lawton, until 1934 when Rev. T. B.
Holcomb returned to Shawnee to be a district missionary. It should
be noted that at the 1934 Baptist General Convention of Oklahoma
Annual Meeting, Dr. Andrew was elected corresponding secretary-treasurer of the Convention. Rev. T. B. Holcomb and Rev. G.
M. Ford of Konowa were selected as the dignitaries to escort Dr. and
Mrs. Potter to the stage for acknowledgment by the annual meeting
delegates.[60] Reverend Holcomb was later appointed as the Oklahoma
state general missionary. In parallel to serving as Oklahoma state gen-

eral missionary, Dr. Holcomb also served as Pottawatomie-Lincoln Baptist Association director of missions from 1934 to 1935.[61] Dr. Holcomb's tenure as state general missionary was short-lived. In February 1936, Dr. Holcomb was tragically killed in an automobile accident.

Reverend Holcomb received generous praise from all across the Oklahoma Baptist family for his service at Oklahoma Baptist University; Draper Street Baptist Church; First Baptist Church, Lawton; and as Oklahoma state general missionary. In a tribute to Dr. Holcomb, Dr. John W. Raley—Oklahoma Baptist University President from 1931 to 1961—said,

> It is difficult to believe that Tom Holcomb has gone on to claim his reward. I can see him now—smiling, happy, optimistic, a heart filled with real passion for the unsaved. His going is a personal loss. It would be possible to write a long tribute, but perhaps the greatest tribute which could be paid is to point out the influence he has had in the lives of a number of our Oklahoma pastors. I have been told that T. B. Holcomb was the first to discover the great possibilities in Marvin Cole. Marvin's great evangelistic heart is a greater eulogy than I could ever pay. I could name a number of other graduates of Oklahoma Baptist University who owe a great deal to Tom Holcomb. He had a genius for finding diamonds in the rough. Every man was his brother. They will rise up and call him a true friend and a true Christian. The denomination has lost a real champion. His place will be hard to fill.[62]

Marvin Cole, of whom Dr. Raley spoke, was a classic example of the influence that T. B. Holcomb had on pastors within Oklahoma while he was a professor at Oklahoma Baptist University. Marvin Cole was born in rural Oklahoma southwest of Ardmore in 1899. He was saved and called to preach in 1918. When he was twenty years old, he enrolled in Oklahoma Baptist University without an eighth grade education.

T. B. Holcomb attempted to place him in the eighth grade but shortly decided it was wiser to place him in seventh grade classes and found him a tutor. Marvin Cole was a capable student, however, and finished both his seventh and eighth grade classes in one year. Reverend Holcomb also found Marvin a job as a janitor. Reverend Cole did supply preaching on weekends. He excelled in his classes and soon received a job as pastor of First Baptist Church, Asher, where he met and married his wife. After nine years (one in elementary school, four in high school, and four in college), he graduated from Oklahoma Baptist University. Reverend Marvin Cole went on to be a very successful pastor and evangelist. He remained forever grateful to T. B. Holcomb and Oklahoma Baptist University for his success.[63]

Figure 1.10. Rev. T. B. Holcomb, the Lawton days

Rev. Thomas Jefferson Doss, who was the pastor of Immanuel Baptist Church at the time, understood the contribution of Dr. Holcomb during those early years at Draper Street Baptist Church. Reverend Doss said this:

> The funeral for Rev. T. B. Holcomb was held from the auditorium of the Immanuel Baptist Church on February 27, 1936. The crowd was large and representative. More than 50 pastors from over the state were present. This large and representative crowd and the most beautiful floral offerings, the many telegrams and countless other words and deeds of kindness expressed the deep and abiding appreciation for this tireless, capable, and sacrificial soldier of the Cross. Brother Holcomb organized the Immanuel Baptist Church on September 16, 1917, with 62

charter members. From this small beginning under his wise and capable leadership, the church grew rapidly in numbers, in favor with the people, and in the missionary spirit. No preacher is loved more sincerely than is T. B. by these charter members and hundreds of others who have come into the membership of this church through his ministry. Our hearts are yielded and our prayers are that God will raise up another great and good leader to take the important place left vacant by this heroic herald of the Gospel. Our deepest sympathies are for the bereaved family, and those who worked with him.

In his tribute, Rev. O. G. Matthews, district missionary from Shawnee, Oklahoma, and the pastor who served briefly at Draper Street Baptist Church, stated,

I am sorry to learn of the untimely death of Brother Holcomb. We have lost a valuable man in the Lord's work. His work has been very important in the Debt-Paying Campaign. He loved his Lord and was always ready to aid his brethren and give his best to the denomination. We have lost a great worker.

The article concerning Dr. Holcomb's death from *The Baptist Messenger* states,

The tragic death of Missionary T. B. Holcomb is a distinct shock not only to all of the Baptist people of Oklahoma, but to the denominational life of the state. Brother Holcomb had served the Baptist cause in Oklahoma for some twenty-three years. For nine years, he was intimately associated with Oklahoma Baptist University as a student and later as a teacher. During this time, he organized the Draper Street Baptist Church that later changed its name to the Immanuel Baptist Church of Shawnee. This church is now one of the strongest churches in the state. On leaving the University, Brother Holcomb went to the pastorate of the First Baptist Church, Lawton, where he served until his coming to the office of General Missionary two years ago. Brother Holcomb had perhaps the greatest hold upon the young preachers of Oklahoma of any man of the state, having taught them while in the University. One did not always agree with T. B. Holcomb as to plans, but one was always compelled to admire his ruggedness and his valuable philosophy of life. This rugged mountaineer carried beneath his somewhat abrupt attitude, a heart that was as gentle as a woman's, and a simple faith in God that defied all onslaughts of doubt. The missionary cause of Oklahoma has lost a great leader, and a host of us have lost a genuine friend. All who knew T. B. Holcomb knew that when he was a friend, he was one who could be depended upon to the utmost limit. Our hearts go out in sympathy to his bereaved ones among whom are: his widow, Mrs. Ruby Holcomb; a son, T. P. Holcomb; a daughter, Ruby Lee Holcomb, Dallas; three brothers, Lee Holcomb, St. Louis; Sammie Holcomb, Paris, Tennessee; and Jim Holcomb, Paris, Tennessee; two sisters, Mrs. Annie McKennon, Paris, Tennessee; Mrs. Cora Swindell, Camden, Tennessee; a grandchild, Marne Glynn Holcomb, Shawnee; and his father, J. W. Holcomb, Paris, Tennessee. At the time of this writing, funeral arrangements have not yet been completed, but we understand that a memorial service is to be held in the OBU chapel as a tribute to his relationship to the University."[64]

Dr. Holcomb's wife, Ruby, was born in 1879, the same year as her husband. She died in 1941. She and Dr. Holcomb are buried in Fairview Cemetery in Shawnee.[65]

35

CHAPTER 2

The Move to Main Street

Rev. Dan Brinkley, March 1926–November 1929

Introduction

Rev. Dan S. Brinkley was the fourth pastor to serve Immanuel Baptist Church. Rev. T. B. Holcomb served two terms as pastor of Draper Street Baptist Church, the forerunner of Immanuel Baptist. His first term of service was from September 1917 to October 1922, and his second term was from January 1924 to March 1926. For the purposes of counting pastors in this book, Rev. T. B. Holcomb is considered to be one pastor serving a split term. Prior to Rev. Dan Brinkley coming to Draper Street Baptist Church, Rev. T. B. Holcomb, Rev. O. G. Matthews, and Rev. William Smith had served as pastors, making Rev. Dan Brinkley the fourth pastor.

Reverend Brinkley was known for successful church-building programs and was called as pastor in March 1926. Reverend Brinkley was called "a man of vision and faith" by Immanuel Baptist Church members. He visualized a large Baptist church on East Main Street and led the congregation into a massive and successful building program.[1] He was criticized for promoting such a large building, but his faith and vision never wavered. Although the final work on the building was not completed during his tenure, he did see his dreams for a beautiful large church facility come true. During his years at Immanuel Baptist Church, Reverend Brinkley was able to do great work among the young people of the church.[2]

The world scene during the years that Rev. Dan Brinkley served Immanuel was one of economic boom and bust. Hyperinflation and massive unemployment hit Germany and soon spread around the world.[3] In 1927, the German economy collapsed. The Russian Communist Party expelled Leon Trotsky from membership. He was later assassinated in Mexico in 1940. Also in 1927, to the joy of millions around the world, Charles Lindbergh made the first nonstop, solo transatlantic flight.[4] In 1928, the first of Joseph Stalin's five-year plans began. One aspect was the collectivization of agriculture in the Soviet Union. Millions of Soviet citizens would die as the collectivization of agriculture resulted in a massive decline in food production.[5] In August 1929, Arab Muslim mobs began attacking Jews in Jerusalem and surrounding towns and villages.[6] The massacre lasted several days, and 133 Jews were killed by Arabs and 339 others were injured, while 110 Arabs were killed and 232 were injured.[7]

The national scene during the years Reverend Brinkley served Immanuel (March 1926–November 1929) paralleled the world scene of economic boom and bust. In 1926, Henry Ford announced a forty-hour workweek and Route 66 was established. In 1927, Babe Ruth made a new home run record that stood for many years. Also in 1927, the first talking movie, *The Jazz Singer*, was released.[8] In November 1928, United States voters elected Herbert Hoover as president over Alfred E. Smith, governor of New York.[9] In February 1929, the St. Valentine's Day massacre in Chicago occurred. Seven members of the George "Bugs" Moran gang were killed allegedly by members of the Al Capone gang. In late 1929, the New York Stock Exchange plunged nearly 50 percent. Securities on Wall Street lost twenty-six billion dollars, marking the first financial disaster of the Great Depression.[10]

Rev. Dan S. Brinkley, the Years before Immanuel

Rev. Dan S. Brinkley first appears in the minutes of the annual meetings of the Baptist General Convention of Oklahoma in 1916. The annual meeting was held at First Baptist Church, Oklahoma City, that year. Reverend Brinkley was a leader in the Custer Baptist Church and attended the annual meeting as a messenger from Custer, Oklahoma.[11] On November 16, 1916, he was an elder in the church and served as moderator for a presbytery that ordained three new Deacons for the Custer Baptist Church.[12] Custer, Oklahoma, now known as Custer City, is a town in Custer County, with a population of 375 at the 2010 census. In 1916, Custer was a much larger town with approximately 875 people.[13]

In 1917, Rev. Brinkley moved from Custer to Wewoka and pastored a church there and initiated a new ten-thousand-dollar building there.[14] The church soon doubled in attendance.[15] Concerning Rev. Dan Brinkley's service in Wewoka, the November 14, 1917, *Baptist Messenger* records,

> Evangelist Elmer Ridgeway writing from Wewoka, says, "We are in the midst of a real revival here in Wewoka. The power of God is upon the people. Even the day crowds nearly fill the house. There are conversions and additions at every night service, deep and pungent conviction is manifested over the entire city. There were 15 professions and 13 additions last night. Geo. W. Reynolds, of Birmingham, Ala., is leading in song. Dan Brinkley is the most popular pastor in town. We go on another week."[16]

The successes of Rev. Dan S. Brinkley were echoed by Oklahoma Baptist University professor and administrator J. W. Jent in one of his regular articles summarizing Oklahoma Baptist life. In his April 3, 1918, "Jent's Jottings" article in *The Baptist Messenger*, Dr. Jent states,

I was with Pastor D. S. Brinkley at Wewoka for a busy day the third Sunday in March. Fine congregations morning, afternoon and evening. They had already made their offering, but they gave me a good hearing on education and our denominational life. Brinkley is doing a great work at Wewoka. He is receiving additions right along. The Sunday School has run the house over and a campaign for a new $10,000 house of worship is on. Every department is flourishing.[17]

In 1918, Reverend Brinkley made one more move—this time, to Purcell to become the pastor of First Baptist Church, Purcell. First Baptist Church, Purcell, was the very church whose pulpit was recently vacated when Rev. T. B. Holcomb moved to Shawnee and became pastor of Draper Street Baptist Church. Having successfully conducted a new building campaign in Wewoka, Reverend Brinkley immediately initiated a new building campaign in Purcell. In the June 4, 1919, issue of *The Baptist Messenger*, Editor C. P. Stealey reported,

Figure 2.1. First Baptist Church, Purcell, 1910

In addition to a most hearty welcome, we enjoyed going over the splendid new building just being completed. They will hold their first service in the auditorium next Sunday. We have been over a good portion of the country and do not remember to have seen as fine a building or so well arranged church in a town the size of Purcell. The auditorium is a thing of beauty; also commodious. The Sunday School department [uses the latest methods]. The church is well located; the people are happy, the pastor and [his] wife [are] in high favor, and more of the members are going to read the Messenger. They begin a revival meeting next Sunday with Pastor Butler aiding Brother Brinkley. We predict a new day for the work at Purcell.[18]

Reverend Brinkley stayed at First Baptist Church, Purcell, for several years and grew in stature within the Oklahoma Baptist community, especially for his work with the $75 Million Fund Campaign.[19] With the return of peace after World War I, the Southern Baptist Convention

Figure 2.2. First Baptist Church, Purcell, 1935

looked to new ways to fund its ministries. Wanting to use a nation-wide approach, the Southern Baptist Convention initiated the $75 Million Fund Campaign in 1919 to raise and allocate $75,000,000 for Baptist causes. Oklahoma's goal was $2,500,000, an aggressive goal for a small rural state.

By 1920, seventy-five million dollars in pledges were received. However, it proved easier to obtain pledges than to collect those pledges, especially with falling farm prices.[20] Pastor D. S. Brinkley of First Baptist Church, Purcell, was at the forefront of soliciting and fulfilling pledges. The October 8, 1919, issue of *The Baptist Messenger* noted,

> "We are in the association getting campaign ammunition to the people," Brother Brinkley says. "The tithe will take the pain out of campaign. I know that we would go over one hundred million if Baptists would pay up their back debts to the Lord, and believe me, prayer will take the pain out of [the] campaign. [We just] closed a meeting last week at Pleasant View Church. That splendid singer and Gospel preacher W. A. Wilcoxon doing the preaching for us. There were a number of additions. It has never been our

pleasure to work with a nobler, more devoted man than he. Purcell Church has received forty-nine members since January and paid into the Lord's treasury over $13,500.00 in the last six months."[21]

As his work at First Baptist Church, Purcell, continued, Rev. Dan Brinkley continued to grow in stature within Oklahoma Baptist life. In 1918, the Baptist General Convention of Oklahoma saw a great need to improve its organization and its communications flow. The state office sought leaders to ensure information reached the remotest church and every Baptist member. The BGCO wanted to include in its records the name of every church and every member. Rev. Dan Brinkley of First Baptist Church, Purcell, was selected to be the leader of this effort for the McClain Association.[22]

At the 1919 Annual Meeting of the Baptist General Convention of Oklahoma, Reverend Brinkley was elected to be a trustee of the New Orleans Bible Institute, now known as the New Orleans Baptist Theological Seminary.[23] In 1920, Reverend Brinkley moved to Sand Springs where he pastored a church. His wife was active in the Baptist youth program at their church. The minutes of the 1920 BGCO Annual Meeting held at the First Baptist Church, Blackwell, records the following: "Greetings from [the] Junior Baptist Youth Program Division, Sand Springs, Oklahoma. [Our] average attendance is one hundred (100). Signed, Mrs. D. S. Brinkley." At the 1921 annual meeting held at First Baptist Church, Oklahoma City, Rev. D. S. Brinkley, Sand Springs, was listed on the $75 Million Fund Committee.[24] At the 1923 BGCO Annual Meeting, Rev. D. S. Brinkley, Sand Springs, served on the Obituaries Committee. In the 1924 BGCO Annual Meeting, Mrs. D. S. Brinkley led the Woman's Missionary Union devotional on Tuesday morning, November 11, 1924. Her devotional was entitled "The Hour Is Come."

While at Sand Springs, Reverend Brinkley tried his hand at poetry. The following is a poem that he wrote while at Sand Springs:

Give Me the Book
D. S. Brinkley

A great man lay dying, life going fast,
He thought of the Bible and scenes of the past,
And whispered ere reaching, the Great Divide,
"Give me the Book, in its truth I abide.
Give me the book, God's message to men.
Teaching deliverance, sweet freedom from sin,
Give me the book, tho' ages shall roll
Its truth is forever, a guide to man's soul.
Give me the Book, the love letter from Him
The Word made flesh and dwelt among men,
Give me the Book, the story of thee
Dying for men on Calvary's tree,
Give me the book, great multitudes cry,
Oh children of God, pass them not by,
Give them the book, until the earth shall ring
With songs of redemption, and Praise to our King.[25]

Rev. Dan S. Brinkley, the Immanuel Years

With the second resignation of Rev. T. B. Holcomb on March 17, 1926, the church quickly formed a Pulpit Committee and, on March 24, 1926, called Rev. Dan S. Brinkley from Sand Springs to be the new pastor. Reverend Brinkley was offered a salary of two hundred dollars per month plus the use of the parsonage.[26] Reverend Brinkley continued the high level of activity that the church had experienced under Reverend Holcomb. The growth in the church had long since exceeded

Figure 2.3. Rev. Dan Brinkley, the Immanuel years

the small three-hundred-seat capacity of the white frame building that was Draper Street Baptist Church.

As noted in the introduction, Rev. Dan S. Brinkley had a reputation for successful church-building programs. The Draper Street Baptist Church members later called him "a man of vision and faith." As he looked at the crowded facilities on Draper Street, he envisioned a large and elegant Baptist church at Main and Eden, a facility that would be large enough to hold the growing congregation for the near future and for years to come. With this vision, he inspired the congregation and led them into a massive building program.[27]

During his years at Immanuel, Rev. Brinkley continued to be active in Baptist life around the state. The June 16, 1926, *Baptist Messenger* recorded the following:

> Brother Brinkley, who recently resigned the Pastorate at Sand Springs to accept the [pulpit] at Draper Street Church, Shawnee, is assisting Pastor C. H. Bell, Temple Church, Oklahoma City, in a [revival] meeting. Last week, there were about 21 conversions with 14 additions [to the church rolls]. Brother Brinkley reports his work at Draper Street starting off in a fine way and says that the great need of the field is more room to accommodate the growing organizations.[28]

Church activities continued at a brisk pace during Rev. Dan Brinkley's early months as pastor of Immanuel Baptist Church. In the June 17, 1926, business meeting, Rev. Earl Hatchet was called as assistant pastor and Choir Director at a salary of forty dollars per month. By November 3, 1926, the membership of Immanuel Baptist Church was sufficiently pleased with Reverend Brinkley's service that his salary was increased to $250 per month.

The feelings of progress continued through the rest of 1926 and early 1927. In a called business meeting on Sunday, January 23, 1927, the church voted to purchase the Milstead property at the southeast corner of Main Street and Eden Street with the intent of selling the Draper Street property and erecting a new church on the new property. In February 1927, Rev. Earl Hatchet felt called into full-time ministry and resigned his positions. He was succeeded by Brother Tolliver as choir director at ten dollars per month. Bro. Tolliver continued as choir director until December 1927 when he was succeeded by F. C. Blosche at fifty dollars per month. In January 1928, however, F. C. Blosche received a salary reduction to twenty-five dollars per month. At the March 7, 1928, business meeting, the Deacons proposed that two committees be formed—one of men and one of women "to see some members of the church with regards to the way they have been living." The church voted to create the two committees.

By May 9, 1928, the church's activities associated with the purchase of the new property for the new building, the raising of funds for the new building, the selling the present property, and the day-to-day running the church had reached a level that the church decided to have two treasurers. One treasurer would be in charge of the building program funds, and one treasurer would be in charge of the regular budget. W. B. Richardson served as the regular treasurer, and Henry Goodson was the building fund treasurer.

By August 1928, sufficient progress had been made in planning and fund-raising for the church to borrow an additional $17,500 from R. A. Cowden, bringing the total borrowed to $25,000. As the move to the new facility progressed, Draper Street Baptist Church decided to change its name. At the February 6, 1929, business meeting, several names were proposed, including *Pilgrim's Rest, Temple,* and *Immanuel.* By vote of the church, *Immanuel* was selected as the new name. At that same meeting, the church voted to send 10 percent of each church offering to Dr. J. B. Rounds, state BGCO secretary, for statewide and Southern Baptist Convention–wide missions and ministries.[29]

Rev. Dan S. Brinkley was well received in Shawnee, and his reputation grew across the state of Oklahoma. In the June 22, 1927, issue of *The Baptist Messenger,* T. C. Carleton, a regular columnist from Oklahoma City, wrote,

> I worshipped with Pastor Brinkley and his Draper Street Church at the evening service. He is a good preacher, doing well, and leading his people in build-

ing a suitable church house for his growing congregation. Brother Brinkley sounds the evangelistic note in his preaching in a fine way. The excellent record he made at Sand Springs has helped to give him high standing among his people and the citizenship of Shawnee.[30]

The actual construction of the Main Street facility was a marvel to behold. Reverend Brinkley led the congregation in building one of the most beautiful buildings in Oklahoma. Twelve train car loads of native rock, picked up in western Arkansas, were used to veneer the outside of the building. Artistic designs were used inside and outside to enhance the worship atmosphere. Dedication ceremonies for the new building were held on September 1, 1929. The growing congregation moved into the basement of its new facility and looked forward to years of growth.[31]

The October 31, 1929, issue of *The Baptist Messenger* contained this description of Immanuel Baptist Church:

> The Draper Street Baptist church, the name of which was changed a few months ago to the Immanuel Church, was organized in September, 1917, with Rev. T. B. Holcomb, now of the First Church, Lawton, as pastor. He was followed by Brethren O. L. Matthews and Bill Smith. Pastor Dan S. Brinkley came to Shawnee from Sand Springs, four years ago. There have been additions [to its membership] almost every Sunday. During this time, the membership has trebled and the church now has a membership of over 600. The Sunday School has grown in proportion to the church membership. Eight hundred by Christmas has been set as [the] goal for Sunday School enrollment. A beautiful church building has been erected during the past year and was formally opened the first Sunday in September. Pastor Brinkley says that the most far-reaching and most sacred gift of all those received was $5.00 in pennies, nickels, and dimes

put into his hand last winter by little Mildred Burger, just a few hours before she died. Pastor Brinkley says that so far as he knows there is not a member of that church that dances or plays cards–although the church is made up largely of young people.[32]

The 1975 Dedication history described the atmosphere of the church under the leadership of Rev. Brinkley:

Figure 2.4. Immanuel Baptist Church, 1930

The congregation then–as now–was busy with building and enlistment programs. Just as there had been enthusiastic support and opposition earlier [to the establishment of the church], there was enthusiastic support and enthusiastic opposition to the building program presented by Bro. Brinkley. "Too large." "Too expensive." "This building is good enough." "You'll never get enough people to fill it up." All these phrases and many more were bounced about. Bro. Brinkley communicated his vision of a large and beautiful Church to the people, and the building program began at Main and Eden. We moved into the basement and changed our name to "Immanuel Baptist Church"–and then came the "Crash of '29."[33]

Reverend Brinkley remained active in local and statewide Baptist life. On August 27–28, 1929, he was one of twenty-four Messengers who attended the Pottawatomie Baptist Association Annual Meeting at First Baptist Church, McLoud. E. C. Routh, editor of *The Baptist Messenger*, also attended that Annual Meeting. Concerning the opening of the new facility, *The Baptist Messenger* editor, E. C. Routh, in the September 5, 1929, recorded,

> [I spent] Sunday morning [at] the Immanuel Church, Shawnee, of which the beloved Dan S. Brinkley is pastor. [The church] celebrated the formal opening of their new house of worship. They have a magnificent building with provision for every department of the church. The new house is built on the same general lines as the Immanuel Church, Tulsa. Pastor Brinkley has been with this church four years. Before coming to Shawnee, he was at First Purcell, then at Sand Springs. At each of [these] places, he had much to do with the building of new houses of worship. He is one of our best pastors and preachers. It was a joy to have fellowship with his people and to partake of the hospitality of his home.[34]

The financial picture of America changed dramatically with the stock market crash of October 1929. As a farming and small business community, the financial picture in Shawnee and Oklahoma began to dim far before the 1929 stock market crash. At the September 11, 1929, business meeting, two motions were made to pay no bills other than regular expense unless the finance committee or a church vote had approved the expense. Both motions failed. Faced with mounting financial problems, Pastor Brinkley resigned in November 1929, leaving an elaborate building and an almost-insurmountable debt.[35]

Rev. Dan S. Brinkley, the Years after Immanuel

After leaving Immanuel Baptist Church, Rev. Dan S. Brinkley moved to Rogers, Arkansas, where he pastored a Baptist church.[36] In the June 12, 1930, issue of the *Baptist Messenger*, editor E. C. Routh noted that evangelists E. A. Petroff and B. H. Elsey were conducting a three-week revival with Pastor D. S. Brinkley in Rogers, Arkansas.[37]

In February 1933, Rev. Brinkley was called to the Picher Church in the Northeast Association.

The Sunday School at Picher Church ran around 275 in attendance.[38] Picher is currently a ghost town in far northeastern Ottawa County. Picher was once a major national center of lead and zinc mining. However, more than a century of unrestricted mining dangerously undermined most of Picher's buildings and left giant piles of toxic waste heaped throughout the area. In 1933, when Dan Brinkley was called as pastor, the town's population was about 7,500.[39] After arriving in Picher, Rev. Brinkley dramatically decreased his involvement in Oklahoma Baptist life. He stopped attending BGCO Annual Meetings. He is not listed as an active pastor in the BGCO Annual Meeting minutes for the next several years. After 1933, Rev. Dan Brinkley was not mentioned in either the BGCO Annual Meeting minutes or *The Baptist Messenger.*

CHAPTER 3

Into the Heart of the Depression

Rev. H. H. Burton, January 1930–February 1934

Introduction

On September 1, 1929, the growing Immanuel Baptist Church congregation moved into the basement of its new facility on Main Street. The church had just changed its name from Draper Street Baptist Church to Immanuel Baptist Church and looked forward to years of growth. However, the financial picture of America changed dramatically with the stock market crash of October 1929. Massive unemployment occurred across the country. Pastor Dan S. Brinkley, the driving force behind the construction of the Main Street facility, resigned in November 1929, leaving an elaborate building and an almost insurmountable debt. The next pastor, Rev. H. H. Burton, faced the lean years of economic depression and financial hardship.[1] Rev. Burton was a great and powerful, spiritual-filled preacher. He not only loved and was loved by the congregation, but he also loved everyone he knew. He came at a time when the Immanuel Baptist Church family needed to be lifted up and given new faith in a time of discouragement due to the Depression and the massive church debt.[2]

The world scene during the years that Reverend Burton served Immanuel was a scene of severe economic depression and the prelude to war. In 1930, the world saw a glimmer of hope for peace when

Great Britain, the United States, Japan, France, and Italy signed a naval disarmament treaty. Japan proceeded to ignore the treaty. In Germany, the Nazi Party gained power in German elections, amid a deepening German financial crisis.[3] In the Soviet Union, Communist efforts to collectivize farming led to massive shortfalls in production with widespread famine across the nation.[4] The year 1933 saw upheaval and confusion in Germany. Hitler became German chancellor in January but without a majority, and the Reichstag (German Parliament) was disbanded. A Nazi reign of terror began in late February.[5]

The national scene during the years that Reverend Burton served Immanuel paralleled the world scene of severe economic depression. In 1930, unemployment soared as factories closed.[6] In 1931, "The Star-Spangled Banner" officially became the national anthem.[7] In May 1932, Amelia Earhart became the first female flyer to make a solo crossing of the Atlantic. In November 1932, Franklin Roosevelt won a decisive victory over Herbert Hoover.[8] Roosevelt was inaugurated in 1933, declaring that "the only thing we have to fear is fear itself." He quickly launched the New Deal, a series of domestic programs designed to reverse the tragedy of the Depression. Also in 1933, Prohibition was repealed.[9]

Rev. H. H. Burton, the Years before Immanuel

Henry Hale Burton was born in 1871. Throughout his life, he was known as H. H. Burton and not Henry Burton. Before coming to Immanuel Baptist Church, Rev. H. H. Burton was a very successful pastor from Altus, Oklahoma. Altus is the county seat of Jackson County down in the southwest corner of Oklahoma. Altus is home to Altus Air Force Base and has a population of approximately twenty thousand people. In the early 1900s, when Rev. H. H. Burton was pastor there, the population was around five thousand people.

The town was originally named Buttermilk Station by cowboys driving herds northward who bought buttermilk from a local farmer there. Unfortunately, the fledgling town was nearly destroyed in a flash flood in 1891, and the townspeople moved two and a half miles eastward to higher ground and renamed the town Altus from the Latin word for *high*.[10] Reverend Burton became pastor of First Baptist Church, Altus, on January 1, 1913, at the age of forty-two. He remained in Altus more than six years and then moved to Arkansas in 1919. After holding two short pastorates in Arkansas, he returned to Altus in 1925 and served again at First Baptist Church, Altus, for four years.[11]

Reverend Burton first appeared in the 1913 minutes of the Baptist General Convention of Oklahoma (BGCO) annual meeting held in Chickasha. He was listed among the new pastors who had just arrived in the state. However, from his role at the annual meeting, it was clear that Reverend Burton was already a well-respected pastor. He was selected as the alternate preacher for the annual sermon at the next BGCO annual meeting. He was also placed on the Christian Education Committee and led the evening devotional service on the evening of the first day and the morning, afternoon, and evening devotional services on the second day.[12]

By the 1914 BGCO Annual Meeting, Reverend Burton had secured positions on the BGCO board of directors and on the board of directors of Western Baptist College in Mangum, Oklahoma. He was also the chairman of the Foreign Mission Committee and did a special symposium on Sunday School attendance entitled "How to Secure Attendance of Members of the Church in the Sunday School and of the Sunday School in the Preaching Service." He was also selected for the Program Committee for the next annual meeting.[13]

At the 1915 Annual Meeting in Tulsa, Reverend Burton was placed on a special committee to investigate the status of Western Baptist College in Mangum, Oklahoma. It was determined that Western Baptist College was unable to function as an institute of higher education and should be dissolved with its outstanding debts paid by the BGCO and its library transferred to Oklahoma Baptist University. Reverend Burton also delivered a special message at the Annual Meeting on "The Method of Soul Winning." The minutes of the annual meeting note, "The message held the attention and interest of the great Convention whose sole existence is for the purpose of soul winning."[14]

In addition, at the 1916 Annual Meeting of the BGCO, Reverend Burton was placed on two special committees. The first was the Apportionment Committee to see how funds should be raised and allocated. The second was a special committee appointed by J. C. Stalcup, president of the Baptist General Convention of Oklahoma, to bring the question of providing a fund for aged ministers, their widows, missionaries, and others before the next meeting of the Southern Baptist Convention, which was to be in New Orleans.[15] (This effort eventually led to the formation of the Southern Baptist Annuity Board, known by the name GuideStone today.)

In 1917, the BGCO annual meeting was held in McAlester, and Rev. H. H. Burton again played a prominent role. He continued his service on the Apportionment Committee and as a BGCO director but was added as a trustee to Southwestern Baptist Theological Seminary as the Oklahoma State Home Mission Board representative. He also addressed the conference on the subject "Walking with God."[16]

At the 1919 BGCO Annual Meeting, he continued his service on the Apportionment Committee and as a BGCO director and also delivered a special message to the messengers and served on the Resolutions Committee.[17]

Between 1919 and 1922, Rev. H. H. Burton served two pastorates in Arkansas. The first was in Fayetteville, Arkansas. While there, he had Rev. A. N. Hall, a pastor from Tulsa, preach a revival for his church in Fayetteville in early May 1920. Reverend Hall reported to *The Baptist Messenger* that Rev. H. H. Burton was well known and respected in Fayetteville. Reverend Hall stated, "Brother Burton seems to have a grip on things in that community. The circuit judge called him by long distance telephone and asked him to open circuit court with prayer." Brother Hall was later asked to speak for half an hour to the circuit court.[18]

Although successful in Arkansas, Rev. H. H. Burton returned to Oklahoma in 1922 to again become pastor of First Baptist Church, Altus. During his four-year absence, First Baptist Church, Altus, underwent a building program and erected a new facility. However, the church was mired in a thirty-thousand-dollar debt that Reverend

Burton vowed to pay off.[19] He also quickly reengaged with state Baptist life. At the 1923 BGCO Annual Meeting in Ada, Reverend Burton was again appointed to the BGCO board of directors, the Oklahoma State Home Mission Board, and the Committee on Committees. He also delivered one of the morning devotionals at the annual meeting.[20]

The month of March 1924 had five Sundays. A Baptist tradition of the time was to have an associational meeting on that fifth Sunday to discuss Sunday School, Baptist Youth Program Union, Women's, and Laymen's Work. Attendance at these meetings was strongly encouraged, and a significant number of people attended the fifth Sunday events. The attendance figures were often very impressive, given the poor roads and shortage of motor vehicles at the time. At the March 30, 1924, Jackson–Greer Baptist Association Fifth Sunday Meeting, there were 507 people present. Every pastor in Jackson County, except Bro. H. H. Burton, was present. Brother Barton was recovering from an operation for appendicitis and could not attend.[21]

At the 1925 BGCO Annual Meeting, Rev. H. H. Burton continued to be active in Oklahoma Baptist life and also assumed a new and significant role. Depressed farm prices in the mid-1920s resulted in depressed giving to local churches and hence depressed giving to the Baptist General Convention of Oklahoma. The minutes of the 1925 Annual Meeting held in Chickasha contained the following statement about the financial straits of the BGCO:

> The financial embarrassment of the Board of Directors has greatly hindered the work of our Denomination for the past year. It has been a serious problem facing every meeting of the Board, has consumed a large portion of the State Secretary's time, and greatly hindered him in the work he is anxious to do. It has forced retrenchment to a serious and alarming degree. This embarrassment comes at a time when we are presented with the greatest opportunity in all the history of our beloved denomination. Every department of the work shows remarkable results, and the fields

were never more inviting. The Efficiency Committee
was appointed by the State Board for the purpose of
making a survey of our conditions, financial and oth-
erwise, to find some method of relieving our financial
embarrassment, and make recommendations to this
Convention on the policies, organization, and methods for the work of the denomination during the year.

One of the key members of the Efficiency Committee was Rev.
H. H. Burton of Altus. Reverend Burton took his work on the committee and for the convention so seriously that he made a personal
loan to the BGCO for $1,000 at 7 percent annual interest. In the
1920s, $1,000 represented the equivalent of a working man's salary
for one year. At the 1925 Annual Meeting, he also led the devotional
message for one of the morning sessions.[22]

In the 1926 and 1927 BGCO Annual Meetings, Rev.
Burton took a very active role in the Oklahoma Baptist University
Endowment Committee.[23, 24] In 1926 and 1927, Rev. H. H. Burton's
status with the state and within Jackson County was sufficiently
high that he was selected to be the moderator of the Jackson County
Baptist Association Annual Meeting.[25, 26]

As part of his role as an Oklahoma Baptist state leader, Rev. H.
H. Burton led revivals in and out of state. In September 1915, Rev.
Burton led a revival at Eldorado Baptist Church, where eighteen peo-
ple accepted Christ as their Lord and Savior.[27] In May of 1916, Rev.
H. H. Burton assisted Pastor Sebe J. Thomas in a revival meeting at
New Castle, Texas. Seven people were received for baptism.[28]

In the September 14, 1927, issue of *The Baptist Messenger*,
Pastor A. F. Whitlock of Manitou, Oklahoma, reported on an August
30, 1927, revival led by H. H. Burton of Altus with Bro. Earl Stark of
Anthony, Kansas, in charge of music. Pastor Whitlock stated,

Our hearts were stirred many times by the wonderful
messages of Brother Burton. Brother Stark is an able
and consecrated leader of song. Our work was very
ably wrought by these good brethren. We had nine

additions both [by] statement and baptizing. Our
people were greatly inspired.[29]

Rev. Burton continued to be very active in supporting state
Baptist endeavors and in 1928 made a second personal loan to the
BGCO for $1,000 at 7 percent annual interest, making a total loaned
by him to the convention of $2,000.[30] On September 18, 1928, Rev.
H. H. Burton from First Baptist Church, Altus, served as moderator for the Jackson–Greer Baptist Association Annual Meeting.[31] In
1929, Rev. H. H. Burton left First Baptist Church, Altus, and was
listed as an out-of-state visitor to the BGCO Annual Meeting that
was held in Shawnee. Before he left First Baptist Church, Altus, he
succeeded in retiring the $30,000 church building debt.[32] He was
also listed in the minutes of the annual meeting as having made a
third personal loan to the BGCO for $1,000 at 7 percent annual
interest, making a total loaned by him to the convention of $3,000.[33]

Rev. H. H. Burton, the Immanuel Years

In November 1929, with the new Immanuel Baptist Church building
just completed in September, Rev. Dan S. Brinkley abruptly resigned
for a pastorate in Rogers, Arkansas. The church voted that the
Deacons should constitute the Pulpit Committee, and the search was
begun for a new pastor. Contact was made with Rev. H. H. Burton,
formerly of First Baptist Church, Altus.
He quickly accepted the empty pulpit
at a salary of three hundred dollars per
month plus the use of the parsonage.
Pastor Burton was fifty-eight years old
when he arrived in Shawnee in early
January 1930.

One of his first acts was to preside
over the Wednesday, January 8, 1930,
business meeting. At that meeting,
Otto Williams was hired as a janitor at
forty dollars per month. Otto Williams
also served as the Sunday School direc-

Figure 3.1. Rev. H. H.
Burton, the Immanuel years

tor. Despite the weakening finances of the church, the Immanuel Baptist Church members voted in March 1930 to take over a mission Sunday School effort on South Harrison Street that had been started by the Oklahoma Baptist University extension band.

Other church work proceeded as normal. The old parsonage near the Draper Street facility was sold to the city. A special Training Union workshop was set up for summer 1930 and a revival for the fall. In the November 2, 1930, business meeting, the Finance Committee proposed a special program to increase church revenues, whereby 50 members would pledge an additional $1.50 per week, 50 members would pledge an additional $1.00 per week, and 50 members would pledge an additional $0.50 per week for a period of 16 weeks.[34]

While at Immanuel Baptist Church, Rev. H. H. Burton continued to be active in the Baptist General Convention of Oklahoma. He and Mrs. Burton attended the 1930 Annual Meeting as a messenger from Immanuel Baptist Church, and because of his prior interest in Oklahoma Baptist University and his residence in Shawnee, he was appointed to the Christian Education Committee. Reverend Burton also delivered the devotional message on the first evening of the annual meeting. Despite its financial woes, Immanuel Baptist Church provided $224.32 for the BGCO annual fund, which was typical of Oklahoma churches for 1930.

It is worth noting that First Baptist Church, Shawnee, provided the second largest contribution in 1930 with an offering of $12,880.77. The largest contribution in the state came from First Baptist Church, Oklahoma City, with an offering of $17,217.31.[35] Also, in 1930, Rev. H. H. Burton continued his practice of preaching revivals. He led a very successful revival in Cordell, Oklahoma, in May of 1930. The pastor of the church, Pastor D. C. Stringer, stated,

> We have just closed a very fruitful revival with Brother H. H. Burton of Shawnee and Brother C. M. Curb of Enid assisting us. Brother Burton preached the first week and [until] Thursday of the second week, and he certainly did some wonderful preaching. Brother Curb led in personal work and did the preaching after Bro. Burton had to return to his own field [at

Immanuel Baptist Church in Shawnee]. The revival
spirit continued to the last service. There were about
40 professions of faith and some 35 additions to the
church. Twenty have been baptized to date with others [having been] approved [for baptism]. This was
one of the most spiritual revivals it has been my privilege to work in for a great while.[36]

At the 1931 Annual Meeting, Reverend Burton continued his
practice of making personal loans to the BGCO. He was sympathetic
to the deep financial problems of Oklahomans and renewed his 3
$1,000 loans, rather than asking the convention to redeem them.[37]
At the 1932 Annual Meeting, Reverend Burton served on the
Credentials Committee and the Religious Literature Committee.[38]
In 1933, he served on the Obituaries Committee. Despite the dif-
ficult financial situation that Immanuel Baptist Church was in, the
Cooperative Program received $337.33 from the church.[39]

In parallel to Rev. H. H. Burton's continued service to Immanuel
Baptist Church and the Baptist General Convention of Oklahoma,
the national, state, and local economies continued to suffer. The economic downturn of the general economy was especially hard felt by
Immanuel Baptist Church with a new building and a large debt. At
the January 7, 1931, business meeting, Pastor Burton asked that his
salary be cut by twenty-five dollars per month to help with the financial problem. Eventually, his salary was reduced from three hundred
per month to two hundred per month.

In the February 4, 1931, business meeting, the church voted to
form a committee to revise the roll. Also in that February 4, 1931,
business meeting, Robert Patterson proposed that coupon books be
sold to help raise funds for the church. A committee was formed to
pursue this idea. Finances continued to be a matter of concern. In the
May 8, 1931, business meeting, the church voted that the endors-
ers of the fifty-thousand-dollar note be responsible for the note payments, interest payments, and insurance premiums on that note. The
church also voted that moneys received by the church be prorated to
the creditors as funds came in.

At the June 10, 1931, business meeting, the continuing financial problems prompted Rev. H. H. Burton to tender his resignation. The church voted not to accept his resignation. At the August 5, 1931, business meeting, the church voted that the treasurer pay no more bills unless he had written orders from the church clerk. In summer 1932, Immanuel Baptist Church submitted paperwork to the state of Oklahoma to be incorporated formally as an entity within the state.

As finances of the church continued to weaken, Rev. H. H. Burton voluntarily had his salary cut from $200 per month to $150 per month at the August 10, 1932, business meeting. Several months later at its May 31, 1933, business meeting, the church instructed the finance committee to offer 25 percent on the dollar to all creditors. Feeling his salary was a burden, Brother Burton tendered his resignation on August 9, 1933. His resignation was rejected by the church, however. He again tried to resign on August 23, 1933, and his resignation was again rejected.

The last business meeting over which Rev. Burton presided was on February 14, 1934. Lay leader J. F. Shirey presided over the next several business meetings. Finally, in the May 9, 1934, business meeting, the church met to call Rev. E. W. Westmoreland of Heavener as pastor. The pulpit committee proposed a salary of two hundred dollars per month plus the use of the parsonage. Reverend Westmoreland declined the church's offer, and Rev. Thomas Doss was called as the new pastor of Immanuel Baptist Church on July 11, 1934. The first business meeting over which Rev. Doss presided was the September 8, 1934, business meeting.[40]

Rev. H. H. Burton, the Years after Immanuel

Rev. H. H. Burton remained in the Shawnee area from August 1934 through June 1937. He served as pastor of Calvary Baptist Church for part of that time.[41] Reverend Burton continued to attend BGCO annual meetings but did not take as active a role as he had in the past. In particular, he did not attend the 1935 Annual Meeting but did attend the 1936 Annual Meeting.[42, 43] He was, however, active in state Baptist life in other ways.

In July 1935, he led revivals at First Baptist Church, Tecumseh, with Rev. M. C. Steward[44] and at First Baptist Church, Henryetta, with Rev. Kenneth Marshall.[45] Rev. H. H. Burton had always had a deep interest in the functioning of the Sunday School system and attended the March 1935 Sunday School Convention in Tulsa as an unaffiliated pastor from Shawnee. He presented one of the morning devotional messages.[46] In addition to these endeavors, Rev. H. H. Burton attended the Rural Pastors' Conference held at Fairview Baptist Church, located just east of Shawnee, in early June 1937. The conference leader was Dr. J. W. Jent of Oklahoma Baptist University.

Many prominent Baptist leaders were in attendance, including Dr. Andrew Potter, president and corresponding secretary of the Baptist General Convention of Oklahoma; Pastor S. M. Scantlan of Fairview Baptist Church; former Immanuel pastor and Pottawatomie Baptist Association director of missions O. G. Matthews; and Oklahoma Baptist University president John Wesley Raley. At the conference, attendees were encouraged to enlist as rural missionaries or as pastors available to serve a small, rural church. Rev. H. H. Burton was one of the attendees who volunteered to serve the BGCO in such a manner.[47]

In the late summer of 1937, Rev. H. H. Burton took the pulpit of Martha Baptist Church in Martha, Oklahoma, and attended the annual meeting in November as a messenger from Martha Baptist Church along with his wife.[48] Martha is a small farming community in southwestern Oklahoma, about nine miles northwest of Altus. In 1937, its population was about three hundred people.[49]

The 1938 BGCO Annual Meeting was held in Shawnee, and Rev. and Mrs. Burton attended as messengers from Martha Baptist Church. However, neither took an active role.[50] At the 1939 BGCO Annual Meeting, an unusual thing happened. Rev. H. H. Burton was on program to preach at the opening morning session but deferred to Oklahoma Senator Josh Lee who addressed the convention on the subject of "Christianity and Churches in Civilization." Reverend Burton did lead in the closing prayer.[51] He also did a devotional message entitled "Going through the Gates" from Isaiah 62:10 for the afternoon session.[52]

In 1941, Rev. H. H. Burton retired from Martha Baptist Church at the age of seventy and moved to Oklahoma City.[53] In 1945, First Baptist Church, Tahlequah, granted their current pastor, Rev. James Hogg, a year's leave of absence to finish his college degree. According to the First Baptist Church, Tahlequah, website,

> During this intermission, the pulpit was being ably filled by Reverend H. H. Burton of Oklahoma City. Reverend Burton formerly preached at Altus, Shawnee, and other prominent churches in the state. He was described as a consecrated servant of the Lord and as being well liked by the congregation.[54]

In 1945, although 74 years old, Reverend Burton remained a pastor at heart when he took the pulpit of West Tenth Street Baptist Church, Oklahoma City.[55] In 1952, at the age of 81, Rev. H. H. Burton was still going strong. He was the founding pastor of a new church in Tulsa called Memorial Baptist Church. The church had approximately 125 charter members.[56]

Mrs. H. H. Burton died on November 6, 1947, of a heart attack while attending the Baptist General Convention of Oklahoma Annual Meeting. The 1947 BGCO Annual Meeting was held in Tulsa, Oklahoma, where the Burtons lived.[57] Pastor Henry Hale Burton died on August 12, 1959, in Houston, Texas, at the age of eighty-eight. Funeral services were held at First Baptist Church, Tulsa, on August 14, 1959. Reverend Burton was survived by a daughter, Mrs. Mary Haden of Houston, three sons—Harold of Denver City, Texas, Leroy of Muskogee, and Paul of Tulsa—and ten grandchildren. His survivors also included a nephew, Joe Burton, who was editor of both *The Baptist Messenger* of Oklahoma and the national *Home Life* magazine.[58]

CHAPTER 4

A Light Shines through the Depths of the Depression

Rev. Thomas J. Doss, July 1934–July 1937

Introduction

Rev. Thomas Jefferson Doss was the seventh pastor of Immanuel Baptist Church. He came to Immanuel when the Great Depression in the United States in general and Oklahoma in particular was at its greatest depths. Unemployment was high, jobs were scarce, and income was low. Many families were just barely able to make ends meet. Oklahoma was suffering through a drought known as the Dust Bowl, and many Oklahoma families had fled the state.[1]

Immanuel Baptist Church faced some difficult times also. Under Rev. Dan Brinkley, a costly new building was constructed at a cost of one hundred thousand dollars. However, a month after the new facility opened, the stock market collapsed in a selling frenzy known as Black Friday. Reverend Brinkley resigned one month later. Rev. H. H. Burton, a very capable and active pastor, accepted the call to the pulpit of Immanuel Baptist Church two months later and guided Immanuel Baptist Church for four difficult years. However, feeling his salary was a burden, Rev. Burton resigned in August 1933. The church asked him to stay until January 1934 when Rev. Thomas J. Doss came as the new leader of Immanuel Baptist Church.

Reverend Doss worked with the banks to develop a plan to refinance the debt. Under his leadership, things began to look brighter. Some members of Immanuel Baptist Church at the time described Reverend Doss as "a financial wizard." Payments on the great debt were reduced, and much-needed repairs on the church buildings were made.[2] All of this helped the church weather the worst days of the Depression. Because of the wonderful faith and determination of Reverend Doss and his leadership, the church was inspired to persevere and to pay its debts as they came due.[3]

The world scene during the years that Reverend Doss served Immanuel was a scene of severe economic depression and the prelude to war. In 1934, in Germany, Adolf Hitler assumed the title of *Führer* (Leader) and united the offices of chancellor and president. In October, Chinese communist leader Mao Zedong began his Long March with one hundred thousand soldiers.[4] In 1935, the German government under Adolf Hitler repudiated the Versailles Treaty and began the militarization of Germany. Germany also enacted the Nuremberg Laws against Jews to prevent "racial pollution." Also in 1935, Benito Mussolini of Italy invaded Ethiopia.[5]

World tensions increased in 1936 when the Rome-Berlin Axis was proclaimed. Japan would join the Axis in 1940. Also in 1936, the Spanish Civil War began. Hundreds of Americans joined the Lincoln Brigades to fight with the loyalists against Francisco Franco's fascist forces. Franco was supported by Germany and Italy. The loyalists were also supported by Russia. Franco defeated the loyalist forces by 1939 when Madrid fell.

In Asia, war broke out between China and Japan. That conflict continued through World War II.[6] In 1937, tensions between Japan and the United States escalated greatly when the Japanese sunk the American gunboat USS *Panay* on the Yangtze River.[7]

The national scene during the years that Reverend Doss served Immanuel paralleled the world scene and concentrated on federal actions to expand the scope of government in hopes to improve the economy. In 1934, the Securities Exchange Act was passed, establishing the Securities and Exchange Commission. In Kansas, Texas, Colorado, and Oklahoma, massive dust storms ruined about a hundred million acres and damaged another two hundred million acres of cropland, creating what was known as the Dust Bowl.[8]

In 1935, President Franklin Roosevelt opened the second phase of the New Deal. The program established the Social Security System and established programs for better housing, equitable taxation, and farm assistance.[9] In 1936, Franklin Roosevelt was reelected in a landslide.[10] In May 1937, the German dirigible *Hindenburg* exploded at Lakehurst, New Jersey. Thirty-six people were killed. Also in 1937, Amelia Earhart and copilot Fred Noonan vanished over the Pacific Ocean on their round-the-world flight.[11]

Rev. Thomas J. Doss, the Years before Immanuel

Thomas Jefferson Doss was born on February 10, 1888, in Decatur, Texas.[12] His wife Lula Alice Doss was born on January 25, 1892, in South Carolina. Thomas and Lula had two children, a son named Doyle and a daughter named Tammy Lou. Reverend Doss served as a pastor for several years prior to coming to Immanuel Baptist Church. The first time that Rev. Thomas J. Doss appears in the minutes of the annual meeting of the Baptist General Convention of Oklahoma or in *The Baptist Messenger* is in 1923 when, as a thirty-five-year-old pastor, he attended the BGCO annual meeting as a Messenger from First Baptist Church, Waurika.

He was recognized as a messenger but not as a pastor. However, in the 1924 BGCO Annual Meeting, he was recognized as a new pastor for the convention from Waurika.[13] Waurika is the county seat of Jefferson County in far southern Oklahoma, along the Red River. Its current population is just under two thousand, but its population in the 1920s when Rev. Doss served there was just over three thousand.

Reverend Doss was evidently an active and progressive pastor while at First Baptist Church, Waurika. The October 31, 1923, issue of *The Baptist Messenger* stated,

> Bro. Thos. J. Doss, the pastor of the Waurika Baptist Church, writes in that he is beginning a class in *The New Convention Normal Manual*. This is the first time in many months that any Knowledge Training Work

has been attempted in the Waurika church, and we
are delighted that this pastor is leading his people in
this forward movement for the betterment of workers in Christian service. There are literally hundreds
of Baptist churches in Oklahoma whose people need
similar training. If your church is one of them, won't
you be responsible for starting this work in your own
local church? Let's march forward! Let's sound no
Sunday School retreats! Let's train for greater service![14]

In the last decade of the nineteenth century, the leadership of
the Southern Baptist Convention became concerned that the members of Southern Baptist churches did not know and were not learning the doctrines that made Southern Baptists uniquely Southern
Baptists. In 1891, the Sunday School Board commissioned John
Broadus to produce a catechism that could be used to teach sound
doctrine to children. That same board published *The New Convention
Normal Manual* in 1913 as an instruction manual in Baptist doctrine
for Sunday School teachers.[15] Pastor Doss and the Waurika Baptist
Church was one of the first rural Oklahoma Baptist Churches to use
The New Convention Normal Manual and its associated Knowledge
Training program. This type of training lives on today in Immanuel
Baptist Church through the Discipleship Training classes of Rev.
Scott Schooler.

While at Waurika Baptist Church, Reverend Doss was active
in revivals. The December 5, 1923, issue of *The Baptist Messenger*
stated,

> Pastor Thomas J. Doss, Waurika, writes that their
> revival is growing in interest and power. Evangelists
> Winsett and Hiett are leading. Miss Danny Gatlin,
> sister of Brother Gatlin of the Central Baptist Church,
> Oklahoma City, is playing [the piano] for them.[16]

Two weeks later, *The Baptist Messenger* reported,

Pastor Thomas J. Doss, Waurika, reports a three weeks' [revival] meeting in which he was aided by Evangelists Winsett and Hiett. So far, thirty have been received for baptism and seventeen additions by letter. [Pastor Doss reports], "We feel that a constructive work has been done."[17]

Rev. Thomas Doss continued to grow in his status within the local Baptist association. In March 1925, the Baptist General Convention of Oklahoma had a fund drive for the Oklahoma Baptist Children's Home in Oklahoma City and other state Baptist ministries. Reverend Doss enthusiastically supported that fund drive and raised over $320 in cash and $180 in pledges for the children's home from Waurika Baptist Church. This was the largest amount raised by any church in the Jefferson Baptist Association and one of the largest raised at that point in the state.[18]

That following December, Reverend Doss was part of a group of distinguished Oklahoma Baptists that signed a pledge to raise three hundred thousand dollars for the Oklahoma Baptist University, Baptist hospitals, foreign missions, the old ministers' relief fund, and state missions. The group also pledged to raise two hundred thousand dollars for Baptist work in Oklahoma and across the South.[19] Reverend Doss's wife, Lula, was also active in Oklahoma Baptist life and was evidently a very capable woman. The May 3, 1925, issue of *The Baptist Messenger* has a summary of a major Sunday School training activity that took place in several churches in Oklahoma City. Lula Doss was listed as one of the faculty members of the training event that took place at Exchange Avenue Baptist Church under the leadership of L. W. Wiley of Du Quoin, Illinois.

Brother Wiley was the Illinois State Sunday School and Baptist Young People's Union secretary.[20] In August 1925, Reverend Doss held sufficient status within the Jefferson Baptist Association to be selected as the moderator for their Annual Meeting.[21] However, in June 1926, after three years of serving as pastor at Waurika Baptist Church, Reverend Doss resigned to take a pastorate at Bowie, Texas. He said the three years at Waurika were the happiest years of his ministry. He described the people of Waurika Baptist Church as being intelligent lovers of God, the Bible, and Baptist work. In following the call to preach at Bowie Baptist Church, he wished for the people of Waurika Baptist Church the highest possible well-being.[22]

Rev. Thomas J. Doss, the Immanuel Years

On Wednesday, July 11, 1934, after several months without a pastor and having been turned down by Rev. E. W. Westmoreland of Heavener, the members of Immanuel Baptist met in a business meeting to hear the Pulpit Committee's report on Rev. Thomas J. Doss of Bowie, Texas. Since there was no pastor for Immanuel Baptist Church at the time, J. F. Shirey, a lay leader within the church, moderated the meeting. E. G. Boatman served as the clerk for the meeting. The Pulpit Committee gave a favorable report on Reverend Doss.

Church members Mr. and Mrs. Winsett had a letter from Pastor Doss to them. The church voted that the letter be read. Mrs. C. C. Peebles read the letter, and a vote was taken on whether or not to call Pastor Doss. The vote was affirmative to call him, and a second vote was taken to make the call unanimous. In a subsequent business meeting on July 18, 1934, the church voted to make repairs to the parsonage and to pay Brother Smedley five dollars per Sunday to preach until Pastor Doss was in place.

On August 1, 1934, the church voted to pay Reverend Doss a monthly salary of two hundred dollars plus the use of the parsonage. The first business meeting over which Reverend Doss presided was the September 5, 1934, business meeting. At that meeting, the church voted to dedicate that Sunday afternoon, September 16, 1934, to taking a religious census of the area surrounding Immanuel Baptist Church. The church also voted to select Reverend Thomas and Mrs. Lula Doss as the leaders of a fifteen-member team to be messengers for the Pottawatomie-Lincoln Baptist Association Annual Meeting to be held at Calvary Baptist Church in Shawnee.[23]

Rev. Thomas J. Doss came to Immanuel Baptist Church with a strong record from his service at Waurika Baptist Church and at Bowie Baptist Church. He was forty-six years old at the time. He served as a capable pastor and was well received within Immanuel Baptist Church, the Pottawatomie-Lincoln Baptist Association, and Oklahoma Baptist life. A measure of his acceptance within the local Baptist community can be illustrated by the fact that, after just one year in the pulpit at Immanuel, he was selected to serve as the moderator for the next three Pottawatomie-Lincoln Baptist Association annual meetings held in 1935, 1936, and 1937.[24]

While pastor of Immanuel Baptist Church, Rev. Thomas Doss served as an active member of the Baptist General Convention of Oklahoma. At the November 13–15, 1935, annual meeting held in Enid, Oklahoma, Rev. and Mrs. Doss attended as messengers from Immanuel Baptist Church. Immanuel Baptist Church continued to experience difficult financial times but was able to contribute $526.83 to the Cooperative Program in 1935, an increase of roughly $200 from the year before.[25]

Both Rev. and Mrs. Doss attended the 1936 BGCO Annual Meeting as messengers. In addition, Reverend Doss delivered the closing prayer at the Wednesday afternoon session. He was selected for the Christian Education Committee, and his wife was selected for the Woman's Missionary Union Recommendation Committee. In 1936,

Figure 4.1. Rev. Thomas J. Doss, the Immanuel years

Immanuel Baptist Church contribution of $560.78 to the Cooperative Program was essentially unchanged from the previous year.[26]

Rev. Thomas and Mrs. Doss attended the 1937 BGCO Annual Meeting. Lula Doss delivered reports from the Recommendations Committee and the Apportionments Committee, both of which she served as chair. Reverend Doss was scheduled to present a message at the Tuesday, November 16, 1937, session, but he did not attend that session since he had resigned from Immanuel Baptist Church and had taken a church in Terrell, Texas. T. B. Lackey, Baptist General

Convention of Oklahoma General missionary, spoke on "State Missions" in the absence of Rev. Doss.[27]

While pastor at Immanuel, Reverend Doss was active in supporting the ministry of and the students of Oklahoma Baptist University. The February 27, 1936, issue of *The Baptist Messenger* reported that the week of February 18–22, 1926, was designated as special evangelistic week for the university. An evangelical discussion group met each afternoon in the Baptist Student Union room on campus.

Floyd North, the third vice president of the Baptist Student Union, led a discussion group of about twenty students. His program was entitled "How to Become Fishers of Men" and attempted to make a practical application of the teaching on the OBU campus. In preparation for this week's work, a special class on "How to Bring Men to Christ" was taught by Reverend Doss, pastor of Immanuel Baptist Church.[28]

The greatest accomplishment by Rev. Thomas J. Doss during his service at Immanuel Baptist Church was to address the crushing debt of the newly constructed building. The facility on Main Street cost one hundred thousand dollars to build. Much of the building had been paid for, but a fifty-thousand-dollar note remained in place. Reverend Doss worked with the banks to develop a plan to refinance the debt. Loan payments were reduced in size, and money was made available to complete needed repairs on the church buildings. Under Reverend Doss's leadership, the church survived the worst years of the Great Depression.[29] In July 1937, Rev. Thomas Doss resigned to take a church in Terrell, Texas.

Rev. Thomas J. Doss, the Years after Immanuel

After leaving Immanuel Baptist Church, Rev. Thomas Doss continued as a pastor. His first post-Immanuel pastorate was at Terrell, Texas, just east of Dallas. While there and for the next three decades, he conducted revivals in Oklahoma and Texas. In the May 18, 1939, issue of *The Baptist Messenger*, editor Dr. E. C. Routh wrote,

> Rev. Thos. J. Doss, Terrell, Texas, closed a [revival] meeting recently with Pastor R. E. Bell at the First Baptist Church, Decatur, Texas. There were 23 additions to the church. Brother Doss closed a meeting April 9 with his own church, during which there were 38 conversions and additions.[30]

In the September 21, 1939, issue of *The Baptist Messenger*, Pastor Lee Aufill of Geary, Oklahoma, reported this:

> A glorious revival came to a close in our church on September 10. Reverend T. J. Doss, First Baptist Church, Terrell, Texas, preached, and Rev. S. B. Nichols, First Baptist Church, Hennessey, Oklahoma, had charge of the music. These men were a blessing to our people. The meeting encountered many hardships. Brother Doss stayed in the middle of the road, preached the gospel with power, and the Lord blessed [the revival] in a pronounced way. Ten were received for baptism, eight [were received] by letter, [and] two [were received] by statement [for a total of 20 additions to the church], and others were saved whom we think will come later.[31]

The November 29, 1956, issue of *The Baptist Messenger* noted that "Noble Avenue Church, Guthrie, had 10 additions, eight by baptism, in a one-week meeting led by Evang. Thomas J. Doss, Fort Worth, Texas. There was one decision for special service."[32] The September 15, 1960, issue of *The Baptist Messenger* noted that First Baptist Church, Thackerville, held a revival led by Evang. Thomas Doss of Fort Worth, Texas. There were seven additions by baptism and two by letter.[33] In his January 12, 1961, "As I See It" column in *The Baptist Messenger*, executive secretary-treasurer of the Baptist General Convention of Oklahoma, T. Bert Lackey, wrote that Pastor Tom Doss had returned to First Baptist Church, Waurika, on New Year's Day, Sunday, January 1, 1961. He participated in the dedication of a completed church plant by First Baptist Church, Waurika.[34]

As with his years at Immanuel Baptist Church, Reverend Doss was well respected everywhere he served. The November 13, 1975, issue of *The Baptist Messenger* reported that Meadowbrook Church in Fort Worth would be honoring Rev. Thomas J. Doss and his wife Lula on November 16, 1975. The article noted that Reverend Doss was a former pastor of Immanuel Baptist Church in Shawnee and served there from 1935 to 1937. Reverend and Mrs. Doss had been members of Meadowbrook Church since 1952. He served as interim pastor there in 1954, 1956, and 1962. He also served as associate pastor in charge of outreach. Lula Doss had been a Sunday School teacher, Woman's Missionary Union leader, and part of the church visitation team during the same years.[35]

Rev. Thomas Doss died in Fort Worth, Texas, on July 18, 1976, at the age of eighty-eight. He is buried in Mount Olivet Cemetery in Fort Worth.[36] His wife, Lula, died in Fort Worth, Texas, on July 16, 1979, at the age of eighty-six. She is buried beside her husband in Mount Olivet Cemetery in Fort Worth.[37]

CHAPTER 5

Out of the Depression and through the War

Dr. H. Tom Wiles, January 1938 to August 1945

Introduction

Dr. H. Thomas Wiles was the seventh pastor of Immanuel Baptist Church. He served during the final years of the Great Depression and throughout World War II. Dr. Tom Wiles was a very accomplished pastor before coming to Immanuel Baptist. His service at Immanuel was superb. His pastoral career after leaving Immanuel was one great distinction.[1]

Dr. Wiles came in January 1938 and set out at once to enlarge the programs of Immanuel Baptist Church and to improve the facility. He led the church from victory to victory in both material and spiritual areas. Under his leadership and with personal sacrifices in both funds and labor by the congregation, the church remodeled the parsonage, completed overdue projects on the church facility, and furnished and decorated portions of the building as part of the completion of those projects.

Under his leadership, temporary education buildings were erected for junior and senior Sunday School classes. In addition, new heating and cooling systems were installed, and a general upgrading of the appearance of the property occurred. While these improvements were being made, Dr. Wiles's heart was set on liquidating the burdensome debt on the church. The church steadily made payments on the debt and a note-burning ceremony was held on March 19, 1944.[2]

The world scene during the years that Reverend Wiles served Immanuel was a scene of great turbulence. The much of the world was still in the grips of the Great Depression. Adolf Hitler, Benito Mussolini, and Showa Hirohito plunged the world into the greatest carnage that mankind had ever seen.

World War II began when Germany and Russia jointly invaded Poland on September 1, 1939. Germany quickly conquered half of Poland, Belgium, the Netherlands, Denmark, France, Norway, the Balkans, Greece, and North Africa. Russia conquered the other half of Poland and parts of Finland, but Germany soon invaded and conquered a large portion of Russia. In the Orient, Japan had maintained a brutal and barbaric war against China. On December 7, 1941, Japan attacked the United States Naval Forces at Pearl Harbor, Hawaii, destroying much of the American Pacific Fleet. Before long, Japan had conquered most of the European and American possessions in the Pacific. After several years of difficult and costly warfare, the Allied Powers of the United States, England, France, and the Union of Soviet Socialist Republics defeated the Axis Powers of Germany, Italy, and Japan.[3]

The national scene during the years that Reverend Wiles served Immanuel paralleled the world scene. When Reverend Wiles assumed the Immanuel pulpit, the United States was still within the financial crisis known as the Great Depression. Industrial production was still down, and farm prices were brutally low.

As World War II progressed in Europe and Asia, President Roosevelt maintained a policy of neutrality but one of friendship and support for the Allied powers. That neutrality ended swiftly on December 7, 1941, with the Japanese attack on Pearl Harbor. Shortly thereafter, Japanese forces invaded the Philippines and quickly defeated American and Philippine forces. The last of the American and Philippine forces surrendered on the island of Corregidor.

The captives were subjected to a brutal evacuation known as the Bataan Death March in which hundreds of American and thousands of Philippine soldiers died. With the onset of war, millions of American men and women joined the armed forces, rationing of commodities went into effect, and millions of women joined the workforce. America's military and industrial power soon produced victory in Europe and Asia.[4]

Dr. H. Tom Wiles, the Years before Immanuel

Howell Tom Wiles was born in the foothills of southwestern Missouri in 1904 and was reared by a farm family in the Ozarks. Dr. Wiles left Missouri when he was 16 and moved with his family to Ralston, Oklahoma, in a covered wagon.[5] Ralston is a small town on the Arkansas River in Pawnee County in northeastern Oklahoma. Ralston currently has about 300 people living there. Its population peaked at 725 people in 1923, a few years after the Wiles family moved there.[6]

Figure 5.1. Tom Wiles, the OBU days

"My earliest memories of childhood center around the preacher," Dr. Wiles recalled. "In those days, the preacher came a-visiting on Saturday night, and everyone went to church on Sunday morning.

The preacher would accept an invitation for Sunday dinner, and all the children wished the preacher could eat at their houses every Sunday. When the preacher came, it really was a feed." Dr. Wiles left home when he was seventeen in 1921. He had just graduated from high school and went off "to make my fortune."

He went north to Kansas, and he served as a sample boy for the National Pipe Company during the day and attended school at night.

Figure 5.2. Hattie Fae Wiles, the OBU days

The oil company job was the only nonpulpit job Tom Wiles had. He served as a minister all of the rest of his adult life.

H. Tom Wiles accepted Christ as his Lord and Savior as a child in Missouri. He was ordained to preach at First Baptist Church, Blackwell, on September 14, 1921, the second Wednesday night in September that year. He was seventeen years old at the time.

Reverend and Mrs. Wiles (Hattie Fae) were married September 12, 1923, the second Wednesday in September that year.[7] Hattie Fae and Tom were both students at Oklahoma Baptist University at the time.[8] As a coincidence, his son John was ordained to the ministry on September 12, 1944, the second Wednesday in September that year.[9] Rev. Tom Wiles's first full-time pastorate after he completed college at Oklahoma Baptist University was at Kingfisher, Oklahoma, where he served five years. He also served Oklahoma Baptist churches in Prague, Carney, Piedmont, Hinton, and Caddo during his early ministry.[10]

In 1921, Reverend Wiles was a full-time student at Oklahoma Baptist University and a part-time pastor at Prague. Under his guidance, First Baptist Church, Prague, had a very successful revival led by Rev. O. G. Matthews of Chandler.[11] Two years later, Reverend Matthews would be called as the pastor of Draper Street Baptist Church. While at First Baptist Church, Carney, Reverend Wiles, who was still a student at Oklahoma Baptist University at the time, was elected as the treasurer of the Lincoln County Baptist Association at their annual meeting on August 1 and 2, 1923, in Stroud.[12]

In 1932, Rev. Tom and Hattie Fae Wiles moved to Seminole where he became the pastor of the First Baptist Church, Seminole. While he was there, the respect that the Oklahoma Baptist community had for him grew greatly. In the 1932 Baptist General Convention Annual Meeting held in Ponca City, he attended as a messenger from First Baptist Church, Seminole, and was appointed to the BGCO board of directors and served on the Committee on Committees.[13]

In the 1933 Baptist General Convention Annual Meeting held in Tulsa, he again attended as a messenger from First Baptist Church, Seminole, and served once more on the Committee on Committees.

He also successfully nominated John T. Daniel for recording secretary of the convention.[14] While at First Baptist Church, Seminole, his church led all other Oklahoma Baptist churches in baptisms during two of the four years he served there. The Sunday School enrollment for his Seminole church grew from three hundred to one thousand during the four-year period that he was there. Following a short stay at Exchange Avenue Baptist Church, Oklahoma City, and twenty months as an evangelist in Oklahoma, Texas, Arkansas, and Missouri, Dr. Wiles accepted the pastorate at Immanuel Baptist Church in January 1938.[15]

Dr. H. Tom Wiles, the Immanuel Years

Dr. H. Tom Wiles came to Immanuel Baptist Church in January 1938 as the Depression was waning. Immanuel Baptist Church, however, was still experiencing financial stress. The church had significant debts and overall finances were difficult. Pastor Wiles was hired at a salary of two hundred dollars per month plus use of the parsonage. The business minutes include letters to creditors, including the Home Mission Board, asking for a restructuring of their debts or providing payments for their debts. The Home Mission Board granted a one-year moratorium on payments.

However, his hard work and cheerful disposition brought not only stability but also growth. Sunday School attendance grew from 324 in 1937 to 650 in 1939. Training Union attendance grew from 75 in 1937 to 200 in 1939. Membership grew from 700 in 1937 to 1,200 in 1939. In 1939, on his one-year anniversary, Dr. Wiles's salary was increased first to $240 per month and then a few months later to $270 per month. He served Immanuel until the end of World War II in August 1945.[16]

As a new pastor at Immanuel Baptist Church, Dr. Tom Wiles was ably supported by Mr. Gene Spearman as choir director and assistant to the pastor. Brother Spearman was finishing his work at Oklahoma Baptist University at the time. Mrs. Spearman, a graduate of Ouachita Baptist University, was the secretary of Immanuel Church.[17] In 1941, Rev. Donald McCollum was the music minister and assistant pastor. Reverend McCollum was replaced in 1942 by Rev. John Wiles, an Oklahoma Baptist University student and Tom Wiles's son.[18]

Structural problems continued to plague the Immanuel facility, and Reverend Wiles began a remodeling and renovation effort immediately after joining Immanuel Baptist Church. His first challenge was the basement and its water problems. The 1975 Dedication Program for the remodeled facility noted:

> Some of the time, we knew how Noah felt – all that water. We rarely prayed for rain because the basement leaked. After a rain, the Sunday School Superintendent and others would arrive early to sweep out the water. The coming of Bro. Wiles in 1938 remedied that. One member said he could 'charm' money from Scrooge. Charm money from everyone—Baptist or not—he did. The basement was waterproofed, a Sunday School building completed, an organ acquired and other improvements made. The congregation suffered and sorrowed together as we lost friends and family members during World War II.[19]

The waterproofing of the basement was one of Dr. Wiles's first priorities as the new pastor. He accomplished this in the summer of 1938 through a product called Hydrozo. Dr. Wiles was very diligent in his search for the proper waterproofing agent. The minutes contain several letters to the Hydrozo Products Company and to customers of the company seeking endorsements. The Hydrozo product greatly reduced the amount of water leakage into the basement. However, throughout Dr. Wiles's years at Immanuel Baptist Church, water problems in the basement area were a constant worry, and many letters were exchanged with the Hydrozo Products Company seeking additional applications or alternative approaches to the leakage. In addition to waterproofing the basement in 1938, Dr. Wiles oversaw the installation of new pews, a new podium, and an offering table manufactured by the Southwest Church Furniture Manufacturing

Company of Shawnee. Also in 1938, new ceiling fans and ductwork for air-conditioning were installed.[20]

In addition to addressing the water problems of the basement, a considerable amount of Dr. Wiles's time was invested in addressing other financial problems of the church. One problem that consumed a significant amount of his time concerned the heating system. In 1929, nine years before Dr. Wiles joined Immanuel Baptist Church, the E. K. Campbell Heating Company of Kansas City installed a heating system. That system never seemed to work properly, and several letters were exchanged between the company and Reverend Wiles concerning how to resolve the problem.

Several letters from the company requesting that the outstanding balance on the system be paid were received by the church. Also, Dr. Wiles conducted a series of correspondence with the Home Mission Board in Atlanta, Georgia, requesting a deferment of payments on a note held by the Home Mission Board for a period of one year starting at July 1, 1939, while the church did some needed repairs and remodeling to the church structure, the parsonage, and some Sunday School rooms. After several exchanges of letters, the deferment was granted. In the midst of obtaining the deferment, an issue related to the paving of streets, and lots around Immanuel Baptist Church complicated the loan deferment process.

In 1929, when the church was built, the city of Shawnee paved certain streets in the area with asphalt. The city assessed Immanuel Baptist Church for part of the cost of this paving. Immanuel Baptist Church used paving bonds to fulfill their obligation to the city. However, in 1935, the contractor who did the paving sued the city for payment. In March 1935, a mandamus order (Latin for "we order") was issued by the court requiring the city of Shawnee to accept the paving bonds as payment for the taxes.

On September 16, 1936, Dr. Wiles negotiated a loan with the Home Mission Board of the Southern Baptist Convention to pay the existing mortgage at a local bank and to reduce the church's interest rate and lower the church's monthly payments. As part of the terms of the Home Mission Board loan, an escrow account for $1,284.59 was set up with American National Bank of Shawnee to settle the back-paving taxes against Immanuel. On September 10, 1937, the Home Mission Board directed American National Bank of Shawnee to pay the taxes and close the account.

Somehow, the payment was not made, and in the summer of 1940, the city of Shawnee sued Immanuel Baptist Church, the Home Mission Board, and 39 individuals and organizations for the back taxes. By then, penalties and interest had brought the city's claim to $2,469.61. The lawsuit dragged on until January 5, 1942, when Immanuel Baptist Church settled for $1,185.00.[21]

While at Immanuel Baptist Church, John C. Wiles, the son of Dr. Wiles, was ordained into the ministry in September 1944. Dr. Elmer Ridgeway, longtime Oklahoma pastor and denominational worker, preached the ordination sermon. In 1917, Dr. Elmer Ridgeway was pastor of First Baptist Church, Blackwell, in northern Oklahoma. While at First Baptist Church, Blackwell, Dr. Ridgeway had the honor of preaching the ordination sermon for Dr. Tom Wiles. Thus, Dr. Ridgeway was instrumental in the ordination of both father and son.

Figure 5.3. Dr. Elmer Ridgeway

In 1944, Dr. Ridgeway was pastor of Immanuel Baptist Church in Oklahoma City. Later, Dr. Ridgeway was elected by the Baptist General Convention of Oklahoma as the state evangelist. Others assisting in the ordination of John Wiles were Don Bergeron, Oklahoma Baptist University graduate and longtime Oklahoma pastor; Dr. John W. Raley, Oklahoma Baptist University president; J. F. Shirey, member of Immanuel Baptist Church; and W. T. Short, Oklahoma Baptist University mathematics professor and member of Immanuel Baptist Church.

Following his ordination, Rev. John Wiles served as pastor of First Baptist

Figure 5.4. Dr. Tom Wiles, the Immanuel days

Church, Tupelo, Oklahoma. [22] He was also pastor of First Southern Mission Church in Del City before serving churches in Kentucky, Arizona, New Mexico, and Texas. Reverend John Wiles died at age fifty-seven in 1983 while serving as pastor of First Baptist Church, Graham, Texas.[23]

Several church members were active in the functioning of the church during Dr. Wiles years at Immanuel. These included J. F. Shirey, Harry Merritt, W. B. Richardson, Roy Stewart, Ed Hicks, and W. T. Short.[24]

During his service at Immanuel Baptist Church, Dr. Wiles grew in stature within the Baptists of Oklahoma. The first BCGO annual meeting that Dr. Wiles attended was in 1938 when he attended as a messenger from Immanuel Baptist Church. Dr. Wiles was evidently able to improve the Immanuel Baptist Church financial situation, and the church gave $873.26 to the Cooperative Program, an increase of $300 from the previous year.[25] In the minutes of the 1940 Annual Meeting of the Baptist General Convention of Oklahoma, Dr. Wiles was listed as a vice president. He presided over the Thursday afternoon session on November 14.[26]

At the 1941 BGCO Annual Meeting, Dr. Wiles served on the Credentials Committee and led in the closing prayer of the Thursday, November 6, afternoon session of the Convention. At the 1942 BGCO Annual Meeting, Dr. Wiles was placed on the Program Committee for the 1943 annual meeting. The strain placed on churches and associations by World War II and the rationing of gasoline and rubber was made clear by a BGCO move to lessen statewide events and encourage local events.

More responsibility was given to associations. Several associations elected men as moderators to achieve this efficiency. For the Pottawatomie-Lincoln Association, Dr. Tom Wiles of Immanuel was selected as moderator. Hattie Fae Wiles was very active in the 1942 Annual Meeting of the Woman's Missionary Union (WMU) meetings. She served on the Obituaries Committee and delivered the In Memoriam Message to honor departed WMU members. Her talk was entitled "When the Silver Cord is Snapped" and was taken from Ecclesiastes 12:6. She also did the closing prayer for that session.

In 1943, Dr. Tom Wiles was placed on the board of directors of the BGCO and on the Committee on Committees. He also delivered the keynote message of the Wednesday, November 17, session. In his message, Dr. Wiles summarized the advancements and achievements of the ten years of Sec. Andrew Potter's leadership. John Wiles, son of Dr. Wiles, sang "Beneath the Cross of Jesus." John Wiles and the Oklahoma Baptist University Men's Quartet also sang "'Tis the Savior Calling Thee" for the WMU meetings.

In 1944, Dr. Tom Wiles was elected president of the Baptist General Convention of Oklahoma at the annual meeting held in Tulsa on November 14–16, 1944. Naturally, he and his wife attended that annual meeting as messengers from Immanuel Baptist Church. His son John attended as a messenger from First Baptist Church, Tupelo. John Wiles was also part of the male quartet from Immanuel Baptist Church, Shawnee, which sang "Shall I Crucify My Savior?" during the Wednesday, November 15, 1944, afternoon session. Other members of the quartet were Kenneth Myers, Bill Van Wye, and Raymond Hopper.[27]

Although World War II brought considerable anguish and suffering among the families of Immanuel Baptist Church, the war brought increased employment opportunities for members who were not members of the military. In addition, many of the military personnel sent back part of their monthly salary to parents and loved ones. As a result, Immanuel Baptist Church was able to hold some special offerings to reduce the debt. By the summer of 1944, these special offerings had amounted to $5,499.12. The treasurer, W. B. Richardson, took these funds and purchased World War II Series G bonds made payable to the Home Mission Board and settled the debt to the Home Mission Board in full. This debt was approximately $10,000.00 in the summer of 1940, so Reverend Wiles, and the members of Immanuel Baptist Church made huge sacrifices to become debt free.

After six and a half years of steadfast service and growth through some very difficult times, Dr. Wiles left Immanuel Baptist Church in August 12, 1945, to become the pastor of First Baptist Church, Lawton.[28] During his service at Immanuel Baptist Church, Dr. Wiles was especially noted and remembered fondly by the congregation for his concern for the young members who were called into the military to serve their country in World War II and their families.[29] Immanuel Baptist Church experienced strong growth during Dr. Wiles's tenure. Membership grew from 796 members to 1,792 members. Sunday School reached a peak attendance of 1,200.[30]

Dr. H. Tom Wiles, the Years after Immanuel

After leaving Immanuel Baptist Church, Dr. Wiles went to First Baptist Church, Lawton, where he preached his first message as pastor on September 6, 1945. He remained very active in the Baptist General Convention of Oklahoma. Dr. Wiles served as president of the Baptist General Convention of Oklahoma for just one year from 1944 to 1945. In November 1945, Reverend and Mrs. Wiles attended that convention as messengers from First Baptist Church, Lawton. Mrs. Wiles was active in the 1945 BGCO Annual Meeting, serving on the Woman's Missionary Union Nominating Committee and the Courtesy Committee.[31]

In 1949, he and Mrs. Wiles attended the BGCO Annual Meeting as messengers from First Baptist Church, Lawton. During that year, he served as the chairman of the board of trustees of the Baptist Children's Home and delivered the home's annual report. He was also the chairman of the Stewardship Committee of the Comanche–Cotton Baptist Association and delivered a pledge for twenty-three thousand dollars toward the unified budget for the year. He also served on the Nomination Committee and was the chairman of the Evangelism Visitation Committee. Reverend Wiles's wife, Hattie Fae, served on the Nomination Committee for the Woman's Missionary Union in 1949.

At the 1955 BGCO Annual Meeting in Tulsa, Dr. Wiles was again very active. First Baptist Church, Lawton, was the tenth strongest giver to the Cooperative Program with $20,557 in offerings. It is worth noting that the strongest giver was First Baptist Church, Oklahoma City, under the leadership of Rev. H. H. Hobbs at $61,424. Immanuel Baptist Church under Rev. Frank Baugh was 27th with an offering of $11,306.

Dr. Wiles also served several terms as a member of the board of trustees of Oklahoma Baptist University; served on the relief and annuity board; and served on the board of Carver School of Missions, Louisville, Kentucky, for eight years. During his years at First Baptist Church, Lawton, autographed photographs of many of the most widely known past and present leaders of the Southern Baptist Convention and the Baptist General Convention of Oklahoma covered the walls of Dr. Wiles's office. Also dotting the walls were photos of baptismal services including a group of seventy-five persons baptized during one service at Shawnee. Many photos show Allied officers who became Christians through attending services here during their training at Fort Sill.

During his twenty years and four months at First Baptist Church, Lawton, Dr. Wiles baptized more than 3,400 persons and received more than 7,000 new members by transfer from other Baptist churches. In the same period, Sunday School enrollment at First Baptist Church, Lawton, increased from 1,014 to 2,953, with church membership climbing from 1,564 to almost 3,000. Under his leadership, the church established a Baptist student center building at Cameron College, Lawton.

In 1947, Dr. Wiles oversaw the erection of a two-story dormitory and two cabins at Falls Creek Assembly. While at First Baptist Church, Lawton, Dr. Wiles led the church in starting six mission churches, four of which are now fully organized churches. He also built a new educational building and auditorium and an all-purpose recreation and educational building.

Despite the many accomplishments under his leadership, Dr. Wiles shunned any credit for himself. "For 20 years, I have been privileged to be pastor of the greatest congregation of people I have ever known or heard of," Dr. Wiles commented. "The Deacons have worked with me fervently, and the church has followed its leadership wholeheartedly. The truth is, there have been only one or two dissenting votes on anything in these 20 years." Concerning his twenty-year service in Lawton, Dr. Wiles said he and his family have been blessed by the citizens in many ways. "The entire city has been more than kind and generous to me and my family," he stated, "so much so that as far as we are concerned, there is no place on earth more like home than Lawton."

Dr. Wiles served First Baptist Church, Lawton, for more than twenty years when he ended his pastorate. He then went to Jerusalem where he spent a year as a missionary in the Holy Land. Mrs. Wiles worked beside her husband in a special assignment for the Southern Baptist Convention, just as she has worked with him during his forty-four years in the ministry. "She has worked every day I have worked," Dr. Wiles said of his wife. "She has served as a Sunday School teacher, Training Union leader, and Woman's Missionary Union worker. She has won many people to Christ."

As to the special assignment that he has accepted with no salary or compensation other than transportation expenses, lodging, and the use of a car, Dr. Wiles said the Southern Baptist Convention actually made the choice for him. "There were three special assignments to be filled," Dr. Wiles explained. "When they told me the assignment in Jerusalem was the most urgent, I accepted it." Dr. Wiles, who toured the Holy Land in 1954, spending 30 days in Palestine, Egypt, Israel, Lebanon, and Jordan, said, "Around 250,000 people travel through Jerusalem each year between Easter and Christmas. I *will* [editor's italics] conduct English services each Lord's Day and work with our missions and churches in Jordan, Lebanon, and Egypt." Dr. Wiles went on to say, "It seems like an impossible job, but God can make it succeed." Concerning their upcoming trip to Jerusalem, Dr. Wiles said, "I have never had any marks of greatness, but have been privileged to number among my personal friends some of the greatest men of our time. What little there is good in me, outside of the grace of God, has been absorbed from these great men."[32]

After he and Hattie Fae had served one year for the Southern Baptist Convention in the Middle East, Dr. and Mrs. Wiles retired in Lawton. H. Tom Wiles died on January 13, 1981, in a Lawton nursing home. He was eighty-three at the time. A memorial service was held on January 15 by Forrest Siler, pastor of First Baptist Church, Lawton, and Richard Hopper of First Baptist Church, Ardmore. Dr. Wiles's burial was in Lawton.

Ordained to the ministry at First Baptist Church, Blackwell, in 1921, Wiles served more than 50 years in the ministry. During his 20-year pastorate at First Baptist Church, Lawton, from 1945 to 1965, the church was a leader in number of baptisms among state churches. Under Wiles's leadership, the church recorded 3,414 baptisms and 7,058 additions by letter.

Wiles also served as pastor of churches in Prague, Sumner, Carney, Piedmont, Hinton, Coalgate, Caddo, Kingfisher, Seminole, Oklahoma City, and Shawnee. After his retirement, he and Mrs. Wiles served a year under special appointment by the Foreign Mission Board in Jerusalem. Survivors include his wife, Hattie Fae; a son, John; and two daughters, Mrs. Mary Ida Needham of Lawton and Mrs. Bettye Fae of Ferguson, Kansas City, Missouri.

At the time of his death, Dr. Wiles had twelve grandchildren and five great-grandchildren.[33] Their son, Rev. John Wiles, was a graduate of Southwestern Baptist Seminary and pastored several churches in Oklahoma and Texas. One daughter, Mrs. Milton Ferguson, was the wife of professor Milton Ferguson at Southwestern Baptist Seminary, Fort Worth, Texas.[34]

Dr. Milton Ferguson eventually served as president of Midwestern Baptist Theological Seminary in Kansas City, Missouri. He retired in 1995. Bettye Fae Ferguson died March 6, 2014.[35] The other daughter, Mrs. Mary Ida Needham, was the wife of Wyatt Needham, an insurance man. Both Mary Ida and her husband Wyatt were active in First Baptist Church, El Paso, Texas. All of Dr. and Mrs. Wiles's children were graduates of Oklahoma Baptist University.[36]

CHAPTER 6

Recovery and Growth after World War II

Dr. Claybron Deering, September 1945–November 1949

Introduction

Rev. Claybron Deering was the eighth pastor of Immanuel Baptist Church. He spent four years working, loving, and helping church families adjust from the turbulence and disruption of World War II. During his pastorate, the Immanuel family gave spiritual support to many who had served and who had loved ones who served in the armed services. The youth building was dedicated in honor of those who served and sacrificed during the war.

During the Deering pastorate, two mission churches were established.[1] In November 1946, Temple Baptist Church was started as a mission church in the home of the late Mrs. Darrell Norman.[2] The mission church continued in her house until a church building could be erected at 1234 Highland Street. In October 1947, Immanuel began a mission church that is now Sharon Baptist Church.[3]

The world scene during the Deering years was one of euphoria after the end of World War II. However, most of Europe and much of Asia had been ravaged by the war. Europe saw the advance of Soviet Communism when a series of Communist puppet states were established in the areas conquered by the Soviet Union. The United Nations was established in 1945. In 1946, Winston Churchill gave his Iron Curtain Speech at Westminster College in Fulton, Missouri, warning the world of the threat of Communism.

In 1947, the United States, through the Marshall Plan, gave thirteen billion dollars in economic support to rebuild European economies devastated by World War II. The Marshall Plan was named for named for United States Secretary of State George Marshall. Also in 1947, the Dead Sea Scrolls were discovered, verifying the accuracy of much of the text of the Bible.

In 1948, the Berlin Airlift broke the Soviet Union's blockade of West Berlin. Also in 1947, the state of Israel was founded, providing the Jewish with a homeland. In 1949, Mao Zedong defeated the last Chinese Nationalist Army, and China became a Communist nation. Also in 1949, the North Atlantic Treaty Organization (NATO) was created to counter the threat of the Soviet Union and her allies (known as the Warsaw Pact).[4]

Within the United States, the end of World War II brought home millions of young men and women who had been serving in the military. The baby boom occurred right after World War II as young men and women who had postponed marriage and family now had the opportunity to do so. The G.I. Bill allowed large numbers of young veterans to enroll in college. As the only industrialized nation whose factories and infrastructure had escaped the ravages of war, the United States soon became the dominant economic power in the world.[5]

Rev. Claybron Deering, the Years before Immanuel

Claybron Deering was born on January 15, 1910,[6] in Newlin, Texas, and grew up in the Shamrock, Texas, area. He accepted Christ at a young age and was licensed to preach at fifteen by Riverview Baptist Church of the North Fork Baptist Association in north Texas. He preached his first sermon there. He was ordained by the same church in 1927.[7] After graduating from

Figure 6.1.
Claybron Deering,
the OBU days

Wayland Academy in Texas, he matriculated at Oklahoma Baptist University in 1929 at the age of nineteen. At the Annual Meeting of the Baptist General Convention of Oklahoma that was held in Shawnee in November 1929, he was listed as a Messenger from Shawnee.[8]

In the May 9, 1929, issue of *The Baptist Messenger*, he is identified by editor E. C. Routh as the pastor of Fairview Baptist in the Shawnee area.[9] He is also listed in the minutes of the 1930 Annual Meeting of the BGCO as being a pastor from Shawnee.[10] While a student at Oklahoma Baptist University, Reverend Deering took a pastorate at Alfalfa, Oklahoma. Alfalfa is currently an unincorporated town in Caddo County, about one hundred miles west of Shawnee.[11]

In the March 13, 1930, issue of *The Baptist Messenger*, J. B. Edward's wrote the following in an article entitled "The Ministerial Alliance of O. B. U.": Rev. Claybron Deering is doing good work with his church at Alfalfa, Oklahoma. Last Sunday, there were three confessions of faith and three additions in the regular service."[12] Reverend Deering evidently continued his relationship with First Baptist Church, Alfalfa, for some time, since he and his wife Lucille were listed as messengers from Alfalfa, Oklahoma, at the 1931 Annual Meeting held in Okmulgee.[13]

While a student at Oklahoma Baptist University, he majored in Christianity with a minor in education. On August 2, 1931, Claybron Deering married Lucille Roberson, who was also an Oklahoma Baptist University student. Claybron Deering was a very active student at Oklahoma Baptist University and held his first position as a pastor at Victory Baptist Church in Shawnee.[14] Victory Baptist Church was constituted as a Baptist church in 1928 at 1315 North McKinley Street. Rev. Claybron Deering was the pastor of Victory Baptist Church from 1932 to 1935. He attended the Pottawatomie-Lincoln Baptist Association Annual Meeting for each of those years.[15]

Victory Baptist Church was evidently a very active church under Reverend Deering's leadership. In June of 1933, the church had a revival in which there were thirty-two professions of faith and twenty-one requests for baptism. Rev. Charles Curb was the evangelist.[16] In the April 12, 1934, issue of *The Baptist Messenger*, editor E.

C. Routh wrote an article entitled "What Pastors Say and Do about the O. B. U. Campaign." The article covered several pastors who were actively supporting a BGCO campaign to raise money to pay faculty and staff salaries at Oklahoma Baptist University and to pay general expenses. After mentioning several prominent pastors, editor Routh stated the following about Victory Baptist Church:

> Much of the finest work that is accomplished is done by student pastors. They are co-operating in a gratifying way. Word from Brother Claybron Deering assures us that his people believe in O. B. U. [Pastor Deering said,] "Everyone with whom I have discussed our offering is enthusiastic and confident that by April 22 we shall have gone over the top by more than reaching our goal."

In addition, the July 11, 1935, issue of *The Baptist Messenger* had a very informative and lengthy letter from Ms. Ardell Watkins to T. H. Farmer, Baptist General Convention of Oklahoma secretary for Sunday School and Baptist Training Union. Ms. Watkins was a special worker for the Sunday School and Baptist Training Union and was reporting on her activities for the prior week to T. H. Farmer, who was her supervisor. During the week, she visited twelve churches and their pastors to help with Sunday School and Baptist Training Union projects. Often, she spoke at the church where she visited and did training in the church. The most active church of the week was Victory Baptist Church, where she spoke at the Sunday evening services, giving the congregation the Baptist Training Union Challenge.

On Thursday, she was back at Victory Baptist Church for a Woman's Missionary Union meeting. During the week, Ms. Watkins met with four Shawnee pastors, including Pastor Deering, to conduct a Sunday School and Baptist Training Union survey for her part of the overall Sunday School and Baptist Training Union report. She also planned the monthly Baptist Training Union business meeting for Victory Baptist Church and secured Oklahoma Baptist University student volunteers to help with the meeting and the follow-on work.[17] In 1947, Victory Baptist Church changed its name to Trinity Baptist Church.[18]

While a student at Oklahoma Baptist University, Reverend Deering had an active campus life. He was part of the Ministerial Alliance and served as its vice president his sophomore year and as president his senior year. In his senior year, he was the Ministerial Alliance representative on the Baptist Student Union Council. He was also a member of the Elean Men's Social Club. His wife, Lucille, was a member of the Yathian Women's Social Club. The two clubs held many joint events during Reverend Deering's senior year, including the Tri-Club County Carnival on September 25, 1934; the Yathian-Elean Circus Party for new students on October 23, 1934; the Yathian-Elean Italian Ball on December 4, 1934; and the Yathian-Elean joint end-of-the-semester meeting at the home of fellow student Jack Baxter on December 18, 1934. The Elean Men's Social Club also held an open house for Oklahoma Baptist University alumni during homecoming on November 11, 1934.[19]

In 1935, Rev. Claybron Deering graduated from Oklahoma Baptist University. One of his last activities before leaving Shawnee was to preach a revival at South Persimmon Church in Sharon, Oklahoma. Sharon, Oklahoma, is near Woodward. Baptist General Convention of Oklahoma secretary-treasurer Andrew Potter described that revival in his August 29, 1935, column in *The Baptist Messenger*, saying,

> Rev. Claybron Deering of Shawnee is conducting a very successful meeting at the South Persimmon Church in the Northwestern Association, where Rev. Haskell Beck is pastor. Large crowds are attending and Brother Deering is preaching the Gospel with convincing power.

In that same issue, Reverend Deering of Victory Baptist Church wrote an "Item of Interest" note to the editor. Reverend Deering stated,

Last Sunday was enlistment day at Victory [Baptist Church], Shawnee. Every church officer and Sunday School teacher together with the B. T. U. and W. M. U leaders signed the "Prove Me" card. Our people are enthusiastic about this plan. My assistant pastor [is] *The Baptist Messenger* [and he] makes fifty-nine regular weekly visits to homes of our members, and I feel that [*The Baptist Messenger*] has done most of the work in informing the members about this movement. You are giving us a good paper. May the Lord bless you in this much needed work."[20]

On Wednesday, September 25, 1935, Rev. Claybron Deering resigned as pastor of the Victory Church in Shawnee to accept the pastorate of Graham Baptist Church. While at Graham, he attended the Southwestern Baptist Theological Seminary in Fort Worth, earning a master's degree and began working on a doctorate.[21] He finished his doctor of divinity degree later while at Immanuel Baptist Church.[22] Graham, Oklahoma, is currently an unincorporated town in Carter County in south central Oklahoma, about thirty miles northwest of Ardmore.[23]

Reverend Deering was evidently a successful and loved pastor at Graham. One of the unusual events that occurred during Reverend Deering's years at Graham was a six-church brush arbor revival. In the September 8, 1938, issue of *The Baptist Messenger*, T. P. Haskins reported:

The Lord has been good to me in giving me the privilege of laboring with six churches and their pastors in the heart of the oil field east of Duncan and north of Ardmore. The churches and pastors engaged in the revival were Pike City, J. L. Dodson; Graham, Claybron Deering; Eaves City, Melvin Walker; Pernell, V. W. Sears; County Line, Jesse Northcutt; Velma Church, R. L. Miears. This meeting was sponsored by the laymen of these six churches. A large brush arbor, well lighted and seated, was constructed three quarters of a mile south of Ratcliff Corner. Although the seating capacity was 1,100 people, there were nights when all the seats were filled and many people were standing outside or sitting in their cars. J. L. Collins, music and educational director of Kelham Avenue Baptist Church, conducted the music for the meeting. Because of two associational meetings, I was compelled to be out of the meeting the first week. The local pastors cared for the morning service and Claybron Deering preached each evening the first week. Under the leadership of Mr. Birdwell of County Line [Baptist Church], the men took the initiative in a visitation program. By the middle of the second week, a mighty spirit of conviction prevailed throughout the entire community. Over 80 people came forward during the meeting. There were approximately 80 additions to the churches. Many young people surrendered their lives for special service. One young man surrendered to the call of the gospel ministry. Of those who were saved and reclaimed during the revival, [many were] children who were just entering the world of sin. [Many] fathers came who had wandered far away from God. All the churches were revived in their membership, and they very enthusiastically accepted the recommendation of' the committee that they have such a meeting another year.[24]

Reverend Deering remained in Graham until 1941 when he took a pastorate in Lindsey, Oklahoma, about twenty-five miles northwest of Paul's Valley.[25] A year later in 1942, however, he and Lucille Deering attended the annual meeting held in Oklahoma City as messengers from First Baptist Church, Marlow.[26] A year later in 1943, Reverend and Mrs. Deering attended the annual meeting again held in Oklahoma City but as messengers from First Baptist Church, Drumright.

After several years of being an active local pastor in the state, Reverend Deering began to be active in the leadership of the Baptist General Convention of Oklahoma. He was placed on the board of directors of the Baptist General Convention of Oklahoma, the Promotional Committee for the Baptist Children's City funding campaign, and the Foreign Missions Committee.[27] A year later, in his "Building Institutions and the Denomination through the Brotherhood" column in the March 2, 1944, issue of *The Baptist Messenger*, Brotherhood secretary Dr. Elmer Ridgeway stated:

On Friday night, February 17, the Pawnee Creek Associational Brotherhood met with the First Baptist Church, Drumright. The attendance, despite the rain, was excellent. Many of the churches were represented with large delegations present. Pastor Claybron Deering and his fine group of men had made the utmost preparation for this meeting. It was one of the finest from the standpoint of attendance and spirit we have attended in the state this year. Associational Brotherhood President J. W. McCloud is leading in a grand way in that section. The First Baptist Church, Drumright, under the gallant leadership of Pastor Deering is being molded into one of the mightiest organizations for conquest in Oklahoma. He and his people have wrought wonders in the brief time he has been there. It was a pleasure to speak to that grand group of men of the Pawnee Creek Association."[28]

In 1944, Reverend and Mrs. Deering attended the BGCO Annual Meeting as messengers from First Baptist Church, Drumright; however, neither was active in that particular annual meeting activities.[29] Nonetheless, Reverend Deering continued to be active in Oklahoma Baptist Life. *The Baptist Messenger* reporter Sophia Duerksen in a December 4, 1944, wrote:

A very pleasant and profitable week was spent with the Teachers and Officers at [First Baptist Church,]

Drumright, November 19-24, as we studied together "Building a Standard Sunday School." Pastor Claybron Deering is leading his people from one victory to another. Strange but true, their Sunday School enrollment exceeds their resident church membership, and their average Sunday School attendance of more than 300 is about 60% of the enrollment. Another unusual thing about this good church is that 40% of its members are tithers! These people are really "abounding in the work of the Lord.[30]

Rev. Claybron Deering, the Immanuel Years

Rev. Claybron Deering became the pastor of Immanuel Baptist Church in September 1945. His first duty day was Monday, October 1; and he preached his first message on Sunday, October 14. The church had a reception for Reverend and Mrs. Deering on Monday evening, October 15.[31] One of his first activities at Immanuel Baptist Church was to meet with the Deacons on November 6, 1945, to give his enthusiastic assessment about the future progress and his vision for Immanuel Baptist Church.[32]

Figure 6.2. Rev. Claybron Deering, the Immanuel years

Rev. Claybron Deering's ministry at Immanuel Baptist Church was highlighted by the years of working, loving, and helping church families adjust from the turbulence and disruption of World War II. Military personnel were returning home and were getting married and having children. Some families had loved ones who died or were seriously injured, both physically and mentally, during the war. All of this required a loving and caring pastor. His pastorate centered around the Immanuel church family and giving spiritual support to many who had been in the armed services. The youth building was dedicated in honor of those who served and sacrificed during the war.[33]

Rev. Claybron Deering was a very active pastor at Immanuel Baptist Church. On November 23, 1945, the Deacons met with Reverend Deering to discuss the purchase of the W. W. Wickes property for a parsonage and the conversion of the current parsonage into a Sunday School class facility. As with the Wileses' years at Immanuel Baptist Church, the water leakage problem in the basement of the church plagued Reverend Deering during his years at Immanuel. In the February 13, 1946, Deacons' meeting, the Deacons voted to provide seventy-five dollars per month to Rev. Maynard Campbell for rural missionary work.

Two revivals were scheduled at that Deacons' meeting. The first was for October 1946, with Dr. Robert Naylor of Enid as the evangelist. The second was for January 1947 with Dr. Willis Howard of Springfield, Missouri, as the evangelist.[34] Being a relatively young pastor at age thirty-five when he started at Immanuel Baptist Church and having very strong Oklahoma Baptist University roots, Reverend Deering had a very strong ministry to the Oklahoma Baptist University students. He was very popular with the students and had very large numbers of students attending Immanuel Baptist Church. To support the transportation needs of the students, Reverend Deering used shuttle buses to take the students to and from the Oklahoma Baptist University campus.[35]

Under Rev. Claybron Deering's leadership, Immanuel Baptist Church continued to be one of the strongest churches in the state, especially given the size of Shawnee at the time. In the March 21, 1946, issue of *The Baptist Messenger*, Immanuel Baptist Church was listed as the thirteenth largest church in the state for Sunday School and Training Union attendance, averaging 632 participants weekly in Sunday School and 231 participants in the weekly Training Union.[36] At the February 4, 1947, Deacons' meeting, the Immanuel Baptist Church Deacons voted to send Reverend Deering to the Baptist World Alliance Congress that would be meeting in Copenhagen, Denmark, in July 1947.[37] The Baptist World Alliance Congress was a

IMMANUEL BAPTIST CHURCH

major event in 1947, and 5,000 Baptist from all corners of the world came to the congress.[38]

At the June 10, 1947, Deacons' meeting, the Deacons approved a motion that was very dear to the heart of Reverend Deering. Reverend Deering spent several years of his early ministry in the pulpit of small rural churches. He always had an affinity for pastors of small rural churches. At the June 10, 1947, Deacons' meeting, the Immanuel Baptist Church Deacons voted to sponsor a rural pastor to the Oklahoma Baptist University Preacher's School.[39] The preacher's school was scheduled for June 17–27 and was designed to be an informational course, Woman's Missionary Union at Work. The school was offered to both pastors and their wives. A course in Problems of a Pastor's Wife by Those Who Know was also available for pastors' wives.[40]

A year before, on May 27–29, 1946, the Baptist General Convention of Oklahoma held an evangelism conference at First Baptist Church, Shawnee. Dignitaries at the conference included executive secretary Dr. T. L. Holcomb of the Baptist Sunday School Board, executive secretary-treasurer T. B. Lackey of the BCGO, and past executive secretary-treasurer Dr. Andrew Potter, of the BCGO.[41] Rev. Claybron Deering of Immanuel Baptist Church was one of the dignitaries on the agenda and chaired a panel on "Conserving the Fruit."[42] Having been a pastor on several occasions at a small, poor, rural church, Reverend Deering extended a cordial invitation to all rural pastors to be the guests of Immanuel Baptist Church for bed and breakfast during the three-day conference. Each guest, however, was advised to provide his own bed linens and covers.[43]

Reverend Deering and Immanuel Baptist Church played a major role in the 1946 Annual Meeting of the Pottawatomie-Lincoln Baptist Association. Immanuel Baptist Church associate pastor Rev. W. E. Russell preached the annual sermon, and Reverend Deering served as the clerk for the annual meeting. He was also elected vice moderator of the upcoming associational year.[44]

During the Deering pastorate, two mission churches were established. On Sunday, November 24, 1946, Immanuel Baptist Church established a Sunday School mission in the Capps Addition

95

of Northeast Shawnee. Undeterred by not having a building in which to meet, the Sunday School was organized in the home of Mrs. Darrel Norman, a member of Immanuel.[45] Mrs. Norman later sold lots from her property for the mission building.[46]

Plans were made to provide a building in the near future, and Rev. James Drake, an Oklahoma Baptist University student who was ordained by Immanuel Baptist Church, was elected as the first mission pastor. Rev. Claybron Deering held a formal opening ceremony of the new mission church on March 7, 1948.[47] The mission church continued in Mrs. Norman's house until a church building could be erected at 1234 Highland Street.[48] The mission church was formally constituted as an independent church in 1951.[49]

Earlier in 1946, Immanuel Baptist Church began a mission church called South Mission Church that grew into what is now Sharon Baptist Church. By the year's end in 1946, Immanuel Baptist Church had completed a mission building for their South Mission Church. The facility regularly had over sixty in Sunday School and preaching services. Rev. Louis A. Haddock was the pastor of the South Mission Church.[50] Reverend Haddock was a member of Immanuel Baptist Church and the head of the Repair and Maintenance Department at the Oklahoma Baptist University.[51] Reverend Haddock served for about a year and then resigned. Rev. Eugene Herndon was then called as the pastor of Sharon Mission Church. After about a year, Rev. Joe Bill Peltaway was called as their pastor.

At the September 2, 1947, Deacons' meeting, the Deacons voted to proceed with the erection of a missions building. The building was to be built in the Capps Addition of Shawnee and was to be thirty-six feet wide and fifty feet in length. It was to be made of yellow tile with a concrete floor. This building would eventually become the home of Temple Baptist Church. A special offering was taken at the spring revival to help Temple Baptist Church get started strongly.[52]

On September 12, 1948, Reverend and Mrs. Deering received a special honor from Dr. John Wesley and Mrs. Helen Raley, president and first lady of Oklahoma Baptist University. As was their custom, Dr. and Mrs. Raley hosted an annual formal reception given at Oklahoma Baptist University on Thursday night of the first school week. Approximately 1,200 people, including students, faculty, and friends, attended. Several special guests attended, including Shawnee City manager and Mrs. Robert C. Hutchinson and Rev. and Mrs. Claybron Deering, as pastor and first lady of the Immanuel Baptist Church. The pastors of First Baptist Church, Shawnee, and University Baptist Church and their wives were also honored guests.[53] Also in fall 1948, Reverend Deering received a second honor. He was selected to deliver the annual sermon at the Pottawatomie-Lincoln Baptist Association Annual Meeting held at First Baptist Church, Davenport.[54]

Reverend Deering served Immanuel Baptist Church lovingly and well, and Immanuel Baptist Church responded well to his leading. In November 1947, he was given a raise from $3,900 per year plus the use of the parsonage to $4,200 per year plus the use of the parsonage. It is worth noting that a larger and more modern parsonage was purchased during the Deering years. Also worth noting is that at the January 14, 1949, Deacons' meeting, the Deacons voted to give Reverend Deering three months leave without pay to finish his doctorate.[55]

Although active at Immanuel Baptist Church, Dr. Deering did not take an extremely active role in Baptist life outside of Immanuel, either at the Pottawatomie-Lincoln Baptist Association level or the Baptist General Convention of Oklahoma level. He and Mrs. Deering attended the Annual Meeting of the Baptist General Convention of Oklahoma that took place from November 6 to 8, 1945, in Oklahoma City, a short drive from Shawnee. However, neither took an active role in the annual meeting.[56] This may have been due to Lucille Deering's advanced stage of pregnancy.

She gave birth to her second daughter, Susan, shortly after Dr. Deering assumed the pulpit of Immanuel Baptist Church.[57] At the 1946 Annual Meeting of Baptist General Convention of Oklahoma, Dr. Deering attended as a Messenger from Immanuel Baptist Church and was placed on the Social Service Committee. Mrs. Deering did not attend, even though the annual meeting was in nearby Oklahoma City. Perhaps she did not attend because she had a one-year-old child for whom she was caring.[58] In 1947, Dr. Deering attended the BGCO Annual Meeting held in Tulsa and helped to present the Social Service Committee report. The committee concluded the following:

1. The Liquor Industry is hurting the American public and stripping it of dignity and money.
2. The home was ordained and established of God as the foundation of the human social order and is being stripped and wounded by the constant increase of immorality and divorce.
3. Minority groups, both racial groups and religious groups, are still being stripped and wounded in America.
4. Since "the love of money is a root of all evil," many Americans are stripped and wounded and left bleeding by the economic wayside by both businesses and labor unions.[59]

In 1948, Dr. Claybron Deering and his wife Lucille attended the Baptist General Convention of Oklahoma Annual Meeting. The meeting was held in Muskogee, but neither Deering took an active role.[60]

On November 6, 1949, Dr. Claybron Deering resigned as pastor of Immanuel Baptist Church to take the pulpit at Exchange Avenue Baptist Church in Oklahoma City.[61] His resignation caused some confusion at the November 7–10, 1949, Annual Meeting of the Baptist General Convention of Oklahoma since he was in the process of transitioning from being the pastor of Immanuel Baptist Church to being the pastor of Exchange Avenue Baptist Church. He was listed as a messenger from Immanuel Baptist Church in Shawnee and as the moderator at the Pottawatomie-Lincoln Baptist Association Annual Meeting that was held in August 1949 but was also listed as being a pastor from Exchange Avenue Baptist Church in Oklahoma City.

Dr. Claybron Deering, the Years after Immanuel

Dr. Claybron Deering's years at Exchange Avenue Baptist Church were very successful. While at Exchange Avenue Baptist Church, Dr. Deering greatly increased his activity in the Baptist General Convention of Oklahoma. For example, at the 1952 Annual Meeting of the Baptist General Convention of Oklahoma, Dr. Deering served as a messenger from Exchange Avenue Baptist Church. He was selected to be the stewardship chairman for the Cooperative Program campaign for the Oklahoma County Baptist Association.

The stewardship goal for the association was the highest in the state at $273,000. In comparison, the Pottawatomie-Lincoln Baptist Association stewardship goal, which was tied for 3rd highest in the state, was $60,000. The Pottawatomie-Lincoln Baptist Association stewardship campaign was headed by Rev. Frank Baugh of Immanuel Baptist Church.[62]

In the summer of 1954, Dr. Claybron Deering was one of twenty-five Oklahoma Baptist pastors who were selected to initiate a considerably different approach to the way that the annual Falls Creek Assemblies were held. Two sessions occurred, one on July 26 to August 2 and the other from August 3 to August 10 at the campgrounds located south of Davis. Twenty-five of the finest pastors of the state brought messages during the two assemblies. Different speakers were used for each morning and each evening service of the entire camp period. Dr. Deering was one of those pastors.

In November 1955, Dr. Deering had the honor to preach the annual sermon for the Baptist General Convention of Oklahoma Annual Meeting held in Tulsa. His text for the sermon was I Samuel 7:3–12. Dr. Claybron Deering's message was entitled The Eternal Purpose of God Regarding Mankind.

Dr. Deering also had the honor of being one of thirty-nine distinguished Oklahoma Baptists to help prepare the Oklahoma material for *The Encyclopedia of Southern Baptists*. In addition, Dr. Deering served as a member of the board of directors of the Baptist General Convention of Oklahoma and was assigned to the Stewardship-Budget Committee. He was also appointed by BGCO President W.

A. Evan to the ad hoc Insurance Committee to make a thorough study of the insurance needs of all convention property.

Exchange Avenue Baptist Church under Dr. Deering was consistently a strong giver to the Cooperative Program. For example, in 1954, it was the 41st strongest giver in Oklahoma to the Cooperative Program with $7,340 in offerings. It is worth noting that the strongest giver was First Baptist Church, Oklahoma City, under the leadership of Rev. H. H. Hobbs at $61,424. Immanuel Baptist Church under Rev. Frank Baugh was 27th with an offering of $11,306.[63]

During Deering's ministry at Exchange Avenue Baptist Church, there were 2,052 additions to the church, 860 of them by baptism. Total gifts amounted to $857,990, with $139,377 going to mission causes. The church built two educational units, established two mission churches, and organized a third mission church into a full and independent church. During Dr. Claybron Deering's years at Exchange Avenue Baptist Church, he supervised the effort to redecorate and air-condition the auditorium, purchased additional property, and increased the number of Sunday School departments from 17 to 37. An all-church fellowship reception was held on the evening of June 28, 1959, to honor the Deerings.

After ten years in the pulpit at Exchange Avenue Baptist Church, he resigned in June 1959 to devote full time to a business he had established that specialized in church financing. He was forty-nine years old at the time and had been in the ministry for thirty-four years. The firm that Dr. Deering established was called Deering Associates. It helped finance sixteen church building programs between the time it was incorporated on April 12 and his resignation in June.[64] The company name was changed to Western Fidelity Corporation on March 30, 1961.[65]

One of the church finance projects funded by Deering Associates was the building of a small facility called Southern Hills Chapel, Western Hills, Oklahoma City. Groundbreaking occurred on June 30, 1963, at Eighty-Fifth and South Pennsylvania. The chapel was the first facility of a mission church founded by Western Hills Baptist Church. The mission church had been at a home at 2236 Laneway Drive, Oklahoma City. The home would eventually become the parsonage for Southern Hills Chapel Church. Southern Hills Chapel has grown to become Southern Hills Baptist Church, one of the strongest and most influential Baptist churches in the state of Oklahoma.[66]

After several years with his church finance company, the Deerings moved to California where Dr. Deering served several Southern Baptist churches. In February 1971, he was the pastor of First Baptist Church, Sylmar, California, when a devastating earthquake hit southern California. The earthquake damaged both his church and home. Damage to the church was so severe that it was eventually condemned for use. Members and former members of Exchange Avenue Baptist Church, Oklahoma City, gave $1,200 in a love offering to benefit their former pastor.[67]

Lucille Deering died on August 24, 1972, in Glendale, California. She was a victim of Hodgkin's lymphoma. At the time, Dr. Claybron Deering was serving as the interim pastor at First Southern Baptist Church, Glendale.[68] Claybron and Lucille Deering had two daughters—Marilyn Jane, who was born December 2, 1935, and Susan, who was born in November 1942—shortly after Dr. Deering started his ministry at Immanuel Baptist Church.[69]

Following the death of Lucille, Dr. Deering married Muriel Robinson Anderson in California. Muriel Robinson was born in Iowa in 1917 and moved to California in 1929 when she was twelve years old. Prior to marrying Claybron Deering, Muriel Anderson had worked and retired from the General Telephone and Electric Company (GTE). She had two children prior to marrying Claybron. She and Dr. Deering moved to Dover, Delaware, in 1994 to help her son-in-law Rev. William Sturgeon establish a church called Church on the Westside. Dr. Deering died in Dover, Delaware, on January 4, 1996, a few days before his eighty-sixth birthday. Muriel Deering died on March 28, 2009, at the age of ninety-one.[70]

CHAPTER 7

Steady Growth and Babyland

Dr. Frank Baugh, February 1950–August 1959

Introduction

In February 1950, Rev. Frank Oliver Baugh was called as pastor of Immanuel Baptist Church. Under his leadership, there was a steady growth in Sunday School and worship attendance. In the summer of 1952, the auditorium was completely redecorated and air-conditioned, and work was done on the basement. A lovely new parsonage, an education building, and new nursery facilities called Babyland were built during the Baugh years.[1]

Figure 7.1. Frank Baugh, the Hollis days

The world scene when Rev. Frank Baugh was pastor of Immanuel Baptist Church was one of war in Korea and rising tensions between the United States and the Soviet Union. The Korean War began in June 1950 with a massive invasion of South Korea by the communist North Korea and ended in an armistice in July 1953 after the loss of many American lives. In 1952, Princess Elizabeth of England became queen at the age of twenty-five. The worldwide expansion of Communism created a major challenge for the United States. In

1953, Soviet dictator Joseph Stalin died, and Nikita Khrushchev succeeded him as premier. In 1957, the Soviet Union launched a satellite named Sputnik 1, ushering in the Space Race. In 1958, Mao Zedong initiated the disastrous Great Leap Forward program, and Fidel Castro became dictator of Cuba in 1959.

Domestically, the United States entered into a period of great prosperity and growth, with the baby boom continuing. The first organ transplant occurred in 1950, and colored television was introduced in 1951. Jonas Salk introduced the polio vaccine in 1952, and DNA was discovered in 1953. Disneyland, the first McDonald's restaurant, the Hula-Hoop, and Velcro were all introduced to the American public in the 1950s.[2]

Rev. Frank Baugh, the Years before Immanuel

Frank Baugh was born on November 30, 1916, in Jackson, Missouri.[3] Jackson is the county seat of Cape Girardeau County in eastern Missouri with a current population of roughly 14,000. The city was much smaller when Frank Baugh was born, with a population of roughly 2,100 people.[4] He later recalled that he began life in what he called "a simple and happily religious home."

His father was a barber who prospered in life and was well respected in the Jackson community, eventually becoming a magistrate of the county court. His mother was a source of joy for him and consecration for him. Upon graduating from high school, Frank Baugh matriculated at Southwest Baptist College in Bolivar, Missouri, where he received an associates of arts degree. He spent his junior and senior years at Baylor University in Waco, Texas, graduating in 1941 with a bachelor of arts degree.

While at Baylor University, Frank Baugh was inducted as a member of the Sigma Tau Delta honorary English society. During his last year at Baylor, he commuted weekly to Dallas where he served as a part-time assistant pastor at Fair Park Baptist Church. His good work there led to a full pastorate at Fruitdale Baptist Church in suburban Dallas. He received a master of divinity degree from Southwestern Baptist Theological Seminary in Fort Worth, Texas, in

1943.[5] While in seminary, he met Christine Knox, his future wife, who was a student at the Baylor School of Nursing in Dallas, Texas.[6] Christine was born on September 18, 1921, in Lelia Lake, Texas, about sixty miles southeast of Amarillo.[7]

Christine grew up on a farm outside Ashtola, Texas, a town about fifty miles southeast of Amarillo. When Christine Knox was a young girl, Ashtola had about fifty people living there.[8] After graduating from high school, Christine went to the Baylor School of Nursing in Dallas, Texas. While at the Baylor School of Nursing, she met Frank Baugh, her future husband.[9] On January 20, 1943, Rev. Frank Baugh and Christine Knox were married.[10]

Reverend Baugh's first pastorate in Oklahoma was at First Baptist Church, Hollis, in March 1944,[11] when he was twenty-eight years old.[12] Hollis is the county seat of Harmon County in southwestern Oklahoma on the Texas border. The population was listed as 2,060 in the 2010 census. In the mid-1940s, when Reverend Baugh served there, the population was approximately 3,000. The city was named for George W. Hollis, a local businessman, who founded a town in 1898.

The town of Hollis is located in an area that was disputed between Texas and the United States known as Greer County, Texas.[13] The dispute originated with a mapping error from the Adams–Onís Treaty of 1819. In 1896, the United States Supreme Court declared the Texas-Oklahoma border to be ninety miles further west than where Texas claimed. When Oklahoma gained statehood in 1907, Hollis, Texas, became Hollis, Oklahoma.[14]

On May 25, 1944, *The Baptist Messenger* printed his picture and noted that Frank Baugh was the new pastor of the First Baptist Church, Hollis. First Baptist Church, Hollis, was evidently well pleased with Rev. Frank Baugh and his wife, who was pregnant with twins. In fact, in the November 23, 1944, issue of *The Baptist Messenger*, J. H. McCuistion reported that the church recently raised the salary of Pastor Frank Baugh after only seven months in the pulpit. A second joyous event occurred the next day after Reverend Baugh received his raise. Twin boys arrived in the Baugh home when sons, Ronnie and Lonnie, were born. Two daughters, Mary and Becky, were born a few years later.

Three of the four children went to Oklahoma Baptist University. Ronnie Baugh graduated in 1966. [15] Lonnie Baugh graduated with a bachelor of science degree with a major in biology in 1967 and became a scientist. He later received his master's degree in microbiology from Oklahoma University and a doctorate in microbiology from the University of Texas. He did postdoctoral work at the University of California, Berkley, and spent thirty-five years working for several biological and pharmaceutical companies.

Lonnie Baugh was president of Fermentation Consulting. He was awarded a United States patent for Yeast Engineering Design and consulted for a broad base of fermentation projects domestically and internationally. Dr. Lonnie Baugh was a teacher in both the financial and academic world. He was a professor of microbiology at Oklahoma Baptist University from 1992 to 1994. Dr. Lonnie Baugh died on April 9, 2011, at St. Francis Hospital in Tulsa at age sixty-six following a battle with cancer. [16] Frank and Christine Baugh's daughter Mary also attended Oklahoma Baptist University but only for one year. [17]

Rev. Frank Baugh thrived as a young pastor in Hollis and became very active in west Oklahoma Baptist life. In the April 5, 1945, issue of *The Baptist Messenger*, he wrote,

> God is greatly blessing us [here at First Baptist Church, Hollis]. We have had about 27 additions in the last four Sundays, eleven of those for baptism. The people are receptive to the Gospel. Pray for us. [18]

In July 1945, while serving his first term as moderator of the Harmon Baptist Association, Reverend Baugh reported to the Baptist General Convention of Oklahoma that the association planned more revivals than ever before. He also reported the association planned to reach a love offering goal of $2,500 for the revivals. [19]

In August, the Quartz Mountain Baptist Assembly held a session at Lugert Lake, about fifty miles northeast of Hollis. Rev. Frank Baugh was one of seven speakers at the session. [20] In early September

1945, Rev. Frank Baugh led a revival at First Baptist Church, Vinson, Oklahoma. Mornings were devoted to Vacation Bible School led by Ms. Ruth Stone of the Home Mission Board. Later in the month, on September 14, 1945, the Harmon Baptist Association met at Harmony Baptist Church. Reverend Baugh was again elected moderator and delivered the annual sermon. His message was based on the prophecy of Zacharias and was entitled Not by Might nor by Power, but by My Spirit Saith the Lord.[21] In late October 1945, Rev. Frank Baugh led a revival at First Baptist Church, Sayre.[22]

In 1945, Rev. Frank Baugh and his wife, Christine, attended their first annual meeting of the Baptist General Convention of Oklahoma. The annual meeting was held in Oklahoma City. They came as messengers from First Baptist Church, Hollis. He was recognized at the annual meeting as the moderator of the Harmon Baptist Association.[23]

Throughout 1946, Rev. Frank Baugh continued his service to Baptist causes in Hollis, the Harmon Baptist Association, and within southwestern Oklahoma. In March of 1946, Reverend Baugh attended a unique soul winning conference and revival hosted by Pastor J. A. Pennington and director of missions Dorvell Tabb at First Baptist Church, Mangum. Pastors and preachers from all around southwestern Oklahoma spent a week in Mangum. Rev. John Kelly of Anadarko brought the Bible study and spoke on "The Practical Church Problem."[24]

God used Rev. Frank Baugh to grow the membership of First Baptist Church, Hollis. The exciting growth can be illustrated by the May 1946 Vacation Bible School goals for the church. Rev. Frank Baugh set his Vacation Bible School goal at one hundred more students than last year. This goal was reasonable since Sunday School at First Baptist Church, Hollis, averaged more than one hundred participants over last year.

From August 11 to 25, 1946, Reverend Baugh led a revival in Hess Baptist Church in the Jackson-Greer Baptist Association. There were ten baptisms, and eight more individuals joined the church by submitting letters of membership from other Baptist churches.[25] On September 12, 1946, the Harmon Baptist Association met with

Louis Baptist Church, a country church south of Gould. Reverend Baugh served as moderator.

Under Reverend Baugh's leadership, a simultaneous school of missions and a Simultaneous Revival were planned for the association for the coming year. The association was a strong association, and practically every church in the association gave through the Cooperative Program to world missions. The association reached its goal set for last year and increased the goal 10 percent for 1947. The association's 9 churches reported 113 baptisms for the year, an increase over the record that was set last year.[26]

Rev. Frank and Christine Baugh attended the 1946 Annual Meeting of the Baptist General Convention of Oklahoma that was held in Oklahoma City as messengers from First Baptist Church, Hollis. He was becoming better known within the Oklahoma Baptist community and was asked to lead the devotion taken from Ephesians 1:1–14 on Thursday morning, November 7. At the annual meeting, he was appointed to *The Baptist Messenger* and Religious Literature Committee. Christine Baugh was appointed to the Obituaries Committee.[27]

After three years at Hollis, Rev. Frank Baugh moved to Hobart in January 1947 to become the pastor of First Baptist Church, Hobart.[28] Hobart is the county seat of Kiowa County, Oklahoma. The population was 3,756 at the 2010 census, but in the late 1940s, the population was nearly 5,300.[29] Upon moving to Hobart, Rev. Baugh continued his efforts to be active in Oklahoma Baptist Life. He was appointed as the director of the Southwestern Oklahoma Baptist Assembly that took place from June 30 to July 4, 1947.[30]

From March 23 to 30, 1947, just three months after assuming the pulpit of First Baptist Church, Hobart, Rev. Frank Baugh held a youth revival. There were seven additions to First Baptist Church, Hobart, as the result of the youth revival, and two young people consecrated their lives for special Christian service—Harold Stephens and Leonard Hill, son of Chaplain and Mrs. Ralph A. Hill. The first four evenings were devoted to a Training Union Study Course entitled The Bible. The average attendance at the youth revival was 195. The climax of the week was an Oklahoma Baptist University gospel team composed of John Wiles, a ministerial student; Kurt Weiss, an ethnic Jew who had accepted Christ as his Savior and who was a medical student; Jim Bell, a ministerial student; Carl Hallford, a ministerial student; and Harold Inman, a religious education student.[31]

In August 1947, Rev. Frank Baugh was one of the pastors selected to preach at the Falls Creek Youth Assembly. He delivered two different messages, Witnessing for Christ and How It Began.[32]

Soul winning was an important part of Rev. Frank Baugh's life. In his column entitled "I Will, He Said" in the September 25, 1947, issue of *The Baptist Messenger*, columnist C. M. Curb told of a visitation that he and Rev. Frank Baugh had recently made:

> We went nine miles into the country to see [the family.] When we entered the home, the wife said, "We are having an early supper so we can go to church tonight." The husband invited us for a moment into the front room to show us a picture of their son who had been shot down over Germany. As he wept, I said, there is a passage of Scripture that I want you to hear that will comfort you. It is Matthew 11:28, [and] I quoted it. "Come unto me all ye that labor and are heavy laden, and I will give you rest." When I appealed to him to accept Christ, he reached out his hand tremblingly and said, "I will!" As we rejoiced together, Frank Baugh, the pastor, won the man's daughter in the next room. They both came [to Rev. Baugh's church] and were baptized that same night. The man said to one of the workers, "I want to thank you all for coming."[33]

In October 1947, Rev. Frank Baugh held a second revival at First Baptist Church, Hobart, the first being the spring youth revival. There were 66 additions to the church, with 44 people being baptized, 13 by letter, and the rest by profession of faith with baptism to follow. The following Sunday, the church experienced a record attendance with 786 in Sunday School and 200 in Training Union. Rev. Henry Kinkeade from Baton Rouge, Louisiana, was the evangelist.[34]

In his first year as pastor of First Baptist Church, Hobart, Rev. Frank Baugh was selected as moderator of the Concord-Kiowa Baptist Association. Under his leadership, the association set a tithers' goal of 1,500 individuals and a Cooperative Program goal of $16,500.

Rev. Frank Baugh and his wife Christine attended the 1947 Annual Meeting of the Baptist General Convention of Oklahoma held in Tulsa as messengers from First Baptist Church, Hobart. At the meeting, Reverend Baugh was appointed to the board of trustees of Oklahoma Baptist University. Christine Baugh led the Woman's Missionary Union Memorial Service for state officers who had died the prior year. She read from John 12:24–25. Mrs. Baugh was twenty-six years old at the time.

In the March 11, 1948, issue of *The Baptist Messenger*, Rev. Frank Baugh wrote a two-column article explaining why he, as a Baptist, could not support the World Day of Prayer.[35] The World Day of Prayer was started in the United States in 1887 by Mrs. Mary James and a group of Methodist women who called for a day of prayer for home missions. Two years later in 1889, two Baptist women joined them and called for a day of prayer for the world mission for all Christians. The day of prayer expanded to Canada and then to the British Isles in the 1930s.[36]

Reverend Baugh's concerns were based upon the fact that the World Day of Prayer group called for prayer to our "Parent-God for our social and economic betterment." He stated that this call to prayer was not consistent with the Bible's call that we can only become brothers and sisters in Christ and children of God through repentance from sin and faith in Jesus Christ as Savior and Lord.[37]

Rev. Frank Baugh and his wife, Christine, attended the 1948 Annual Meeting of the Baptist General Convention of Oklahoma held in Muskogee as messengers from First Baptist Church, Hobart. At the meeting, Reverend Baugh was again appointed to the board of trustees of Oklahoma Baptist University. He was also appointed to the Program Committee for the 1949 Annual Meeting.[38]

In January 1949, Rev. Frank Baugh had a Sunday School study course scheduled for First Baptist Church, Hobart. Unfortunately, the weather did not cooperate, and January 1949 started out cold and bleak. In spite of howling blizzards, inches of sleet and snow, and near-zero temperatures, an average of fifty-one persons attended a Sunday School study course taught by Reverend Baugh at First Baptist Church, Hobart, from January 24 to 28. Those who were not able to attend because of the weather made extra preparations later to qualify for awards. Over a hundred teachers qualified for credit on the courses taught.[39]

In summer 1949, Rev. Frank Baugh held a very successful revival in Hobart. The renowned Oklahoma pastor Rev. Hugh Bumpus was the evangelist and C. M. Curb, a columnist for *The Baptist Messenger*, served as a personal worker. In his February 23, 1950, column, C. M. Curb tells of an experience that he had with Rev. Frank Baugh. C. M. Curb wrote,

Figure 7.2. 1950s Immanuel Yahnseh advertisement

Finding those who want to be saved is the constant problem of the soul winner. One way to find them is by being led by the Holy Spirit, as Phillip was led to the Ethiopian [in] Acts 8:29. [Frank Baugh and I] were driving along the street when I felt led of the Holy Spirit to speak to a young man who was standing in the back yard. I suggested to Frank that we stop. He was driving so fast that he had passed the house, so we circled the block and came back and the young man had walked out to the street. He came up to my side of the car and I asked him if he was a Christian. He said, "No," and I explained to him how to be saved. He was ready and willing, as the Ethiopian, to be saved. While we were rejoicing over his conversion, his sister-in-law, whom he was visiting, came out to the car and remarked, "I know you Bro. Curb. You held a meeting for us at Headrick." I asked her if she had transferred her church membership to First Baptist Church, Hobart, and she had not. She promised to come that night and did. This story would not be complete without telling the story of the conversion of three young men who lived next door to this family. They had just moved in, and the young lady we were talking to asked us to call on them. Mr. Nash, a Deacon, and I called on them and found there were three young men in the home not saved. We held a service in the home, but we did not win them. A day or two later, Bro. Baugh and Bro. Hugh Bumpas, who was preaching in the revival, called on them and won the two oldest boys. The younger brother would not surrender to the Lord, but he did come to see his brothers baptized. After the service adjourned, by the help of the boys that were baptized, and the mother, we won the youngest brother to the Lord. By following the leading of the Holy Spirit, to stop and speak to the young man in the yard, four young men were saved, and a mother joined the church by letter.[40]

In 1949, Rev. Frank Baugh and his wife, Christine, attended the Annual Meeting of the Baptist General Convention of Oklahoma held in Oklahoma City as messengers from First Baptist Church, Hobart, for the last time. At the meeting, Reverend Baugh was again appointed to the board of trustees of Oklahoma Baptist University. He was also appointed to the board of trustees of the Baptist Orphans' Home and the Committee on Nominations. The minutes of the meeting noted that Reverend Baugh was again the moderator of the Concord-Kiowa Baptist Association, but that their annual Cooperative Program goal had grown to twenty-one thousand dollars.[41]

Rev. Frank Baugh, the Immanuel Years

In February 1950, Rev. Frank O. Baugh became the ninth pastor of Immanuel Baptist Church. His first service in the pulpit was Wednesday, February 15, 1950. His first Sunday sermon was on February 19, 1950. Reverend Baugh was thirty-four years old when he began his service to Immanuel Baptist Church.[42]

As was his pattern with his previous churches and associations, Reverend Baugh did not take long to get involved in activities at Immanuel Baptist Church and the Pottawatomie-Lincoln Baptist Association. On Tuesday, February 15, 1950, Rev. Baugh presided over a specially called Deacons' meeting. At that meeting, arrangements were made to hold a meeting with Rev. Roy Ditmar of Sharon Baptist Church so that the South Mission property could be formally deeded to Sharon Baptist Church. In addition, Thad

Figure 7.3. Associate pastor Rev. William Lutker

Roberts was called as the full-time music director, and Rev. William Lutker was retained as an associate pastor until school was out.

Reverend Lutker was an Oklahoma Baptist University assistant professor of Education and had been doing interim preaching at Immanuel Baptist Church until Reverend Baugh assumed the pulpit.[43] Reverend Lutker went on to become the pastor of First Baptist Church, Harrah,[44] and of First Baptist Church, Weatherford.[45] The Deacons also discussed how to best support the South McKinley Mission Church.

At the May 14, 1950, Deacons' meeting, the resignation of J. P. Hilty as pastor of the South McKinley Mission Church was accepted.

The Deacons appointed Art Dirkie as interim pastor in his place. The Deacons also voted to determine the legality of building an additional room onto the mission.

Figure 7.4. Rev. Frank Baugh, the Immanuel Days

At the June 6, 1950, Deacons' meeting, the need for restrooms at the Temple Mission Church was discussed. The Deacons decided that if the Temple Mission Church was unable to build the restrooms, then Immanuel Baptist Church would build them. The pastor of the Temple Mission Church at the time was Rev. Lewis Krouse. After receiving a report from Reverend Krouse in the October 10, 1950, Deacons' meeting, the Deacons of Immanuel Baptist Church voted in their November 7, 1950, meeting to underwrite three hundred dollars for the construction of the restrooms with the money to be raised with a special offering.

At the July 2, 1950, Deacons' meeting, Rev. Frank Baugh presented a plan to reorganize the church's finances. Some of the key points were the following: (1) Mrs. Mote, the church secretary, would do all check writing and she would maintain the books; (2) the Finance Committee would be dissolved and the Deacons would assume those responsibilities; (3) a finance officer would be elected to work with the pastor, the financial secretary, and the Deacons; and (4) a quarterly financial report would be printed in *The Immanuel Messenger*.

The report would show each budget item, the percent spent year to date, average income for each Sunday, and a comparison of spending at the same point last year. The report also called for a special offering on Sunday, August 20, 1950, to liquidate the debt on the house recently purchased for the Music Director. The Deacons agreed to present the plan to the congregation.[46]

Rev. Frank Baugh and his wife, Christine, attended the 1950 Annual Meeting of the Baptist General Convention of Oklahoma held in Tulsa as messengers from Immanuel Baptist Church. At the meeting, Reverend Baugh was again appointed to the board of trustees of Oklahoma Baptist University. The minutes of the meeting noted that Reverend Baugh was the incoming moderator of the Pottawatomie-Lincoln Baptist Association and that the association's annual Cooperative Program goal was fifty-eight thousand dollars, reflecting the larger association with a larger population density.[47]

Starting in February 1951, Rev. Frank Baugh and the Deacons began developing plans and promoting the construction of an education building for Immanuel Baptist Church. Also at the February 6, 1951, Deacons' meeting, the Deacons voted to hire Byran Abbott as pastor of the McKinley Street Mission Church at a salary of five dollars per week. At the May 8, 1951, Deacons' meeting, the Deacons voted to enlist 200 members to subscribe to an additional fifty cents per week to make up for the deficit in the budget caused by Oklahoma Baptist University students being away for the summer and by the hiring of a full-time music director.

Plans for the education building had progressed sufficiently by the May 1951 Deacons' meeting for the Deacons to vote to hire Noftsger and Lawrence, Architects, to create a plan for a two story, fifty-foot educational building attached to the southeast corner of the building. In the July 17, 1951, Deacons' meeting, the Deacons voted to call J. P. Hilty as the pastor of the McKinley Street Mission Church and to investigate a five-year lease on a South Harrison Street property for the mission.

At the 1951 Annual Meeting of the Baptist General Convention of Oklahoma, Rev. Frank Baugh was appointed to the BGCO Board of Directors. The minutes also noted that Reverend Baugh was elected to be the stewardship chairman of the Cooperative Program effort for the Pottawatomie-Lincoln Baptist Association under the leadership of Rev. W. F. Crow. The associational goal was again fifty-eight thousand dollars, third largest in the state behind the Oklahoma City and Tulsa associations.

Figure 7.5. Dr. Frank Baugh, Immanuel Baptist Church

Also in the minutes of the annual meeting was a report by Dr. John W. Raley of Oklahoma Baptist University on the state of the university. Dr. Raley made special note of Rev. Fred Willhoite and Rev. Frank Baugh who chaired the Scholarship Committee of the Board of Trustees. More than fifty Oklahoma Baptist University students received scholarships from their own local congregations because of the work of Reverends Willhoite and Baugh.[48]

At its February 19, 1951, annual meeting, the Pottawatomie-Lincoln Baptist Association elected its steering committee for the 1951 Evangelistic Crusade. The crusade was a Shawnee-wide event held from April 22 to May 6. Rev. Frank Baugh was elected the chairman for pre-crusade special rallies and Immanuel Baptist Church associate pastor William Lutker was elected census chairman. The first special rally for the crusade was held on February 20 at Immanuel Baptist Church.[49]

In the January 1952 Deacons' meeting, the Finance Committee announced that the debt on the music director's house had been liquidated. By the April 1952 Deacons' meeting, Leroy McClard had begun serving as the education director. He would later resign in December 1952. In the May 13, 1952, Deacons' meeting, J. P. Hilty, who had been hired ten months before as the pastor of the McKinley Street Mission Church, submitted his resignation. Art Dirkie was asked to serve as the interim pastor. Also at that meeting, the Deacons approved the purchase of an attic fan for the parsonage and initiated a cost study to consider air conditioning the sanctuary.

Problems with the foundation of the sanctuary continued. In the July 1952 Deacons' meeting, funds were approved for additional waterproofing the foundation and for painting the basement. Also in the July 1952 Deacons' meeting, the Deacons voted to provide twenty-five dollars per month each to the Foreign Mission Board missionaries sponsored by Immanuel Baptist Church, Jaxie Short and Leslie Williams. Jaxie Short was the daughter of longtime Immanuel member W. T. Short. In the August 1952 Deacons' meeting, the Deacons discussed the need and approach to financing and constructing a nursery building.[50]

At the 1952 Annual Meeting of the Baptist General Convention of Oklahoma, Rev. Frank Baugh attended as a messenger from Immanuel Baptist Church. He was selected to serve on the board of trustees of the Baptist General Convention of Oklahoma. He was also selected to be the stewardship chairman for the Cooperative Program campaign for the Pottawatomie-Lincoln Baptist Association. The stewardship goal for the association was tied for 3rd highest in the state at $60,000. The highest Stewardship Goal in the state at $273,000 belonged to the Oklahoma County Baptist Association whose stewardship campaign was headed by former Immanuel Baptist Church pastor Dr. Claybron Deering.[51]

By the February 2, 1953, business meeting, plans for the nursery building had progressed to a point where a steering committee for the building fund drive was selected. At the August 1952 Deacons' meeting, the Deacons selected two building fund dates to raise funds for the nursery building. These were September 13, 1953, Sealing the Corner Stone Day, and November 1, 1953, Homecoming Day.[52] The plans for Babyland called for a brick building east of the sanctuary with four nurseries and a library on the main floor and two adult Sunday School departments on the second floor.[53] Also in the November 1953 Deacons' meeting, the successful calling of Jack Frost as music director was announced.[54]

At the 1953 Annual Meeting of the Baptist General Convention of Oklahoma held in Tulsa, Reverend and Mrs. Baugh served as messengers from Immanuel Baptist Church. He was again elected to the BGCO board of directors and was appointed to the Ministers' Retirement Committee within the board. Within the baptisms, membership, enrollment, and financial data for the association that was released in the annual meeting minutes, Immanuel Baptist Church was credited with 80 baptisms, 2,229 members, and a total giving to Baptist missions efforts of $16,313.95.[55]

Rev. Frank Baugh and Immanuel Baptist Church continued to be involved in civic, educational, church, and state events in 1954. Reverend Baugh and Immanuel Baptist Church sponsored the visit to Shawnee from January 9 to 14 of Charles A. Wells, a well-known religious cartoonist and journalist. Mr. Wells did a series of conferences on Christ and World Need. He also made appearances before school and civic groups and was on a daily radio broadcast.[56]

The church's involvement in Christian education was illustrated at the January 12, 1954, Deacons' meeting, when the Deacons voted to apply $250 from the scholarship fund to the tuition expenses of church members Richard Kim and his wife, Frances.[57] Richard Kim was a native of Hawaii who moved his family 4,000 miles from Wailuku on the island of Maui to Shawnee in fall 1953 to attend Oklahoma Baptist University and to prepare for the ministry. Kim and his wife, Frances, entered Oklahoma Baptist University as freshmen while their three daughters, Vivienne, Frances, and Wanda, entered the third, fifth, and sixth grades at the Shawnee Woodrow Wilson School.

The Kim family was active in a Baptist church on their home island of Maui. Richard Kim had been a Christian about three years and had served as Sunday School teacher, chairman of the board of Deacons, and youth worker during that time. Richard Kim came from Korean ancestry, and Mrs. Kim was of Japanese descent. He was a second-generation American citizen, and Mrs. Kim was a third-generation citizen. The September 24, 1953, issue of *The Baptist Messenger* noted,

> The [Kim] family noticed differences here, of course, including the people, the climate, and the food. Mrs. Kim added, "We like Oklahoma, but we can't get used to wearing our shoes all the time. We go shopping barefooted in Hawaii." Winter coats, home and car heaters, and high-heeled shoes are also items that the [Kim family] did not use last year. The girls were pleased to find that the Shawnee schools were little different from those at home A World war II veteran, Kim was stationed in the south Pacific during the war. After receiving his degree from OBU, he plans to attend one of the Baptist seminaries. Mrs. Kim expects to complete work for a degree during the time her husband is attending OBU.[58]

Richard Kim was evidently a man of courage and conviction. The September 14, 1954, Deacons' meeting minutes noted that Richard Kim presented to the board of Deacons his conviction of the evil of selling Coca-Cola and other soft drinks on Sunday and requested that the Deacons take the appropriate action. A. V. Daugherty moved and Brother McKerracher seconded that the Coca-Cola machine be moved into the kitchen and that nothing be sold through that machine on Sunday. The motion passed. Brother Daniel then moved and Cap Gardner seconded that the current machine be traded for a more suitable one. The motion passed. Brother Presley then moved and Rev. Frank Baugh seconded that Richard Kim be given a vote of thanks. The motion passed.[59]

In the June 15, 1954, Deacons' meeting, Rev. Frank Baugh presented the need for a new education building based on the growth the church had been experiencing. The Deacons voted that the church should be asked to create a committee to develop plans for an education building. A committee was created, and over the next few months, plans were indeed developed. By January 1955, the church membership was sufficiently pleased with the plans so that a press release was issued. The January 2, 1955, issue of *The Baptist Messenger* reported,

> Immanuel [Baptist] Church, Shawnee, has approved tentative floor plans for an educational unit to be built late this year or in 1956. The addition will provide for 12 departments, from birth through age 17, with a third Adult department. Also approved were plans for a new brick parsonage. Frank O. Baugh will begin his sixth year as pastor in February.[60]

Rev. Frank Baugh served a very active role in the 1954 Annual Meeting of the Baptist General Convention of Oklahoma held in Oklahoma City. He and Christine Baugh served as messengers from Immanuel Baptist Church. He served on the Credentials Committee as chairman and was again elected to the board of directors of the BGCO. He was appointed to the Advisory Council for the Baptist Foundation. During the business session, Rev. Frank Baugh nominated Rev. W. H. Evans, pastor of the Blackburn Chapel Baptist Church, for president of the convention. Rev. Roscoe Miller of Chickasha nominated Dr. H. H. Hobbs, pastor of the First Baptist Church, Oklahoma City, for president. In the subsequent voting, Reverend Evans was elected.[61]

In February 1955, Rev. Ray Johnson was called to be minister of music and education at Immanuel Baptist Church. Rev. Ray Johnson had just spent three years at River Oaks Church, Fort Worth, Texas, in the same position while he worked on a master of music degree at Southwestern Baptist Theological Seminary in Fort Worth. Reverend and Mrs. Johnson had a four-month-old daughter when he was hired.

Part of his hiring package was the use of the educational parsonage at 118 South Eden, just west of the church. Reverend Johnson was a native of Kentucky and held a bachelor of music degree from Georgetown College and master's degrees from both Southern Baptist Theological Seminary in Louisville, Kentucky, and Southwestern Baptist Theological Seminary.[62] Reverend Johnson would later resign in November 1956 to be replaced by Richard Farley as minister of music.[63]

Richard Farley was born May 28, 1925, in Miami, Oklahoma. After high school graduation in 1943, he worked in a shipyard in Portland, Oregon, before enlisting in the US Navy during World War II. Following the war, Richard Farley earned a bachelor of music degree from Oklahoma Baptist University in 1950. He earned a master of music degree from Northwestern University, Evanston, Illinois, and a doctorate of music education degree from the University of Oklahoma. He did additional graduate study at the Eastman School of Music in Rochester, New York.

After serving as minister of music at First Baptist Church, Elizabethton, Tennessee, and at Central Baptist Church, Muskogee, he joined the Oklahoma Baptist University music faculty in 1954. At the time of his retirement in May 1990, he served as degree counselor for the College of Fine Arts. During his career, he served as minister of music in a number of churches, including First Baptist Church,

McLoud; First Baptist Church, Stroud; Wallace Avenue Baptist; Immanuel Baptist; and First Christian Church, Shawnee.[64]

The need for a new education building was a topic of frequent discussion at the 1955 and 1956 Deacons' meetings. At the January 4, 1955, Deacons' meeting, a Building Finance Committee was appointed. In their May 10, 1955, Deacons' meeting, the Deacons agreed to present the education building plans and a proposal to hire an architect to the church. In August 1955, the trustees signed a contract with the architect. In the March and July 1956, Deacons' meetings, final financial arrangements were discussed.

The Immanuel Baptist Church cabin at Falls Creek was also a topic of frequent discussion at the 1955 and 1956 Deacons' meetings. The existing cabin was evidently in disrepair, and at the February 22, 1955, Deacons' meeting the Deacons discussed the need to build a new cabin. The Deacons voted to recommend to the church that a new cabin be built and that the funds for the construction be raised through a special fund drive. Other church events led to the shelving of the plans to build a new cabin.

At the June 19, 1955, Deacons' meeting, a committee was appointed to determine if repairs to the current cabin were feasible and, if so, what the cost of repairs might be. At the November 15, 1955, Deacons' meeting, a proposal to rent a cabin for future use at Falls Creek was referred to the Falls Creek Committee. Finally, at the December 18, 1955, Deacons' meeting, the Falls Creek Committee proposed that Immanuel Baptist Church purchase half ownership in the Nogales Avenue Baptist Church's cabin for five thousand dollars. The Deacons accepted this proposal. The July 15, 1956, Deacons' meeting minutes record that the loan for the new education building would include twenty thousand dollars for a new parsonage and five thousand to complete the purchase of half ownership in the Nogales Avenue Baptist Church's cabin. In August 1956, the old Immanuel Baptist Church cabin at the Falls Creek Assembly was given to the Pottawatomie-Lincoln Baptist Association. [65]

In May 1955, Dr. and Mrs. Baugh became the first husband-wife team to be graduated from OBU in the same commencement exercises when she earned her bachelor of arts degree and he received the doctor of divinity degree. [66]

At the 1955 Annual Meeting of the Baptist General Convention of Oklahoma held in Tulsa, Dr. and Mrs. Baugh served as messengers from Immanuel Baptist Church. He was elected to the executive board and was placed on the Assembly Committee. He was also placed on the Advisory Council of the Baptist Foundation, the Building Committee, and on the Committee on Nominations.

Immanuel Baptist Church had the 25th strongest church in the state in Cooperative Program giving, with an offering of $11,306. The strongest church in the state was First Baptist Church, Oklahoma City, under the leadership of Rev. Herschel Hobbs with an offering of $61,424. First Baptist Church, Lawton, under the leadership of former Immanuel Baptist Church pastor Tom Wiles, was 8th strongest with an offering of $20,557. Dr. Baugh was also selected as the Pottawatomie-Lincoln Baptist Association Cooperative Program Chairman with a goal of $80,000 for the association.[67]

January 1956 started the year strongly. The business meeting minutes for January 11, 1956, noted that the church had 1,493 resident members and 1,036 nonresident members for a total of 2,529 members. Sunday School enrollment was 1,566 attendees, and average church attendance was 815. Receipts for the month were $8,475.32, and regular expenditures were $6,181.86. In addition, $1,000.00 was paid on the building debt, and $950.00 was paid to the architect. The Woman's Memorial Union President, Mrs. Merrill Woods, reported that March 5 through March 9 would be designated as a week of prayer for the Annie Armstrong offering and that the goal for the church's offering was five hundred dollars. At the June 27, 1956, business meeting, Walker Thompson moved, and the church voted to sell the old parsonage that was somewhat in disrepair for a thousand.

At the July 18, 1956, business meeting, problems with the ductwork and the heating system that had existed for several years were again addressed, and bids to correct the problem were solicited. Only 1 company made a bid. The church voted to accept the bid. At the July 25, 1956, business meeting, Kenneth Eyer, the chairman of the Building Committee, announced that three bids for the new parsonage had been received ranging from a low bid of $19,178.00 by Burse Borden to a high bid of $23,440.57 by Elmer Freeman and Company. Mr. Eyer, speaking for the committee, moved that the low bid be accepted with a start date of August 1, 1956 and a completion date of ninety days hence. The motion passed.

At the September 26, 1956, business meeting, Harold Hall and Fred Williams were ordained to the Deacon Ministry. Following the ordination, Dr. Frank Baugh presented a contract with the Attebery Sign Company for twenty-five dollars per month for three years for a sign on Highway 270 west of Oklahoma Baptist University. Burse Borden made a motion that the contract be accepted and signed. The church passed the motion.[68]

An article in the March 1, 1956, issue of *The Baptist Messenger*, noted that Dr. Frank Baugh of Immanuel Baptist Church just observed his sixth anniversary as pastor on February 19. The membership presented him and Mrs. Baugh with a check and other personal mementos from the members. The article noted that under his leadership, the church received 500 new members by baptism and reached an average Sunday School attendance of 815. The church erected one new building and another building in the planning stage. It also built a new parsonage and redecorated and air-conditioned its auditorium. The present budget calls for $86,770 in membership donations, with $16,000, or 18.4 percent, going to the Cooperative Program.[69]

In spring 1956, the Southern Baptist Convention continued its Simultaneous Revivals Initiative Crusade. In the last week of March, the Delaware-Osage Baptist Association conducted twenty-six Simultaneous Revivals. One of those revivals was at Trinity Baptist Church in Bartlesville. Frank Baugh was the evangelist for that revival. The song leader was twenty-two-year-old Rev. John Bisagno, a 1955 Oklahoma Baptist University graduate. Reverend Bisagno would eventually become one of the greatest Southern Baptist evangelical leaders.[70]

About two weeks later from April 8 to 22, 1955, Dr. Baugh held a revival at Immanuel Baptist Church in which he did the preaching. Immanuel had fifty-four additions during the revival. Of those, twenty-nine were by baptism. Dr. Baugh also received two professions for special service. Carlyle Brooks directed visitation, and Joe Trussell served as the guest musician.

Enthusiasm for revival continued that summer at Immanuel Baptist Church. During the week of June 17, 1956, evangelist Billy Graham led a crusade in Oklahoma City. Five busloads of Immanuel Baptist Church members journeyed to the Billy Graham meeting in Oklahoma City on Tuesday, June 19. The trip was organized and sponsored by the church's Brotherhood Ministry.[71] Manoi Adair fondly remembers going on one of those buses with her husband Preston.[72]

The September 13, 1956, issue of *The Baptist Messenger* had a full page with three columns dedicated to the Cooperative Program. Prominent pastors from around the state made enthusiastic endorsements of the Cooperative Program. One of those pastors was Dr. Frank Baugh. He stated,

> You can count on us to increase our Cooperative Program giving to missions [by] at least in the amount of $1 per resident member. We must have some measure by which to grow, and if God will continue to lead the vision of our leadership to larger things, Baptists will continue to lift Christ up before the World.[73]

In the October 25, 1956, issue of *The Baptist Messenger*, editor Jack Gritz wrote an editorial entitled "Kinds of Baptists" in which he outlined several different Baptist denominations that existed within the United States—e.g., Southern, Free Will, Missionary, and Primitive. He also outlined the similarities and differences between the denominations and noted that the differences may cause Southern Baptist churches to decline a membership by letter from another denomination.[74] A letter from Dr. Frank Baugh, responding to the editorial, appeared in the next issue of *The Baptist Messenger*.

Dr. Baugh made two points: First, Dr. Baugh noted that the name Southern Baptist has long ago shed its geographic significance.

The name, he said, stands for a biblical position, which has become a trademark too valuable to lose. Second, Dr. Baugh cautioned that churches need to look carefully at the individual who is wanting to join the church either by profession or by letter. After printing Dr. Baugh's letter, editor Gritz stated that he heartily agreed.[75]

At the 1956 Annual Meeting of the Baptist General Convention of Oklahoma held in Oklahoma City, Dr. and Mrs. Baugh served as messengers from Immanuel Baptist Church. He was again active at the annual meeting. He continued his place on the Advisory Council of the Baptist Foundation and was placed on the Christian Education Committee. Immanuel Baptist Church had the 27th strongest church in the state in Cooperative Program giving, with an offering of $12,822.[76] At the Woman's Missionary Union meetings, Christine Baugh was elected Chairman of the Mission Study Committee.[77]

As newly elected state mission study chairman, Mrs. Christine Baugh presided over the State Mission Study Institute that was held on December 13. At that meeting, the five books of the graded series of home mission study books and teaching helps were presented. There were 206 women present at the institute. Table decorations for the luncheon represented the mission fields presented in the five books. A film entitled *World Missions, USA*, was shown. These 206 women prepared and led in associational institutes for Baptist associations across the state.[78]

At the 1957 Annual Meeting of the Baptist General Convention of Oklahoma held in Tulsa, Dr. and Mrs. Baugh served as messengers from Immanuel Baptist Church. Dr. Baugh served on the Resolution Committee and the Christian Education Committee. He continued to serve on the Advisory Council of the Baptist Foundation.

The minutes of the annual meeting included a report about the Oklahoma Baptist University Summer School for Preachers. The article noted that some of the best teachers in the land were brought in to teach in the school. That last summer, the faculty composed of Dr. J. M. Price of Southwestern Seminary; Dr. Frank and Mrs. Baugh, Immanuel Baptist Church, Shawnee; and Dr. Jack Gritz, editor of *The Baptist Messenger*. There were 123 pastors enrolled in the summer of 1956.[79]

A full-page article written by Dr. Baugh appeared in the January 24, 1957, issue of *The Baptist Messenger*. The article was entitled "Glamorizing the Going." In the article, Dr. Baugh noted that a recent syndicated article entitled "Wanted: 56,000 Clergymen" had appeared in many of the major newspapers across the nation. The article had decried the shortage of pastors for the pulpits of the nation.

Dr. Baugh noted in his article that the Southern Baptists have a slightly different problem. While our seminaries and colleges were filled with some of the finest ministerial students that we have ever had, there was a dire shortage of students for the secondary roles within a church. These roles were ministers of education, music, and youth and many other vocational choices within the sphere of the Christian concept such as counseling, journalism, and directors of recreational programs and religious dramas.

Dr. Baugh said they needed to "glamorize the going" of the work of the Kingdom. Dr. Baugh praised the leadership of Dr. John Raley and the Oklahoma Baptist University administration and noted a strategy meeting was scheduled for the campus at Oklahoma Baptist University on Founder's Day, Friday, February 22, 1957. Dr. Baugh noted the event was a Christian education convention and was the only such meeting of its kind in the world. He stated, "The administration at Oklahoma Baptist University is meeting the problem head-on, realistically, and yet in a daring venture outreach."[80]

When the Christian Education Convention was held, it was a multifaceted event with some of the giants of Oklahoma Baptist and Southern Baptist life in attendance. Not only did the conference include a discussion of the need to glamorize "doing of the ministry" positions, but the conference also included the dedication of Kerr Dormitory and the plans for Raley Chapel were presented. Honored participants at the conference included the following:

- Gene Bartlett, secretary of church music for the Baptist General Convention of Oklahoma;

- Dr. J. Thurmond George, president of the Baptist General Convention of Oklahoma;

- Oklahoma senator Robert S. Kerr;

- Dr. Auguie Henry, executive secretary, The Baptist Foundation;

- Dr. H. H. Hobbs, president of the Oklahoma Baptist University board of trustees and pastor of First Baptist Church, Oklahoma City;

- Dr. T. Bert Lackey, executive secretary of the Baptist General Convention of Oklahoma; and

- Dr. Walter Pope Binns, president of William Jewell College.

As chairman of the Christian Education Commission for the Baptist General Convention of Oklahoma, Dr. Frank Baugh delivered a message entitled Capturing Student Potential. John Stetler, assistant professor of music in the Oklahoma Baptist University, led the Yahnseh Band at the conference; and Dr. Warren M. Angell, dean of the College of Fine Arts, Oklahoma Baptist University, led the Bison Glee Club at the conference.[81]

The Deacons were very active in 1957. In their January 8, 1957, meeting, they voted to allocate five hundred dollars to the Raley Chapel Building Fund in honor of Immanuel Baptist Church missionaries Jaxie Short and Leslie Williams. Certificates of honor were to be produced and given to the mothers of the two missionaries at a special public ceremony on Friday, February 22, 1957. Also at that meeting, structural problems with the east entrance to the church were discussed, but an approach to solving the problem was not determined, so the matter was referred to the Maintenance Committee.

At the February 10, 1957, Deacons' meeting, the Deacons voted to repair the roof. Also, the Deacons were informed by Dr. Baugh that Rev. Vern Baker had accepted the call to be the Immanuel Baptist Church director of education at an annual salary of $4,800 plus an expense allowance of $300. Reverend Baker's start date was set at April 1.

At the April 30, 1957, Deacons' meeting, Charles Hulsey made a motion that the church "get into high gear" on the building program for the education building and the nursery. Ben Aylor seconded the motion, which passed. Fred Williams then led "a good discussion on the need for more reverence in our church services."

At the May 14, 1957, Deacons' meeting, the Building Committee brought a proposal to build the education building in two stages. The committee reported that the American National Bank was receptive to the approach and was willing to loan up to seventy thousand dollars for the first phase. Wilbur Patterson made a motion, seconded by Ben Aylor, to have a cost breakdown of the one-stage approach versus the two-stage approach be made. The motion carried. Cap Gardner then made a motion, seconded by Carl Webb, to have the church hold a "Double Tithe" Sunday to raise the two thousand dollars needed to repair the roof.

At the September 17, 1957, Deacons' meeting, the Deacons were informed that Brother Carley had obtained the civic center for a loyalty dinner. A loyalty dinner was a key component of a Southern Baptist initiative known as the Forward Program of Church Finance. To help secure funding for the general church budget and for special building programs, a series of events culminating in a loyalty dinner occurred at each church participating in the program. In order to secure pledges for the education building, Dr. Baugh used the Forward Program of Church Finance approach.

By the November 18, 1957, Deacons' meeting, the overcrowding of the Immanuel Baptist Church facilities had reached a point where the Deacons appointed a committee to study the feasibility of going to two services—one at 8:30 and one at 11:00, with Sunday School being held at 9:40.[82]

In 1958, the Deacons were also very active. In the February 4, 1958, Deacons' meeting, A. V. Daugherty made a motion, seconded by Ben Aylor, that a hundred thousand dollars in mortgage bonds be issued and sold for the construction of the new education building. The motion passed. At the February 25, 1958, Deacons' meeting, the Deacons voted to have an all-night prayer vigil for the upcoming revival and to pay a bill for one thousand dollars to the Baptist General Convention of Oklahoma for the printing of the mortgage bonds.

At the May 6, 1958, Deacons' meeting, Ben Aylor made a motion, seconded by Fred Williams, that the Maintenance Committee be asked to develop specifications for the needed repairs to the roof and for the waterproofing of the facility. At the June 3, 1958, Deacons' meeting, two estimates for the costs associated with the roof and other repairs and the waterproofing were submitted by the Maintenance Committee. These were $8,500 and $6,550 respectively. The Deacons decided to proceed with the repairs and the waterproofing by borrowing the money from the building fund and paying the fund back at a rate of $100 per week from the general offerings and through special offerings.

At the July 14, 1958, Deacons' meeting, the status of the funding for the education building was discussed. The goal for the church was to have fifty-five thousand raised by June 1958. However, only forty-thousand was raised. The Deacons noted that the church was thirteen thousand, or 23.6 percent, behind schedule.

At the August 5, 1958, Deacons' meeting, Russell Hathcock made a motion and Manuel Ramirez seconded that the Deacons recommend no increase in the general budget but that thirty thousand dollars be allocated for equipping the new education building and redecorating the current building. Any surplus from this allocation would be paid on the education building loan. The motion passed.

By the November 9, 1958, Deacons' meeting, the Deacons were feeling sufficiently confident with the financing and the progress of the education building that plans were discussed for the interior and exterior painting and the types of tile to be used. Also at the Deacons' meeting, Sam Lawson presented some recommendations for a Deacons' visitation program of church members. The recommendations included the partitioning of the church membership among the Deacons for visits, with no church members being assigned to the pastor, staff members, or the chairman of the Deacons. Wives of Deacons were to be included in the visits when possible. The final Deacons' meeting of the year was on December 14, 1958. At that meeting, the Deacons voted that $350 be provided to the church staff as Christmas bonuses.[83]

The last Annual Meeting of the Baptist General Convention of Oklahoma that the Baughs attended as messengers from Immanuel Baptist Church was in 1958 in Oklahoma City. Dr. Baugh again served on the Christian Education Committee. He continued to serve on the Advisory Council of the Baptist Foundation. Christine Baugh was again selected to be the chairman of the Mission Study Committee.[84]

Several of the Deacons' meeting discussions and decisions in the early part of 1959 dealt with getting equipment and materials and securing labor for finishing the education building. For example, $1,185 worth of chairs was purchased from the Pottawatomie County Book Store, and Burse Borden was given a contract for $885 to remodel some classrooms. Also, fire extinguishers were installed, Paul Burns was paid $22 for painting, and S. J. Gollahon was paid $875 for carpentry work.[85]

The key event in 1959 for Immanuel Baptist Church was the completion and dedication of the education building. In his "As I See It" column in the May 14, 1959, issue of *The Baptist Messenger*, BGCO executive secretary-treasurer T. Bert Lackey commented,

> On the evening of May 3, 1959, I was with Immanuel
> [Baptist] Church, Shawnee, for the concluding service
> of a day of dedication for a new educational building.
> This building has made it possible for the church to
> expand from 19 to 28 departments. Frank Baugh
> is the aggressive pastor, Vernon Baker, Minister of
> Education, and Richard Farley, Minister of Music.[86]

The new education building had four beginner departments and a young married couples' department on the first floor and primary departments upstairs.[87]

During the last year of Dr. Frank Baugh's tenure at Immanuel Baptist Church, a major social and political issue occurred. The issue was the sale of liquor at liquor stores. Prior to 1907 statehood, Oklahoma and Indian territories had different liquor policies. Oklahoma Territory laws permitted the sale of alcohol, but in Indian Territory, federal laws prohibited the sale.

For more than a decade before statehood, the powerful Anti-Saloon League and the Woman's Christian Temperance Union forces waged war against the legalized sale of liquor. As statehood neared, prohibitionists—with churches as their key support—were able to select constitutional convention delegates who would frame an anti-liquor law into the new state's constitution. The 1906 Oklahoma Enabling Act mandated prohibition for twenty-one years, and the 1907 state constitution made prohibition the law of the land.

However, in 1958 Democrat J. Howard Edmondson won the governorship. His platform included a pledge for a special election to allow liquor sales.[88] Across the state, Baptist churches solidly opposed allowing liquor sales. Many churches—including Immanuel Baptist Church under the leadership of Dr. Frank Baugh and First Baptist Church, Lawton, under the leadership of former Immanuel pastor Dr. Tom Wiles—campaigned vigorously for the continuation of pro-hibition.[89] However, on April 7, 1959, Oklahomans voted to repeal prohibition and allow liquor stores to open.[90]

The April 23, 1959, issue of The Baptist Messenger included letters by Dr. Tom Wiles and five other prominent Oklahoma pastors lamenting the failure of churches to maintain prohibition.[91] Across the state, many churches including Immanuel Baptist Church, First Baptist Church, Ardmore[92], First Baptist Church, Okmulgee[93], and First Baptist Church, Lawton[94], passed resolutions to drop members who deal in the sale of liquor from their rolls. The First Church, Lawton, resolution stated, "Any member of our church who becomes a liquor dealer shall automatically be dropped from our church roll."

Immanuel's resolution was dated July 7, 1959, and was pre-sented to the church by the Deacons. The resolution stated, "Any member of the church who owns and/or operates a liquor business does automatically, by entry into said liquor business, terminate his membership in Immanuel Baptist Church." The resolution passed as an amendment to the church constitution and bylaws.

At the September 8, 1959, Deacons' meeting, the Deacons voted to form a visitation team to visit a church member, his wife, and his son who had opened a liquor store to discuss their status as mem-bers. The visitation team consisted of three highly respected Deacons,

Burse Borden, Manuel Ramirez, and A. V. Daugherty. The family had been active members of the church, with the wife serving as a Sunday School teacher and the husband serving of several committees. However, at the October 13, 1959, Deacons' meeting, the visitation teams reported that the family did not intend to leave the liquor business. At the October 14, 1959, church business meeting, the church voted to terminate the membership of the three family members.[95]

On August 11, 1959, Dr. Frank Baugh announced his resignation from Immanuel Baptist Church to take a pastorate in Colorado. At the time of his resignation, Immanuel Baptist Church had approximately 1,350 members on its rolls and averaged about 660 people each Sunday in attendance in Sunday School. About 200 people attended Training Union on Sunday evenings.[96] His resignation was summarized in the August 27, 1959, issue of *The Baptist Messenger* as follows:

> After nine and a half years as pastor of Immanuel [Baptist] Church, Shawnee, Frank O. Baugh resigned effective August 23 to become pastor of First Southern [Baptist] Church, Colorado Springs, Colorado. During his Shawnee ministry, the church built a Nursery Building costing about $40,000 and erected the major section of a new educational building at a cost of $125,000. A parsonage valued at $25,000 was constructed, and a partnership in a cabin at Falls Creek, valued at $14,000 was made. Baugh has been a member of the state convention Board of Directors, the OBU Board of Trustees, [and] the Advisory Board of the Baptist Foundation of Oklahoma. For the past four years, [Rev. Baugh] has served as chairman of the Christian Education Committee. He was active in civic affairs. Mrs. Baugh, also active in civic work, has been Mission Study Director for the Oklahoma WMU for several years and a member of the WMU Executive Board.[97]

Dr. Frank Baugh, the Years after Immanuel

After leaving Immanuel Baptist Church in August 1959, Dr. Frank Baugh became pastor of First Southern Baptist Church in Colorado Springs, Colorado. His pattern of leadership and success continued. In late spring 1960, the directors of the Colorado Southern Baptist Assembly Association voted to develop 80 acres of their 1,400-acre site near Monument, Colorado. The 80-acre development would be used for housing for the facility. They elected Dr. Frank Baugh, pastor of First Southern Baptist Church, Colorado Springs, to be president of the site.

Figure 7.6. Dr. Frank Baugh in retirement

The first activity on the newly purchased assembly on Pioneer Week was held from August 1 to 5, 1960.[98] A mission church at Monument, Colorado, near the United States Air Force Academy was constituted as a church in December 1960. Dr. Baugh led First Southern Baptist Church, Colorado Springs, to observe its 10th anniversary in December 1961. The church baptized 108 people in 1961 and adopted a goal of 200 baptisms for that year. The all-time high Sunday School attendance of 749 for First Southern Baptist Church, Colorado Springs, occurred in April 1961. Dr. Baugh served on the board of directors of the General Convention of Southern Baptists in Colorado and on various committees. Mrs. Baugh has been Woman's Missionary Union president in the Pike's Peak Association and held various state Woman's Missionary Union offices in Colorado and Oklahoma.[99]

In its May 16, 1962, issue, *The Baptist Messenger* announced that Dr. Frank Baugh was returning to Oklahoma after three years in Colorado Springs, Colorado, to become the pastor of Exchange Avenue Baptist Church, Oklahoma City. He began his pastorate at Exchange Avenue Baptist Church on June 1, 1962. The family moved to Oklahoma City following the high school graduation of their twin sons, Ronnie and Lonnie. The Baughs had two daughters—Mary

Jeanette, a high school junior, and Rebecca Ann, age nine—when they moved back to Oklahoma.[100]

Mrs. Baugh quickly returned to activity in the Oklahoma Woman's Missionary Union. The August 23, 1962, issue of *The Baptist Messenger* contained an article about a training institute being organized by WMU Executive Secretary Mrs. L. E. Stith Jr. on the new books of the foreign mission series. The institute was scheduled to occur on August 31, 1962, at First Baptist Church, Oklahoma City. The theme for the studies was East Asia. Two of the four teachers had Immanuel Baptist Church connections. Immanuel Baptist Church member Eunice Short taught a book entitled *Fragrant Harbor*. Christine Baugh taught a book entitled *To Tell the Truth*.[101]

Dr. Frank Baugh served as pastor of Exchange Avenue Baptist Church for nineteen years prior to his retirement in 1981. In November 1981, Dr. Frank Baugh was elected to a four-year term on the Oklahoma Baptist University board of trustees at the Baptist General Convention of Oklahoma's Annual Meeting that was held in Tulsa.[102] Dr. Frank Baugh also served as a member of the building committee for Baptist Memorial Hospital in Oklahoma City and as president of the Oklahoma Baptist State Pastors' Conference.[103]

Figure 7.7 Christine Baugh in retirement

Dr. Frank Baugh died on August 10, 2001. He was eighty-four. Funeral services were August 13 at Exchange Avenue Baptist Church in Oklahoma City. Survivors included Christine, his wife of fifty-nine years; twin sons, Ronnie and Lonnie; daughters, Mary Wilkinson and Becky Lasiter; and seven grandchildren and four great-grandchildren.

Throughout their marriage, Frank and Christine Baugh were a team in the ministry, serving Southern Baptist churches in Oklahoma and Colorado. The final years of their ministry were spent at Exchange Avenue Baptist Church in Oklahoma City.[104] Christine Baugh earned a bachelor's degree from Oklahoma Baptist University in 1955. She also earned a master's degree from the University of

Central Oklahoma in Edmond, Oklahoma. Mrs. Baugh retired from Ulysses Simpson Grant High School in Oklahoma City after teaching for twenty-two years.

Initially, she taught standard English classes at US Grant High School but later was assigned to teach college preparatory classes. The capstone of her teaching career was teaching a course entitled The Bible as Literature, an elective course at US Grant High School. Christine Baugh developed the course and wrote the curriculum for the course. Every semester, students were turned away from the course due to lack of space. Many of her students named her as their strictest and most loving teacher.[105] Christine Baugh died on January 6, 2016, in Moore, Oklahoma. At the time of her death, Mrs. Baugh was survived by a son, Ronnie; daughters Mary Wilkinson and Rebecca Lasiter; seven grandchildren and eight great-grandchildren; two sisters Billie Jean Roberts and Charlene Denney; and many nieces and nephews.[106]

CHAPTER 8

A Short Tenure

Dr. Joe Ingram, January 1960–June 1961

Introduction

Rev. Joe Ingram was the tenth pastor of Immanuel Baptist Church. He became pastor on January 25, 1960. Reverend Ingram has been described as "an organizer 'par excellence.'" He was responsible for many refinements in the financial administrative operations of the church. After a pastorate of only sixteen months at Immanuel Baptist Church, Dr. Ingram left to become the assistant executive secretary of the Baptist General Convention. He later became the executive secretary-treasurer, the highest post in Oklahoma Baptist life.[1]

The international scene during the year and a half that Rev. Joe Ingram served Immanuel Baptist Church was one of great tension between the United States and the Soviet Union. Following the election of Pres. John F. Kennedy, an attempt backed by the Central Intelligence Agency to overthrow Cuban dictator Fidel Castro—known as the Bay of Pigs Invasion—ended in failure. Seeking to stem the flow of East Germans fleeing to West Berlin, the Communist East Germans built the Berlin Wall. On April 12, 1961, Soviet cosmonaut Yuri Gagarin became the first human being to travel into space. Also in 1961, the Soviet Union exploded the largest nuclear weapon ever built.

In the United States, during Rev. Joe Ingram's service at Immanuel Baptist Church, a series of four presidential debates occurred between Richard Nixon and John F. Kennedy in 1960. These four debates were the first debates ever between presidential candidates. The debates also had the distinction of being broadcast on both radio and television.[2] John F. Kennedy would go on to be elected President in November 1960. Seeing the advances in rocketry and technology by the Soviet Union, Pres. F. Kennedy gave his Man on the Moon speech to Congress in May 1961. The Peace Corps was also founded in 1961.[3]

Rev. Joe Ingram, the Years before Immanuel

Joe Ingram was born in Russellville, Arkansas, on January 6, 1920. His father was an ordained Cumberland Presbyterian pastor. Being the son of a pastor, Joe Ingram moved several times throughout his childhood. Shortly after his birth, the family moved to Corsicana, Texas, where he spent much of his childhood. The family then moved to Marshall, Texas, where Joe graduated from high school.

At age sixteen, in the fall of 1936, he enrolled in East Texas Baptist College in Marshall, Texas, where he obtained a bachelor of arts degree in the spring of 1940. Joe Ingram attended religion classes and chapel at East Texas Baptist College and began to pick up some of the distinctions in Baptist doctrine and Cumberland Presbyterian doctrine. While at East Texas Baptist College, he met Jacque Nevill.

At the time, Joe worked part-time as a mortician at a funeral home in Marshall, Texas. Jacque worked in the County Assessor's Office for a friend of Joe's named Joe Riley. Joe Ingram went to visit his friend for a cup of coffee and not only got some coffee but also got a girlfriend. The two were married in March 1940, just before Joe graduated.[4]

Joe Ingram accepted Christ as his Lord and Savior at an early age. He was called to preach in Marshall, Texas, in 1941, just after he graduated from college. In fact, Joe Ingram's call to preach came the night before he was to go to Dallas to a mortician college to become a licensed funeral home director. When he excitedly wrote to his father, who was pastoring a church in Dyersburg, Tennessee, his father wrote back a very terse letter, telling him, "If you can be happy doing anything else, you ought to do it."

His first pastorate was at the Olton Cumberland Presbyterian Church in West Texas, about eighty miles south of Amarillo. After several months of service at Olton, Joe Ingram was ordained to the ministry at the Floydada Cumberland Presbyterian Church in Floydada, Texas, about fifty miles east of Olton. After serving as pastor in the Olton Cumberland Presbyterian Church, Rev. Joe Ingram was called to the Corsicana Cumberland Presbyterian Church where his father had served when Joe was a child.

After a few months at Corsicana Cumberland Presbyterian Church, Reverend Ingram was called to the Rose City Cumberland Presbyterian Church in North Little Rock, Arkansas. The church was one of the strongest in the Cumberland Presbyterian denomination in Arkansas and had roughly 200 to 250 attendees in Sunday School each week.[5]

While at Rose City Cumberland Presbyterian Church, Reverend Ingram developed a close friendship with Rev. R. O. Barker, the pastor of North Little Rock Baptist Church, a neighboring Southern Baptist church. Among the discussions that they had were topics of Baptist organizational structure and Baptist beliefs. As the two men chatted, the college experience from East Texas Baptist College (and possibly the urgings of the Holy Spirit) helped to convince Reverend Ingram that the Cumberland Presbyterian doctrines about sprinkling and infant baptism were wrong and that the Southern Baptist doctrines correctly followed the teachings of the Bible.

Reverend Ingram's conviction of the error of the doctrine that he was preaching and teaching was so strong that in 1944, he resigned his position at Rose City Cumberland Presbyterian Church and joined North Little Rock Baptist Church. Both he and Jacque were baptized by immersion as part of becoming members of a Baptist church.

Having resigned his position at Rose City Cumberland Presbyterian Church, Rev. Joe Ingram took a job at a Baptist bookstore and did supply preaching on the weekends to help with the family finances. One of the churches where he preached on a temporary basis was Woodlawn Baptist Church, Little Rock, Arkansas. The congregation was so pleased with his preaching that they called him to be their pastor and ordained him as a Baptist minister.[6]

While serving at Woodlawn Baptist Church, Rev. Joe Ingram decided that he needed to further his theological education and enrolled in Southwestern Baptist Theological Seminary in Fort Worth, Texas. Reverend Ingram would take a weekly train from Little Rock to Fort Worth for his seminary classes. Riding with him on the train was Rev. Charlie Lawrence of First Baptist Church, Little Rock, who was completing his doctoral degree.

The train ride was itself an educational experience for Reverend Ingram who was a pastor of a small church with 150 to 175 in attendance each Sunday. He was able to share experiences and sermon preparation with a prominent Arkansas pastor who had 1,200 to 1,500 in attendance each Sunday. In 1948, toward the conclusion of his seminary study, Rev. Joe Ingram resigned from Woodlawn Baptist Church and moved his family to the Fort Worth area. He took the pastorate of First Baptist Church, Rio Vista, Texas, about 40 miles south of Fort Worth.

In the spring of 1950, Rev. Joe Ingram received his master of religious education degree from Southwestern Baptist Theological Seminary. He resigned from the pulpit at First Baptist Church, Rio Vista, and moved to Okmulgee, Oklahoma, to be the associate pastor and education director of First Baptist Church, Okmulgee. The senior pastor of First Baptist Church, Okmulgee, was Rev. James Ivey, a strong Baptist leader within the state of Oklahoma. Reverend Ingram was thirty years old at the time and ready to start his pastoral career in earnest.[7]

Once he got to Oklahoma, Rev. Joe Ingram became a very active member of Oklahoma Baptist life. He attended his first Baptist General Convention of Oklahoma

Figure 8.1. Rev. Joe Ingram, the Okemah years

Annual Meeting on October 31–November 2, 1950, in Tulsa as a messenger from First Baptist Church, Okmulgee.[8] That annual meeting gave him a vision of Baptist work in Oklahoma and the importance of the BGCO.

Consequently, in late March 1951, Reverend Ingram was part of a large team of approximately seventy-five preachers and singers from all over Oklahoma who visited eleven southeastern states as part of the Southern Baptist Convention's Simultaneous Revival Initiative east of the Mississippi. Many dignataries from the Baptist General Convention of Oklahoma were part of the team, and Reverend Ingram got to know them. Rev. Joe Ingram was assigned to support a revival in Cullman, Alabama. A few months later, in the summer of 1951, Reverend Ingram was selected to be part of the Falls Creek Assembly program.[9]

After two years at First Baptist Church, Okmulgee, as an associate pastor, Reverend Ingram went to Okemah to be the senior pastor at the First Baptist Church there. His first duty day was April 6, 1952. By then, he and Jacque had two children—Stephen, age seven, and Krista Lynn, age five.[10]

He was at First Baptist Church, Okemah, for three years and was a very successful pastor. Sunday School enrollment grew from 381 to 570, exclusive of the extension and cradle roll departments, and average attendance increased from 270 to 380. The church budget increased from $22,000 to $36,000 and Cooperative Program gifts increased from 17 percent to 32 percent.

By 1953, Reverend Ingram was ready to begin serving the BGCO at a higher level. As part of the proceedings of the General Convention of Oklahoma Annual Meeting, Reverend Ingram was selected to serve on the Social Service Commision.[11] Reverend Ingram was one of twenty-five Oklahoma Southern Baptist pastors who were selected in the summer of 1954 to initiate a considerably different approach to the way that the annual Falls Creek Assemblies were held. Two sessions occurred, one on July 26–August 2 and the other from August 3 to August 10, at the campgrounds located south of Davis. Twenty-five of the finest pastors of the state brought messages during the two assemblies. Different speakers were used for each morning and each evening service of the entire camp period. Reverend Ingram was one of those pastors.[12]

Reverend Ingram left First Baptist Church, Okemah, in February 1955 to become the senior pastor at Nogales Avenue Baptist Church, Tulsa. He took up his duties in his new pastorate on Sunday, February 13. The Nogales Avenue Baptist Church designated that day to be "I" Day (*I* for "Ingram") in the church.[13]

While at Nogales Avenue Baptist Church, Rev. Joe Ingram continued to be very active in the Baptist General Convention of Oklahoma and to be recognized for his achievements. For example, at the 1955 Annual Meeting of the Baptist General Convention of Oklahoma held in Tulsa, both Rev. Joe Ingram and his wife Jacque attended as messengers from Nogales Avenue Baptist Church. Reverend Ingram was selected to be part of the Advisory Council of the Baptist Foundation of Oklahoma. He was also selected to be on the Public Relations Committee of the board of directors and on the Christian Life Commission.

Nogales Avenue Baptist Church under Reverend Ingram was consistently a strong giver to the Cooperative Program. For example, at the 1955 Annual Meeting, Nogales Avenue Baptist Church was listed as the seventeenth strongest giver to the Cooperative Program with $14,322 in offerings. It is worth noting that the strongest giver was First Baptist Church, Oklahoma City, under the leadership of Rev. H. H. Hobbs at $61,424. Immanuel Baptist Church under Rev. Frank Baugh was twenty-seventh with an offering of $11,306.[14]

At the 1959 Baptist General Convention of Oklahoma Annual Meeting, Rev. Joe Ingram's level of participation in Oklahoma Baptist life increased. He was appointed to the board of directors of the Baptist General Convention of Oklahoma. Within the board of directors, he was placed on the Executive Committee under the leadership of Oklahoma Baptist giant Dr. Hershel Hobbs of First Baptist Church, Oklahoma City. He was also placed on the Stewardship and Budget Committee, the Hospital and Golden Homes Committee, and the Long Range Falls Creek Planning Committee.[15]

While Reverend Ingram was serving at Nogales Avenue Baptist Church, the Southern Baptist Convention held a series of yearly coordinated revivals across several states. These were called the Simultaneous Revival Crusades. In May 1956, Nogales Avenue Baptist Church was one of the churches that participated in the crusade in Oklahoma, with Rev. Joe Ingram preaching the revival there. The revival was a strong success and twenty-eight individuals came forward for baptism and thirty-seven individuals joined the church.[16]

After four years at Nogales Avenue Baptist Church, Rev. Joe Ingram resigned in December 1959 to become the pastor of Immanuel Baptist Church. Additions to the Tulsa church during Reverend Ingram's ministry there totaled 1,240 individuals, with 490 of them by baptism. Total gifts to the church amounted to $480,000, with some $100,000 of that amount going to missions. The church spent $115,000 on buildings and parking lots and constructed a $25,000 parsonage for the pastor and his family.

Nogales Avenue Baptist Church started two mission churches under Rev. Joe Ingram's leadership. These were Valley View Baptist Mission and Bowen Place Indian Baptist Mission. Reverend Ingram was thirty-nine when he left Nogales Avenue Baptist Church and was a member of the BGCO board of directors, the Southern Baptist Convention Christian Life Commission, and the BGCO Christian Life Commission.[17]

Rev. Joe Ingram, the Immanuel Years

Rev. Joe Ingram became pastor of Immanuel Baptist Church on January 25, 1960, at a salary of $7,300 per year plus an annual expense allowance of $1,836. Reverend Ingram was 40 years old at the time. Also in January 1960, Mrs. Leslie Coats was hired as church secretary at $3,000 per year. Rev. Joe Ingram's service at Immanuel Baptist Church was marked by regular, punctual, and orderly execution of church

Figure 8.2. Rev. Joe Ingram, the Immanuel years

141

business. Key laymen and laywomen during Reverend Ingram's service to Immanuel Baptist Church included A. V. and Lucille Daugherty, Carl Webb, Ben Aylor, Carl Wright, Cap and Wanda Gardner, Roy and Ruby Curtis, and Fred Williams.

Although Rev. Ingram's tenure at Immanuel Baptist Church would be short, he was very active while serving the church. From January 25 to 27, 1960, just as Reverend Ingram was arriving at Immanuel Baptist Church, the Baptist General Convention of Oklahoma held an evangelistic conference in Ponca City. All-night prayer chains were a feature of the state evangelistic conference that met at First Church, Ponca City. Rev. Joe Ingram was on the program for that conference.[18]

The February 11, 1960, issue of *The Baptist Messenger* summarized the conference by saying that over 1,500 pastors and lay members of Oklahoma Baptist churches attended the conference and came away with new inspiration and enthusiasm for evangelism. The conference was held under the direction of J. A. Pennington, state secretary of evangelism. It was one of the largest meetings of the kind ever conducted in Oklahoma. Rev. Joe Ingram was quoted as saying,

> If we are going to lead the people in our churches to win the lost, we are going to have to be soul winners ourselves. We must preach the great doctrines of our faith from the pulpits. We must lead the people to have real experiences in our Sunday worship services.[19]

As his service at Immanuel Baptist Church continued, Rev. Joe Ingram became more involved in various BGCO activities. His involvement in Oklahoma Baptist life reflected the growing confidence that the BGCO leadership had in him. In summer 1960, Reverend Ingram was one of the pastors selected to address Oklahoma Baptist youth at the Falls Creek Assembly. His topic for the youth was "Mastering Life's Problems."[20]

The proximity of Immanuel Baptist Church in Shawnee to the Baptist General Convention of Oklahoma headquarters in Oklahoma City allowed Rev. Joe Ingram to strengthen his personal friendship with executive secretary Dr. T. B. Lackey. As Rev. Ingram became more involved in Oklahoma Baptist life, a natural friendship between these two good Baptist leaders developed and blossomed. In his July 21, 1960, "As I See It" column entitled "Mission Emphasis" in *The Baptist Messenger*, Dr. Lackey stated:

> It is encouraging to note that more and more of our churches are giving special emphasis to our over-all mission program. In recent days, I have had several invitations from pastors to visit their churches and speak on missions. This I love to do. [On] Sunday, July 10, I was with Joe Ingram and Immanuel [Baptist] Church, Shawnee, and presented our Baptist mission program.[21]

Just before the 1960 Baptist General Convention of Oklahoma Annual Meeting, Rev. Joe Ingram led a revival at one of his former churches—First Baptist Church, Okemah—on October 9–16. Through the revival, the church received sixteen additions by baptism and four by letter. The song leader for the revival was Carlos Gruber.[22]

At the 1960 Baptist General Convention of Oklahoma Annual Meeting, Reverend Ingram took a very active role. He and Jacque attended as messengers from Immanuel Baptist Church. Reverend Ingram was selected for the BGCO board of directors. Within the board of directors, he was placed on the Executive Committee, the Brotherhood and Evangelism Committee, and the Auditing and Insurance Committee. Reverend Ingram was also selected for the Advisory Council of the Baptist Foundation.

As Chairman of the Christian Life Commission, Reverend Ingram presented the report of the commission to the messengers. As member of the Hospital and Golden Homes Committee, he presented awards to four nursing students for their excellent work. Certificates were given to each of the students, and Loving Cups with the names of the students inscribed upon them were presented to the hospitals where they were studying. In addition, Reverend Ingram was selected as zone leader for the Pottawatomie-Lincoln Baptist Association Cooperative Program Support initiative.[23]

Immediately following the annual meeting, Rev. Joe Ingram was also one of the speakers at the State Brotherhood Convention held at Trinity Baptist Church, Oklahoma City, on November 14–15, 1960. His topic was "Witnessing and the Baptist Jubilee Advance." He reminded the men at the convention, "New Testament evangelism, which is based on personal witnessing, is the heart of the Baptist Jubilee Advance."[24] The Baptist Jubilee Advance was a five-year program from 1959 to 1964 to celebrate the sesquicentennial (1814–1964) of Baptist associational involvement in the evangelism, culture, and well-being of the United States of America. In 1814, the first national Baptist association, called the Triennial Convention, was established in Philadelphia. The Southern Baptist Convention is a natural outgrowth of the Triennial Convention.[25]

Another Oklahoma state–level activity for Rev. Joe Ingram was the simultaneous associational *M* (Mobilization) Night meetings. As part of its emphasis on revivals and evangelism, the Southern Baptist Convention decided to sponsor a series of annual simultaneous evening mini revivals and informational meetings called Mobilization Nights, or M Nights. The Southern Baptist goal was to have six hundred thousand people in attendance for their December 5, 1961, M Night. Oklahoma's goal for the December 5, 1961, M Night event was to hold forty-two simultaneous events with a total attendance of twenty thousand, making that M Night event the largest ever.

The M Night's purpose was also to launch the Training Union program for the upcoming year. The theme for 1961 was "Be Thou Faithful." An important feature of the evening's program is a preview of goals, objectives, and the calendar of activities. Planning for the M Night took place well in advance.

In the December 1, 1960, issue of *The Baptist Messenger*, a list of the 42 M Night locations was published. Rev. Joe Ingram was listed as the moderator for the Arbuckle Baptist Association event on December 5, 1961, to be held at First Baptist Church, Paul's Valley, with an attendance goal of 692.[26]

At the November 1960 Annual Meeting of the Baptist General Convention of Oklahoma, Rev. Joe Ingram was again selected for the Advisory Council of the Baptist Foundation. The executive secretary-treasurer of the Baptist Foundation at the time was Dr. Auguie Henry. In early December 1960, Rev. Joe Ingram declared December 11, 1960, to be Auguie Henry Day. Reverend Ingram issued a proclamation declaring the need to honor Dr. Henry since he "has served the Kingdom of God for many years as an outstanding pastor of several of Oklahoma's greatest Baptist churches and has for the past several years served our denomination as Executive Secretary-Treasurer of the Baptist Foundation and has a distinguished record as a faithful preacher of the gospel."

Figure 8.3. Auguie Henry in retirement

Rev. Joe L. Ingram, pastor; Cap Gardner, chairman of deacons; and Leon Haddock, clerk, signed the proclamation.[27] Dr. Auguie Henry preached the morning message on December 11. Henry was ordained by Immanuel Baptist Church on December 15, 1920, when it was Draper Street Church. He served as part-time student assistant pastor for Immanuel while he was a student at Oklahoma Baptist University.[28] During Rev. Joe Ingram's service to Immanuel Baptist Church, the normal business activities of the church were conducted predominantly through its monthly business meetings and Deacons' meetings.

In the January 3, 1960, business meeting, the end-of-the-year records showed that Immanuel Baptist Church had a solid 1,182 individuals attending Sunday School and an average Sunday worship attendance of 559. The Lottie Moon offering for the Christmas season was $842.68 against a goal of $1,100. In the April 13, 1960, business meeting, the congregation voted to allow music minister Richard Farley a leave of absence to study at the New York School of

Music. The congregation also voted to spend $7,000 to remodel the office area and $5,000 for organ repairs.

In the June 19, 1960, business meeting, the congregation approved Rev. Robert Audd from Tulsa as the associate pastor and education director with an annual salary of $5,500 and with $2,000 in annual expense allowance. In the August 10, 1960, business meeting, Pottawatomie-Lincoln Baptist Association Annual Meeting messengers were elected. The messengers selected were Reverend and Mrs. Ingram, Reverend and Mrs. Audd, and Bro. Burse Borden; Mrs. Newton Wall, and Mr. and Mrs. Vic Peetoom.[29]

The 1960 Pottawatomie-Lincoln Baptist Association Annual Meeting was held at First Baptist Church, Shawnee.[30] In the November 9, 1960, business meeting, Baptist General Convention of Oklahoma Annual Meeting messengers were elected. These were Reverend and Mrs. Ingram, Reverend and Mrs. Audd, Bro. Burse Borden, Ms. Eunice Short, and Mrs. Jimmy Thompson. The 1960 Baptist General Convention of Oklahoma Annual Meeting was held November 15–17 in Oklahoma City.[31]

On February 2, 1961, Rev. Robert Audd provided the church with a major surprise. A mere seven months after he was hired, Reverend Audd resigned to return to Tulsa to become the pastor of Woodland Baptist Church, Tulsa. Woodland Baptist Church was a newly started church in southeastern Tulsa, and Reverend Audd would be their first pastor.

At the May 3, 1961, business meeting, the congregation voted to seek bids for air-conditioning for the sanctuary, the nursery, and the parsonage. On Tuesday, May 16, 1961, at a very unusual, late-night called Deacons' meeting, Rev. Joe Ingram provided the church with a major surprise. Reverend Ingram had just started a revival in Stroud.

After the evening revival message had concluded, Reverend Ingram called a special Deacons' meeting to be held at 10:15 p.m. He drove back from Stroud to Shawnee for the called meeting. The purpose of the meeting was to discuss his resignation from Immanuel Baptist Church so that he could accept an appointment to become the assistant executive secretary of the Baptist General Convention of Oklahoma reporting to Dr. T. B. Lackey, the executive secretary of the BGCO.

The decision to hire Reverend Ingram had been made earlier in the day by the Executive Committee of the BGCO board of directors. A press release announcing the selection of Reverend Ingram by the BGCO as assistant executive secretary was to be issued on the morning of May 17, and Reverend Ingram wanted the Deacons and members of Immanuel Baptist Church to hear the news directly from him rather than from a press release. After the meeting, Reverend Ingram returned to Stroud to complete the revival.

His last revival message in Stroud was on Sunday morning, May 21, 1961. Reverend Ingram preached the evening message at Immanuel Baptist Church on Sunday evening, May 21, 1961, and explained his new Baptist General Convention of Oklahoma duties and answered questions that evening. The effective date of his resignation was June 18, 1961.

Dr. Joe Ingram, the Years after Immanuel

After Rev. Joe Ingram left Immanuel Baptist Church, he became the assistant executive secretary to Dr. T. B. Lackey, the executive secretary of the Baptist General Convention of Oklahoma. Reverend Ingram served Dr. Lackey and the BGCO with ability and discernment.[32] In 1969, Oklahoma Baptist University granted Rev. Joe Ingram an honorary doctor of divinity degree.[33]

After hiring Reverend Ingram to be his assistant, Dr. T. B. Lackey continued to serve as the executive secretary of the Baptist General Convention of Oklahoma for ten more years. However, Dr. Lackey's health began to deteriorate a few years after he hired Reverend Ingram. As a result, Dr. Lackey began to shift more and more of his duties to Reverend Ingram who quickly learned the operations of the BGCO and the duties of the executive secretary.

By the last years of Dr. Lackey's service to the BGCO, he and Dr. Ingram were in essence coleaders of the BGCO. When Dr. Lackey announced on November 1970 that he desired to retire, it was only natural for the BGCO board of directors to name Dr. Joe Ingram as the successor to Dr. Lackey in their December 15, 1970, board meeting. Because of the timing of Dr. Lackey's official date based on his birth in 1906, Dr. Ingram's official start date was delayed until September 1971. Dr. Ingram was fifty-one years old at the time.

Dr. Joe Ingram served the Baptist General Convention of Oklahoma successfully and well for fifteen years until he retired in June 1986 at the age of sixty-six. The Baptist General Convention of Oklahoma grew under Dr. Ingram's leadership. In 1971, the BGCO had 1,366 churches. In 1986, it had 1,473 churches. The membership of those churches grew from 546,872 to 739,555. Cooperative Program gifts grew from $4 million to $15.7 million. Existing Baptist student union facilities on Oklahoma college and university campuses were modernized and increased in number to 34. The number of Baptist retirement centers increased from 2 to 7, and 6 new Baptist Children's Homes were opened.[34] During his years of service to the Baptist General Convention of Oklahoma, Oklahoma Baptist University reorganized and expanded its Religion Department and named the new entity the Joe L. Ingram School of Christian Service in his honor.[35]

Dr. Joe Ingram died on Sunday, May 8, 1994, in Oklahoma City. He was survived by Jacque, his wife of fifty-four years; his son, Stephen Michael; his daughter, Krista Lynn; five grandchildren; and one great-grandchild. He was buried in Resurrection Cemetery, Oklahoma City.

CHAPTER 9

New Ideas and New Growth

Dr. Alfred Woodard, September 196–August 1964

Introduction

Rev. Alfred Woodard was the eleventh pastor of Immanuel Baptist Church. He served from September 1961 to August 1964. During his time at Immanuel, more building improvements were made, organ repairs were made, and a kindergarten program was begun that has continued for many years.[1] His wife was Gwendolyn Griffitts Woodard. Gwendolyn hailed from Wichita Falls, Texas.[2]

The world scene during the years that Reverend Woodard served Immanuel was one of great tension between the East and the West as the Cold War reached new levels of hostility. In August 1961, East Germany erected the Berlin Wall to divide East and West Berlin and to halt the flood of refugees trying to escape Communism. By year's end of 1961, there were two thousand United States military advisers in South Vietnam working to stop a Communist takeover of South Vietnam. The Woodard years at Immanuel also saw the formal establishment of the Organization of Petroleum Exporting Countries (OPEC).[3]

On the domestic scene, the United States had just entered the manned space race with Alan Shepard's suborbital flight in May 1961 in his *Freedom 7* spacecraft. In June 1963, the United States

Supreme Court ruled that neither the Lord's Prayer nor Bible verses may be recited in public schools, and in August, Martin Luther King delivered his "I Have a Dream" speech in Washington, D.C. In November, President Kennedy was shot and killed in Dallas, Texas, by Lee Harvey Oswald.[4]

Dr. Alfred Woodard, the Years before Immanuel

Alfred Woodard was born June 3, 1930, outside of Fargo, Texas, just across the Red River southwest of Frederick, Oklahoma.[5] In 1930, Fargo was a small farming community with about 150 residents. Fargo was established on a stage line from Wichita Falls, Texas, to Mobeetie, Texas, around 1883. A school known as Richland was built there in 1889, and a post office was added on April 15, 1894. By 1900, the town had grown to include a store and post office, a gin, and several churches, including the Fargo Baptist Church that was established in 1904.[6]

Alfred Woodard's parents were tenant farmers who, at the beginning of the Great Depression, lived in what today would be recognized as poverty. Dr. Woodard recalled, "They lived with integrity and through hard work and honest living made their way through this difficult period."

His parents did not attend church during his childhood, but his grandparents regularly attended Fargo Baptist Church, a small country church where they were charter members. His grandparents took young Alfred to church with them. He accepted Christ as his savior at Fargo Baptist Church when he was nine years of age. Dr. Woodard fondly remembered,

> When I was between the ages of 9 and 12 years of age, I was a member of a Sunday School class taught by Kate Scherer, a dedicated and praying teacher who in her sincerity sometimes would shed a tear when she prayed and who loved the little boys who were in her class. In that class of little boys was Carroll Wayne Shaw, Gerald Doyle, Paul C. Bell, myself, and others. Carroll Wayne grew up, went to Howard Payne

College and Southwestern Seminary, and became a
missionary to South Africa and unfortunately died
when he was about to retire. He was 65 years old at
the time of his death. Gerald Doyle went to Hardin
Simmons University and Southwestern Baptist
Theological Seminary and became a missionary to
Ecuador. Paul C. Bell became a missionary to Costa
Rica.[7]

Reverend Woodard recalled his calling to preach and the support that he received from that little church:

> I hold in my hand a letter that I have kept in my bank
> box for fifty years in memory of a Deacon known as
> "Uncle Jess Parker" to my generation. Uncle Jess, who
> was no kin to me, knew, after I had surrendered to
> preach as a teenager, I did not know where the money
> was coming from to attend college. On a Sunday
> evening after church, he called me aside out of ear-
> shot of everyone else and asked me for the 'privilege'
> of loaning me money if I needed it to complete my
> education. He said we would make out a note, and I
> could decide how long I needed to pay it back, and
> there would be no interest. He commented that he
> had never married and that he had no children, but
> through such loans, he had had a 'kid in college' for
> the past twenty-five years. When I was a sophomore
> in college, the little church at Medicine Mound near
> Quahah called me as their pastor. (I was the ripe old
> age of nineteen.) Because the church was 150 miles
> from Abilene where I was attending school, I had
> to have a car to make the trip each weekend. I bor-
> rowed $600 from Uncle Jesse, took the money to the
> Waggoner National Bank and used it as a down pay-
> ment on a 1949 Plymouth. I made the note to Uncle
> Jesse for a three-year payout. With the Lord's help, I
> was able to pay the note off ten months in advance

of the period when it was due. When I paid it off, I received a letter. It bears a three-cent stamp and is addressed to "Rev. and Mrs. Woodard, 1358 Cedar, Abilene, Texas."

On the occasion when he first made the offer to loan me money, he gave me some of the best advice that I have received. He said, "Alfred, you have surrendered to preach. You should always act and talk and dress in such a way that people wouldn't too quickly recognize that you are a preacher. But," he continued after a brief pause, "you should be careful to act and talk in such a way that they wouldn't be too surprised when they find out." There may have been a few surprises along the way, but I have never heard any better advice.[8]

Alfred Woodard graduated as salutatorian from his high school class in 1948. He enrolled in Hardin Simmons University when he was eighteen.[9] Hardin-Simmons University is located in Abilene, Texas, and was established in 1891 as a private, coeducational, liberal arts university. It is affiliated with the Baptist General Convention of Texas. It currently has an enrollment of about 2,200 students and offers doctoral degrees in ministry, physical therapy, and leadership.[10]

Figure 9.1.
Hardin-Simmons Cowgirl Band

Alfred met his wife, Gwen, while they were both students at Hardin-Simmons University. She was a member of Sigma Tau Delta, the international collegiate honor society for students majoring in English. She was also the master of ceremonies for the Hardin-Simmons Cowgirl Band and served as the social chairman for the Baptist Student Union. Gwen was an honors' program graduate of Hardin-Simmons University.[11]

According to its website, the Hardin-Simmons Cowgirl Band is a high-stepping, rope-twirling cowgirl organization associated at Hardin-Simmons from 1925 until 1974. Willie Rae McDonald, who graduated from Simmons College in 1922 and became a faculty member in 1925, founded the Cowgirl Band. The members' uniforms consisted of a purple skirt, a gold button-up flannel jacket, a purple headband, and tan oxfords with purple ties. Members were required to have exemplary behavior before they could represent the school. Behavior rules included no smoking, no drinking, no gum chewing, and no bad language.[12]

Reverend Woodard and Gwen were married in 1950 and spent part of their honeymoon in Oklahoma. Their honeymoon trip took them to Shawnee, and they were fascinated by the stone structure of Immanuel Baptist Church as they drove down Main Street. Alfred decided to stop and park the car and have Gwen take a honeymoon remembrance picture of him on the north entrance steps of Immanuel Baptist Church, not knowing that one day he would be the pastor there.[13] As Reverend Woodard expressed it as follows:

> I met my wife at Hardin Simmons University where she was the social chairman for the Baptist Student Union, and I was a ministerial student. We were married December 26, 1950, in her home church in Wichita Falls, Texas. At our wedding, we pledged to be married "until death do us part." We were married sixty-three years until we were parted by her death on August 10, 2014. After our wedding, which occurred during the Christmas holidays, we took a brief honeymoon trip through Oklahoma. One place we visited was Shawnee. As we drove down east Main Street in Shawnee, we saw this beautiful Gothic Cathedral type church building that, at first, we thought to be a Catholic church. However, when we stopped to snap my picture on the church steps, we found that it was, indeed, a Baptist church, never even dreaming that I might be the pastor of this beautiful church in the future.

Rev. Alfred Woodard completed his bachelor of arts with majors in Bible and English from Hardin-Simmons University in 1951. Rev. Woodard became pastor of his first church in Medicine Mound Baptist Church, about twelve miles east of Quanah, Texas, when he was nineteen and a student at Hardin-Simmons University.[14] The town of Medicine Mound and the Baptist church no longer exist.[15]

He received his bachelor of divinity degree from Southwestern Baptist Theological Seminary in 1956. While at Southwestern Baptist Theological Seminary, Reverend Woodard served as pastor at First Baptist Church, Gordon, Texas.[16] Gordon, Texas, is a small town of approximately five hundred citizens, about sixty-five miles west of Fort Worth, Texas, on Interstate 20. First Baptist Church, Gordon, was formally organized in January 1879 from an earlier church. For many years, the church was known as the Baptist Church of Christ. The current church structure was built in 1942.[17]

Figure 9.2. First Baptist Church, Gordon

Upon finishing his bachelor of divinity degree in 1956, Reverend Woodard first served at Skyline Heights Baptist Church, Dallas, Texas, and then at First Baptist Church, Hollis, Oklahoma, from 1957 to 1961. Hollis, Oklahoma, is just across the Red River in southwestern Oklahoma, near where Reverend Woodard and his wife Gwen were born and raised.[18] Hollis is the county seat of Harmon County, Oklahoma.

Dr. W. A. Criswell, pastor of First Baptist Church, Dallas, recommended Reverend Woodard to the church. The Hollis church averaged 480 in Sunday School the year that he came and was averaging 530 in Sunday School the year that he left. The church budget doubled the second year that he was there and tripled the third year that he was there.

Under Reverend Woodard's leadership at First Baptist Church, Hollis, the church added ten thousand square feet of educational space, and a new auditorium to seat eight hundred was constructed. One of the largest—if not the largest—number of baptisms in the state in one year up to that time occurred during his ministry there. During his ministry there, Reverend and Mrs. Woodard were fortunate to tour the Holy Land with Dr. Herschel Hobbs, then president of the Southern Baptist Convention and the pastor of First Baptist Church, Oklahoma City.

The tour took them to Rome where they toured the Vatican; Cairo; Luxor including the Valley of the Kings in Egypt; Beirut, Lebanon; Damascus, Syria; Amman, Jordan; Jerusalem; and the Holy Land. Dr. T. B. Lackey, the executive secretary of the Oklahoma Baptist Convention at the time, and Reverend Fuquay, president of the Baptist General Oklahoma Convention and a number of other prominent Oklahoma Baptists were in this tour.[19]

While serving at First Baptist, Hollis, Reverend Woodard quickly became active in Oklahoma Baptist life. The first Baptist General Convention of Oklahoma (BGCO) Annual Meeting

Figure 9.3. Rev. Alfred Woodard, the Immanuel days

that he attended was in Tulsa on November 12–14, 1957.[20] By his second BGCO Annual Meeting—held in Oklahoma City on November 11–13, 1958—Reverend Woodard had gained sufficient stature that he was asked to lead in prayer at the opening of the Thursday afternoon session.

Reverend Woodard was also asked to serve on the Christian Education Committee, on the Promotion Committee as a zone leader for the Harmon Association, and on the Committee on Committees. Rev. Frank Baugh, a former pastor of Immanuel Baptist Church, chaired the Christian Education Committee.[21] The 1959 Annual Meeting of the BGCO was held in Tulsa on November 10–12. Both

Reverend and Mrs. Woodard were listed as messengers. Reverend Woodard was nominated as a representative of the denomination to SANE (Sooner Alcohol Narcotics Education).[22]

At his third BGCO Annual Meeting held in Oklahoma City on November 15–17, 1960, Reverend Woodard was asked to lead the opening prayer on Wednesday morning for the blessings of God upon the work of the Convention. He was also appointed to the Advisory Council of the Baptist Foundation as a representative from the Southwest Association.[23]

Dr. Alfred Woodard, the Immanuel Years

Rev. Alfred V. Woodard was called to be the pastor of Immanuel Baptist Church in August 1961. He began serving in September 1961. The church was large with a membership of 1,168 when Reverend Woodard began serving. The church was near its seating capacity during the years of Reverend Woodard's service.

The church experienced a quick growth in membership after Dr. Woodard assumed the pulpit. Membership peaked at 1,298 in October 1962. Sunday School attendance tended to be between 1,000 and 1,200 people. Reverend Woodard brought several new ideas to Immanuel. In October 1961, the church voted to allow church member and army chaplain Alpha Farrow to perform baptisms in Germany in the name of Immanuel Baptist Church. Each person so baptized would receive a letter of membership.

In January and February of 1962, Reverend Woodard conducted an eight-week, Sunday-evening Training Union program on Doctrines of Our Faith. In the Spring of 1962, Reverend Woodard began Operation Home Study in which one of four books could be studied. The books were *The Christian Life, Building a Better Sunday School, The Ministry of Visitation*, and *Preparing to Teach the Bible*. Classes began on June 1.

In the June 1962 business meeting, the church voted to install air-conditioning in the parsonage and to send Reverend Woodard to San Francisco as a messenger to the Southern Baptist Convention Annual Meeting. In November 1962, the fourth Wednesday-night service was cancelled so the congregation could go to a community-wide Thanksgiving service in Raley Chapel at Oklahoma Baptist University. In the May 1963 business meeting, the church voted to send Reverend and Mrs. Woodard to Kansas City as messengers to the Southern Baptist Convention Annual Meeting.

In the June 1963 business meeting, the church voted to appoint a committee to address the continuing water problems in the basement and to see if a renovation was possible. During 1963, the church participated in two revivals. The first was a citywide revival under Rev. Buckner Fanning, a renowned evangelist from San Antonio, Texas.[24] The second was an Immanuel revival under evangelist Dr. W. D. Lawes, secretary of evangelism at the Arizona Baptist Convention. In preparation for the Lawes Revival, Dr. Othal Feather, a professor at Southwestern Baptist Theological Seminary and author of *Promoting Evangelism through the Sunday School*, was brought in to speak to Sunday School teachers and officers.[25]

In the May 1963 business meeting, the church voted to send Reverend and Mrs. Woodard to Atlantic City, New Jersey, as messengers to the Southern Baptist Convention Annual Meeting. In February of 1964, the Immanuel Baptist Church held a youth revival with Rev. Arty Alexander as the evangelist. [26]

Being relatively young at thirty-one years of age when he became pastor of Immanuel Baptist Church, Rev. Alfred Woodard was able to attract a large number of Oklahoma Baptist University students. At one time, there were approximately 130 Oklahoma Baptist University students in his college department. The students were from all over Oklahoma, across the United States, and around the world. Some of the most outstanding individuals were from Nigeria. One of these Nigerian students was Charles Wade who later became a prominent Texas pastor and eventually became the executive secretary of the Baptist General Convention of Texas. Another outstanding student was Omar Hancock who became a professor at Logsdon Seminary in Abilene, Texas.

Rev. Alfred Woodard continued to be active in Baptist life across Oklahoma. In 1961, he and Mrs. Woodard attended the annual meeting in Tulsa as messengers from Immanuel Baptist Church. At the annual meeting, Reverend Woodard was elected to the Baptist Foundation's Advisory Council for 1962. He was also listed as a zone leader for the Pottawatomie-Lincoln Baptist Association for stewardship, Cooperative Program, and associational missions promotion.[27]

At the 1962 BGCO Annual Meeting held at Raley Chapel at Oklahoma Baptist University in Shawnee, he and Mrs. Woodard again attended as Messengers from Immanuel Baptist Church. Mrs. Woodard was listed as a State Woman's Missionary Union officer and the Christian education representative.[28] At the 1963 BGCO Annual Meeting held in Oklahoma City, Reverend and Mrs. Woodard again attended as messengers from Immanuel Baptist Church. She was again listed as a State Woman's Missionary Union officer and the Christian education representative. Reverend Woodard was listed as a member of the Memorials Committee, serving under John Wesley Raley, longtime Oklahoma Baptist University president. Reverend Woodard was again elected to the Baptist Foundation's Advisory Council.[29]

Immanuel Baptist Church had several excellent staff members during the years that Reverend Woodard served. Rev. Gene Wright was the education and youth minister.[30] Richard Farley was the music minister until May 1963 when he resigned. Rev. Bill Green then became the music director at a salary of two hundred dollars per month and use of the parsonage at 118 South Eden Street. Rev. Bill Green was a senior at Oklahoma Baptist University when he was called.

Figure 9.4. Bill Green and the church choir

In April 1964, Rev. Bill Green was nearing graduation and became full-time music minister with a salary of four hundred dollars per month and the use of the parsonage at 118 South Eden Street.[31] Bill Green's wife, Linda, served as organist for Immanuel during his service as music minister.[32] After leaving Immanuel Baptist Church, Reverend Green went on to be very active in Baptist life across the state, serving for fourteen years as the Falls Creek music director and for many years as the church music director of the Baptist General Convention of Oklahoma.[33]

Several members of Immanuel Baptist Church played key roles during the years that Alfred Woodard served Immanuel, including Cap Gardner, Fred Luckett, Kenneth Eyer, Fred Williams, Manuel Ramirez, Carl Webb, A. V. Daugherty, Woodrow Whitely, and Floyd Corley. Cap Gardner served as the chairman of the Deacons. Fred Williams was the Training Union director. Manuel Ramirez was the head of the Pulpit Committee who selected Reverend Woodard. Carl Webb headed the Personnel Committee. Floyd Corley was the financial secretary. A special BGCO finance and stewardship program known as the Forward Program of Church Finance was adopted by Immanuel Baptist Church shortly after Reverend Woodard joined Immanuel. A. V. Daugherty was selected as the chairman to implement that program.[34]

Deacon and local insurance agent A. V. Daugherty was especially dear to and supportive of Reverend Woodard and Gwen. Reverend Woodard regularly went to A. V.'s office in downtown Shawnee for advice, counsel, and support. One day, Reverend Woodard was visiting A. V.'s office, and an angry female customer came in to A. V.'s office.

The customer proceeded to talk to A. V. in a very harsh and derogatory manner, while A. V. did his best to be agreeable and to calm her concerns. After she left, Reverend Woodard complimented A. V. on how gracious and Christlike his approach to the woman was. According to Reverend Woodard, A. V. chuckled and said, "What you didn't realize is that all the time she was running me down, she was also writing out her insurance payment check."[35]

During his time at Immanuel, improvements were made to the north stairs and the basement. The pipe organ was repaired. Mrs. Gwen Woodard was instrumental in starting a kindergarten program. That kindergarten program has continued for several years. In 1963, a committee was elected to prepare for the observance of the fiftieth anniversary in September 1967. BGCO materials and materials from other churches were helpful in the planning.[36]

While Reverend Woodard was at Immanuel Baptist Church, the church family learned not to believe "old sayings." Lightning did strike twice in 1962, both times hitting the east tower of the church building.[37] George McElhanon, the janitor at the time, was in the auditorium cleaning when the lightning first struck the tower. He exclaimed, "Lord, when you finish your work, then I'll come back and do mine." Then George rushed to the basement.[38] George had a great personality with a great memory for names and a booming voice. He knew all the Babyland parents and all the Babyland children. He would joyously greet them by name.[39]

In July 1964, Rev. Alfred Woodard resigned as pastor of Immanuel Baptist Church, effective August 9. Reverend Woodard had been accepted by the committee on graduate studies of Southwestern Baptist Theological Seminary, Fort Worth, Texas, to begin work leading to a doctor of theology degree. As part of the move, Reverend Woodard accepted the call to the pulpit of Southmayd Baptist Church, a rural church near Sherman, Texas.[40] At a special called meeting of the Immanuel Baptist Church Deacons on July 26, 1964, the Deacons voted to call Dr. Evans Mosely as the interim pastor.[41] Dr. Moseley was the vice president for publicity at Oklahoma Baptist University and became the interim president of Oklahoma Baptist University when Dr. Ralph Scales resigned in September 1965.[42]

Dr. Alfred Woodard, the Years after Immanuel

After leaving Immanuel Baptist Church in August 1964, Reverend Woodard went to Southwest Baptist Theological Seminary to earn his doctor of theology degree in 1967.[43] While working on his doctoral degree, he served as the pastor of Southmayd Baptist, Southmayd, Texas.[44] Southmayd is a town of about a thousand people and is about ninety miles northeast of Fort Worth. The church was founded in 1897.[45]

After finishing his doctor of theology degree, Dr. Woodard went on to have a very distinguished career in the academia. Working through the New Mexico Baptist Convention, he served as the Baptist student director of East New Mexico University in Portales, New Mexico. He also served as a visiting assistant professor in religion and as the registrar at East New Mexico University. His final positions at East New Mexico University were assistant to the graduate dean and assistant to the vice president. While at Eastern New Mexico University, Dr. Woodard earned a master of education in 1977. Dr. Woodard then went to Wayland Baptist University in Plainview, Texas, where he served as assistant to the president.[46]

Dr. Woodard and the late Gwen have three children—Candace, Claire, and Kyle. The children were all young when he served at Immanuel Baptist Church. Immanuel Baptist Church members from the days that Dr. Woodard was pastor may remember that Claire was burned severely while he served at Immanuel Baptist Church. Candace, now Mrs. Chris Moseley, is a certified public accountant. Claire, now Mrs. Jack Ward, lives in a suburb of Philadelphia, Pennsylvania, and is a registered nurse. Kyle lives in the Dallas, Texas, area and is the property manager for one of the largest law offices in the area.[47]

Figure 9.5. Dr. Alfred and Gwen Woodard

CHAPTER 10

Stability, Growth, and Groundwork for the Family Life Center

Rev. Lawrence Stewart, November 1964–July 1973

Introduction

Rev. Lawrence Stewart was the twelfth pastor of Immanuel Baptist Church. He was an outstanding in his evangelistic sermons, and the church experienced a strong growth in membership during his tenure. One of the accomplishments of the church during Reverend Stewart's years was the complete air-conditioning of the church plant.[1] In May 1968, under Reverend Stewart's leadership, the church voted to purchase the Taylor Daniel property adjoining the church on the east. During the Stewart years, efforts were made to purchase the old Shawnee Hospital. That property eventually became the location of the Family Life Center.[2]

The world scene when Rev. Lawrence Stewart was pastor of Immanuel Baptist Church was one of Cold War and hostility between the United States and the Soviet Union and an active war in Vietnam. In 1964, Congress approved the Gulf of Tonkin Resolution after North Vietnamese torpedo boats attacked American destroyers. In the Soviet Union, Alexei Kosygin and Leonid Brezhnev deposed Premier Nikita Khrushchev. World tensions further heightened when China detonated its first atomic bomb.[3] The first US combat troops arrived in South Vietnam in 1965. By the end of the year, 190,000 American soldiers were in South Vietnam.[4]

In 1966, Mao Zedong launched the Cultural Revolution, leading to a massive upheaval of Chinese society and starvation. Estimates of total deaths from the violence of the Cultural Revolution range between five hundred thousand and ten million people. In 1967, Israel defeated a coalition of thirteen Muslim countries in the Six-Day War. In 1968, Soviet Union and Warsaw Pact troops suppressed a prodemocracy uprising known as the Prague Spring in Czechoslovakia.[5]

In 1969, the United States, the Soviet Union, and about one hundred other countries signed the nuclear nonproliferation treaty, and a twenty-seven-year-old colonel named Muammar Gaddafi established an anti-Western Islamic republic in Libya.[6] In 1970, the Aswan High Dam was completed, and a Palestinian terrorist group hijacked five airplanes.[7] In 1971, Richard Nixon and Mao Zedong began trade and diplomatic relations between the United States and Communist China.[8] In 1972, Muslim terrorists attacked at the Olympic Games in Munich and killed eleven Israeli athletes and one policeman. In 1973, the United States withdrew from South Vietnam.[9] In 1974, India detonated a nuclear device, becoming the world's sixth nuclear power.[10]

Amid the world tensions, the United States experienced a period of prosperity. In 1964, The Beatles became popular, and Cassius Clay (later known as Muhammed Ali) won the world heavyweight champion.[11] In 1965, Rev. Martin Luther King Jr. was arrested in Selma, Alabama, during civil rights demonstrations.[12] In 1966, the *Star Trek* television series began airing on NBC. In 1967, the first heart transplant and the first Super Bowl occurred. Also in 1967, Thurgood Marshall became the first African American Supreme Court Justice, and three astronauts—Roger Coffee, Gus Grissom, and Ed White— were killed during a simulated launch. Tragedy also struck in 1968 when Martin Luther King Jr. and Robert Kennedy were assassinated.

In 1969, Neil Armstrong became the first man to walk on the moon, and the *Sesame Street* television series began. Also in 1969, Senator Ted Kennedy left the scene of an accident in which campaign aide Mary Jo Kopechne was drowned.[13] In 1970, computer technology took a major step forward when the floppy disk was introduced. In 1972, Mark Spitz won seven gold medals at the Olympic Games, and pocket calculators were introduced. The year 1973 saw a great tragedy for the prolife community when the Supreme Court ruled in the *Roe v. Wade* case that abortion was legal in the United States. In 1974, President Nixon resigned as part of the ongoing Watergate scandal investigation and possible impeachment proceedings.[14]

Rev. Lawrence Stewart, the Years before Immanuel

Lawrence Reading Stewart was born on December 4, 1919, in Britton, Oklahoma, to Richard Lafayette and Onie Virginia (Davis) Stewart.[15] Britton, Oklahoma is a former town that lies in north central Oklahoma City at the corners of Britton Road and Western Avenue.[16] Lawrence Stewart served his country in the United States Army during World War II as a master sergeant. He married Dennie Florence Hooper on July 9, 1942, in Lawton, Oklahoma, while stationed at Fort Sill.[17] Lawrence Stewart entered Oklahoma Baptist University in Shawnee in 1948 as a twenty-six-year-old freshman and army veteran and graduated with a bachelor of arts degree in religious education in 1950. While at Oklahoma Baptist University, Lawrence Stewart was active in the ministerial alliance.[18]

Figure 10.1. Lawrence Stewart, the OBU days

While a student at Oklahoma Baptist University, Rev. Lawrence Stewart was also the full-time pastor of Morse Baptist Church, Okemah.[19] Morse Baptist Church was about twenty-three miles northeast of Okemah and has been renamed Last Chance Baptist Church.[20] Reverend Stewart was evidently a very effective and loving pastor for the church.

In the October 13, 1949, issue of *The Baptist Messenger*, Floyd Campbell wrote a letter to the editor describing a joint need within the Oklahoma Baptist Community. The joint need was for rural and small-town Baptist churches to have capable pastors and for Oklahoma Baptist University ministerial students to have employment and experience during their college days. He claimed the solution to the two needs was for the leadership of rural and small-town churches to reach out to and employ Oklahoma Baptist University ministerial students. He used Rev. Lawrence Stewart and Morse Baptist Church as an example of how well such an arrangement could work. He stated:

> A good example of this [mutual benefit] is found in the leadership of the pastor of the Morse [Baptist] Church near Okemah. Lawrence Stewart, a student at the University, is full-time pastor of the church. Some of the members of this rural church were in doubt as to the ability of a student to carry on the church work. Brother Lawrence has removed that doubt. Although Shawnee is about 60 miles from this church, Brother Lawrence has not missed an appointment. In a recent revival at the church, 38 new members were received. Although the pastor and his wife are a young couple and haven't been in this work as long as some of our older pastors, they would be in strong competition for some of the preachers in our large cities. They are both good personal workers and a great asset to this rural church.[21]

As Reverend Stewart was nearing graduation, Morse Baptist Church had a membership of 101 people and had baptized 12 people the prior year. Their Cooperative Program offering was $249.82, which was a very respectable offering for a small rural church at the time.[22]

In addition, while a student at Oklahoma Baptist University, Lawrence Stewart had begun his involvement in Oklahoma state Baptist life. He attended the 1948, 1949, and 1950 annual meetings of the Baptist General Convention of Oklahoma. These were held in Muskogee, Oklahoma City, and Tulsa, respectively.[23, 24, 25]

After finishing his bachelor of arts degree in religious education in the spring of 1950, Rev. Lawrence Stewart attended Southwestern Baptist Theological Seminary in Fort Worth, Texas. He received a bachelor of divinity degree and a master of theology degree from Southwestern Baptist Theological Seminary. While working on his two degrees, he served as a Baptist minister for churches in Texas.

Upon finishing his degree work at Southwestern Baptist Theological Seminary in spring 1954, Rev. Lawrence Stewart returned to Oklahoma to take the pastorate of First Baptist Church, Caddo.[26] Caddo is a town in Bryan County, Oklahoma, a few miles from the Red River. Reverend Stewart attended the 1954 Annual Meeting of the Baptist General Convention of Oklahoma held in Oklahoma City as a messenger from First Baptist Church, Caddo, but he took no active role in the proceedings.[27]

After less than a year at First Baptist Church, Caddo, in March 1955, Reverend Lawrence resigned his position and took the pastor- ate of First Baptist Church, Okemah, not far from Morse Church where he had been pastor during his time as an Oklahoma Baptist University student.[28] One of his final duties in the Caddo area was to serve as the evangelist for the Simultaneous Revival that was held in March 1955 at Trinity Baptist Church, Durant, within the Bryan Baptist Association.[29] The church added three members by baptism as the result of Reverend Stewart's preaching at the Simultaneous Revival.[30]

While at First Baptist Church, Okemah, Rev. Lawrence Stewart began to become more active in the area and Oklahoma Baptist life. He attended the 1955 Annual Meeting of the Baptist General Convention of Oklahoma in Tulsa as a messenger from First Baptist Church, Okemah. He was selected to serve on the Advisory Board of the Baptist Foundation.

In terms of Cooperative Program giving, First Baptist Church, Okemah, ranked 40th in the state at $7,441. It is worth noting that Immanuel Baptist Church under Rev. Frank Baugh ranked 26th at $11,306, and Exchange Baptist Church under former Immanuel pastor Rev. Claybron Deering was 41st with $7,340 in offerings. The first-place church in terms of Cooperative Program giving was

First Baptist Church, Oklahoma City, under the leadership of Dr. Hershel Hobbs. In terms of per capita giving, First Baptist Church, Okemah ranked 32nd with $11.06 in Cooperative Program offerings per person.[31]

Rev. Lawrence Stewart also supported Baptist life in other ways. On March 26, 1956, he was the moderator for a father-and-son banquet sponsored by Second Baptist Church, Okmulgee.[32] In May 1956, he served as the evangelist at the Simultaneous Revival held in Blanchard, Oklahoma.[33] In 1958, Reverend Stewart was the North Canadian Baptist Association chairman for the Cooperative Program.[34] At the October 13–14, 1958, Annual Meeting of the North Canadian Baptist Association at Calvary Baptist Church, Okmulgee, Rev. Lawrence Stewart was named as the moderator of the meeting.[35] In May 1959, Reverend Stewart held a Simultaneous Revival at First Baptist Church, Okemah, in which he was the evangelist. Ten people were baptized, and seventeen people were added to the church rolls.[36]

In September 1959, Rev. Lawrence Stewart resigned from First Baptist Church, Okemah, to assume the pulpit at First Baptist Church, Madill.[37] At First Baptist Church, Madill, his music minister, A. L. (Pete) Butler was of great assistance to Reverend Stewart. More than a hundred members were enrolled in four choirs at First Baptist Church, Madill.

A. L. Butler's wife, Jo Ann, directed the primary choir; and A. L. Butler directed the junior, youth, and adult choirs.[38] The Butlers became well known in Baptist music circles. Pete and Jo Ann were both graduates of Oklahoma Baptist University. They directed music at First Baptist Church, Ada, for twenty-three years. They also taught music at Midwestern Baptist Theological Seminary in Kansas City for seventeen years.[39]

Figure 10.2. Rev. Lawrence Stewart, the Madill days

Rev. Lawrence Stewart continued serving his fellow Baptist both at First Baptist Church, Madill, and across the state. At the Annual Meeting of the Baptist General Convention of Oklahoma held in Tulsa in November 1959, Reverend Stewart was elected to the board of directors of the Baptist General Convention of Oklahoma. Within the board, he was placed on the Missions and Falls Creek Committee and the Public Relations Committee. He was also selected to serve on the Advisory Board of the Baptist Foundation.[40] Within the Johnston-Marshall Baptist Association, Reverend Stewart was selected as the chairman of evangelism and sponsored a Simultaneous Revival at his home church—First Baptist Church, Madill. The evangelist for the revival was Bill West and the Worship Leader was Dale Perkins.[41]

In September 1960, Reverend Stewart was elected as moderator of the Johnston-Marshall Baptist Association. Their annual meeting was held at Little City Baptist Church, Madill, on September 12 and 13. Because of his activity within the Johnston-Marshall Baptist Association and because of the prominence of First Baptist Church, Madill, within the community, First Baptist Church, Madill, was selected to be the host to the 1961 Annual Meeting.[42]

From November 27 to December 4, as the year rolled down, Reverend Stewart held a revival at First Baptist Church, Madill. Rev. John Bisagno, who was on his way to becoming one of Oklahoma's greatest evangelists, led a revival team from Tulsa. As a result of this revival, there were twenty-six additions by baptism, six by letter, and ten by professions of faith.[43] As soon as that revival ended, Reverend Stewart led a one-week revival at First Baptist Church, Temple, Oklahoma. There were seven additions, including two by baptism. Rev. Royce Brown, minister of music and education from Oak Avenue Baptist Church, Ada, led the music.[44]

During his last year at First Baptist Church, Madill, Rev. Lawrence Stewart continued to be active in revivals, hosting one at First Baptist Church, Madill, and sponsoring one at First Baptist Church, Madill's mission church, Enos Chapel, both in April of 1964. The revival at Enos Chapel was led by Loyd Ellis, the chapel's pastor and resulted in three baptisms and eight total additions to the chapel's membership. The First Baptist Church, Madill, revival resulted in eight baptisms and eleven new members.[45]

From September 27 to October 4, 1964, Rev. Lawrence R. Stewart was the evangelist for a revival at Immanuel Baptist Church,

Henryetta. There were ten additions by baptism, eight by letter, and one other profession of faith. Music was led by Sidney Thompson, an Oklahoma Baptist University student. This revival occurred a short distance from Shawnee while Immanuel Baptist Church was seeking a pastor to replace Rev. Alfred Woodard.

On September 6, 1964, members of First Baptist Church, Madill, honored Rev. Lawrence R. Stewart on his fifth anniversary as their pastor. Reverend Stewart and his wife were presented a book of letters of appreciation and a service of china. During his ministry, the resident membership of the church increased from 652 to 750, and 422 additions were recorded, with 175 of those by professions of faith. Sunday School average attendance increased from 309 to 405. Total mission giving during Stewart's pastorate reached $49,177. The church built a new parsonage under Reverend Stewart's leadership.

The indebtedness on the parsonage was almost paid off by the anniversary celebration. One hallmark of his first five years at First Baptist Church, Madill, was the broadcasting of Sunday morning services over KMAD, Madill.[46] In October 1964, one month after the fifth-anniversary celebration, Reverend Stewart resigned from First Baptist Church, Madill, to take the pulpit of Immanuel Baptist Church.[47]

Rev. Lawrence Stewart, the Immanuel Years

On October 18, 1964, the Immanuel Baptist Church Pulpit Committee—chaired by A. V. Daugherty and consisting of Cap Gardner, Kenneth Eyer, Carl Webb, Fred Luckett, and Wayne Zorger—documented the employment package extended to Rev. Lawrence R. Stewart. His base salary was $7,280 plus use of the parsonage and moving expenses. He was given an expense allowance of $1,560 for his automobile, parsonage utilities, and Southern Baptist Convention Annual Meeting expenses.[48] Reverend Stewart accepted the pastorate of

Figure 10.3.
Lawrence Stewart,
the Immanuel days

Immanuel Baptist Church, Shawnee, effective November 1, 1964, after five years at First Baptist Church, Madill.

Reverend Stewart preached his first sermon at Immanuel Baptist Church on Sunday, November 8. The move to Shawnee was very natural for the Stewarts. He was born and raised in the Oklahoma City area. Reverend Stewart was also a graduate of Oklahoma Baptist University. In addition, the Stewart's son, Larry, was a sophomore at OBU.[49]

The Stewart family fit in very well at Immanuel Baptist Church and in Shawnee. Immanuel Baptist Church member Pat (McQuerry) Coker recalled that Dennie Stewart became the high school Sunday School director and that Dennie was a delightful person, very stable, very wise, and very mature. The Stewarts and Pat and J. D. McQuerry—Pat's late husband—were great friends.[50] Rev. Lawrence Stewart was a very frugal pastor. If there was a job that was needed and he could do it himself without hiring someone with church funds to do it, Reverend Stewart would happily and cheerfully do the job himself.[51]

The first full year for Rev. Lawrence Stewart was 1965, and the year was a very active year. At the January 12, 1965, Deacons' meeting, the following officers were elected: Fred Williams, chairman; A. V. Daugherty, vice chairman; Clair Hodges, secretary; and Louis McElroy, financial secretary. The Deacons also voted to recommend to the congregation the purchase of a new bus.

In 1965 under the leadership of Rev. Lawrence Stewart and his wife Dennie, Immanuel Baptist Church was very active in the Girls' Auxiliary ministry. The July 15, 1965, issue of *The Baptist Messenger* records a significant Girls' Auxiliary coronation event at the church. Relleen Smith was crowned as a queen regent, only the second such distinction in the church's history. Five queens were also crowned. These were Cindy Bradley, Jenise Williams, Patti Weaver, Merrill Woods, and Patricia Fruit. Also recognized were one princess, three ladies-in-waiting, and three maidens. Mrs. Merrill Woods served as Girls' Auxiliary director, and Mrs. Merle Thompson was the Woman's Missionary Union director.[52]

In November 1965, Rev. Lawrence Stewart and his wife Dennie attended the annual meeting of the Baptist General Convention of

Oklahoma for the first time as messengers from Immanuel Baptist Church. The annual meeting was held in Oklahoma City, just a short drive from Shawnee. The messengers at the annual meeting elected Reverend Stewart to be a member of the Board of Trustees of Oklahoma Baptist University, thus deepening his ties with the University.[53]

Revivals and evangelism continued to be dear to the heart of Rev. Lawrence Stewart. In April 1965, Reverend Stewart conducted a weeklong revival at First Baptist Church, Caddo, his original church in Oklahoma after completing his master of theology degree. In late 1965, he worked with some college-age members at Immanuel Baptist Church to form a youth revival team. The team was composed of Oklahoma Baptist University students who were members of Immanuel Baptist Church. The youth revival team was available for weekend events and youth revivals. The members were evangelist Jim Burkett, song leader and soloist Ken Jones, and pianist Carol Shannon.[54]

The youth revival team enjoyed success in its efforts and soon grew to eleven members. One of their more noteworthy revivals was at First Baptist Church, Skiatook, in April 1966, where the youth revival team ably supported the revival team brought in by Pastor Charlie W. Hargrave. In addition to conducting morning services, presenting music and testimonials at evening services, conducting the Friday evening service, and counseling, the team-led youth activities made an intensive visitation effort to contact every family in Skiatook.

Pastor Charlie W. Hargrave reported the church recorded nineteen additions by baptism and six by letter. In addition, six people at the revival surrendered for special service. Fifty-seven rededications were made during the revival, and twelve other professions of faith were made.[55] The Immanuel Youth Revival Team also had a major success at a revival at Virginia Avenue Baptist Church in Bartlesville from July 7 to 10. There were twenty-two decisions, including three professions of faith. The Immanuel Youth Revival Team conducted a door-to-door soul-winning campaign, a leadership training session, and fellowship sessions. The youth revival team members for the

Bartlesville revival were Jim Burkett, Natalie Brown, Aaron Austin, David Elledge, Jim Westmoreland, Martha Watkins, and Cara Beth Watkins.[56]

The year 1966 was a year of growth and cooperation for Immanuel Baptist Church. Resident membership increased from 1,342 to 1,386. At the January 5, 1966, business meeting, Fred Williams made a motion that the church assist the Shawnee Ministerial Association with a January 23 citywide census. The motion was seconded by L. L. McElroy and was eventually carried. The church also voted that Susan Coker should replace Anna Lewis, who was having health concerns, as librarian and that a letter of appreciation should be sent to Mrs. Lewis. Cap Gardner, as chairman of the Deacons, wrote the letter.

At the February 9, 1966, business meeting, the church voted to have a revival from March 13 to 20 with Rev. Lawrence Stewart as the evangelist and minister of music Rev. John Long providing the music. The revival was evidently successful since the church added ten members by letter, fourteen by baptism, and two by statement. Following the revival, the church leadership seemed to have decided to examine its rolls very carefully and to contact members who were not attending. Over the next five months, 176 members were deleted from the roles by letter and by erasure, bringing the membership down to 1,216 in August 1966. The church experienced strong growth in the fall months and ended the year with 1,386 members.[57]

The year 1967 began with the approval of an $81,154.43 budget. The budget included an increase in the pastor's salary from $7,850 to $8,243 and an increase in his automobile, parsonage utilities, and Southern Baptist Convention Annual Meeting expenses from $2,200 to $2,300. The New Year also saw the resignation of Rev. John Long, minister of music and youth, on January 18, 1967. He was called as minister of music and youth at Baptist Temple Church in Oklahoma City. A search committee consisting of Cap Gardner, Pat Robinson, and Mrs. Wayne Zorger was appointed to search for a new music minister.

On February 1, 1967, Ed Otto was hired as the interim music minister at a salary of thirty-five dollars per week. Jack Pearson, an

Oklahoma Baptist University music professor, was added later in 1967 as the minister of music. At a special called business meeting on April 19, 1967, the members of Immanuel Baptist Church voted unanimously to have the sanctuary and the education building air-conditioned by Harry Drew at a cost of $23,794.61, with $15,000.00 being borrowed at 6 percent interest for five years and the remainder being paid in cash.

At the May 17, 1967, business meeting, messengers to the Annual Meeting of the Baptist General Convention of Oklahoma were elected. These were Reverend Lawrence and Dennie Stewart, A. V. and Mrs. Lucille Daugherty, Kenneth and Mrs. Eyer, and Cap Gardner. The church leadership again appeared to have examined the church rolls during the summer of 1967 for inactive members. Between May and September, 149 members were removed from the rolls due to letters or erasure. Immanuel Baptist Church ended the year with 1,231 members.

The first business meeting in 1968 was on January 10. At that meeting, George McElhanon submitted his resignation as janitor, expressing how much he had enjoyed working in the Lord's house. Fred Williams then moved and E. F. Arnold seconded that Ellis Gregg be hired in Brother McElhanon's place. The motion carried.

At the May 8, 1968, business meeting, the Deacons, the Finance Committee, and the Maintenance Committee made a joint recommendation that the church undergo another waterproofing treatment at an estimated cost of $4,857. The recommendation passed. It is worth noting that the waterproofing cost was about 6 percent of the annual budget.

In a special called business meeting on May 22, 1968, the members of Immanuel Baptist Church voted to purchase the Daniel property just east of the church for four thousand dollars, plus one thousand in legal and city fees. The motion to purchase was made by Joe Russell and seconded by Carl Wright. The vote was unanimous. Also at that meeting, a joint recommendation was made by the Deacons and the Personnel Committee to hire Larry Taylor as an assistant to Reverend Stewart, giving special attention to the youth and education programs. Brother Taylor's salary was set at a hundred per week plus the parsonage at 118 South Eden. Immanuel Baptist Church finished the year with 1,229 resident members.[58]

The year 1969 started with a special request at the January 14, 1969, business meeting from the Finance Committee and the Deacons that three thousand dollars be moved from the general fund to the maintenance fund for the repair of the roof of the sanctuary. At the February 11, 1969, business meeting, A. V. Daugherty read a special report from the Music Committee outlining that the church organ could be used by members without charge for practice and by anyone for weddings and funerals also without charge.

In May 1969, thirty-three youth and six sponsors made a youth choir trip to Memphis, Tennessee. Funds for the trip were generated by the individuals, fund-raisers, and special offerings. A small amount of general fund money was used to cover additional expenses.[59] In November 1969, Immanuel Baptist Church honored Rev. Lawrence and Dennie Stewart with a reception, honoring their fifth anniversary with the church. They were presented with a new color television.[60]

In the November business meeting, the need for a new church bus was discussed. It was noted that both current buses were in poor condition and that on the last two youth trips, the bus taken had failed to run properly, requiring the bus to be towed back to Shawnee for repair. The result greatly dampened the success of the trip. The church voted to spend up to $8,500 for the purchase of a new bus.[61]

In December 1969, an unusual pair of baptisms took place at Immanuel Baptist Church when Rev. Lawrence Stewart baptized Willis F. Marrs and his wife, Eva. The baptismal ceremony was held near the beginning of the service. Following his baptism Marrs, who was seventy-six, still dressed in his baptismal garments, slumped over dead in the robing room. Stewart waited until the close of the service to inform the congregation, and then he said to them, "Willis Marrs has stepped into heaven tonight." Reverend Stewart added,

> When I stand in that place of silent voices with memory fresh of the broken cords of earth's deepest love, I ask, "Is there a sign that our-loved ones shall live again?" Quickly, comes the answer. Yes, there is a sign.

> There is a symbol. Christ left it for us. That symbol is
> baptism. Baptism tells us, "They shall live. O marvel-
> ous picture! O voice of promise! What better way to
> say, 'Good bye, earth!' and 'Good morning, Heaven!'
> than by coming out of those baptismal waters reveal-
> ing to a waiting congregation?" This [is the] hope that
> is ours through our Savior, and finding it [must be] a
> reality for you.[62]

A very special event in the life of Immanuel Baptist Church occurred on Sunday afternoon, October 24, 1971, when Mrs. K. R. (Ruby) Sands was honored for forty-eight years of teaching Sunday School class at Immanuel. The Mary and Martha Class and the Adult III Department hosted a reception in her honor. The event also marked her birthday.

Mrs. Sands was born in Alma, Arkansas, and moved to Shawnee in 1922. Upon arriving in Shawnee, she joined Draper Baptist Street Church and was part of the move to Main Street and the renaming of the church to Immanuel Baptist Church. She taught beginner, young people, and adult classes and served with twelve of Immanuel's pastors—T. B. Holcomb, O. G. Matthews, Bill Smith, Dan Brinkley, H. H. Burton, Thomas Doss, H. Tom Wiles, Claybron Deering, Frank O. Baugh, Joe L. Ingram, Alfred Woodard, and Lawrence R. Stewart.

Mrs. Sands spent two years in Africa with her daughter, her son-in-law William Williams, and their family, while they served as missionaries. While in Africa, Mrs. Sands taught at the Newton Memorial School for Missionary Children in Nigeria. Upon her return to Shawnee, she began a kindergarten at Immanuel Baptist Church and taught four years, retiring in 1963.[63]

While at Immanuel Baptist Church, Rev. Lawrence Stewart was active in the Pottawatomie-Lincoln Baptist Association. In a March 1967 event that was reminiscent of his days as a young ministerial student at Oklahoma Baptist University, Reverend Stewart assisted in the ordination of Larry Paul Taylor, an Oklahoma Baptist University ministerial student from Yukon. The ordination occurred at Pearson Baptist Church where Brother Taylor served as pastor.

Rev. Arlis A. Brady, director of missions in Pottawatomie-Lincoln Baptist Association, was the moderator. Rev. Lawrence Stewart led the questioning of Brother Taylor. Rev. Bob Helmich, pastor of First Baptist Church, Paul's Valley, and the former pastor of Brother Taylor from his days as a youth in Yukon, brought the special music. Rev. Leon Christiansen, pastor of First Baptist Church, Yukon, brought the message.[64]

Pearson was a small rural church southeast of Asher. The church disbanded around 2004. Rev. George Bone was pastor there for a very long time.[65] Reverend Stewart's leadership role in the Pottawatomie-Lincoln Baptist Association also included being elected as moderator for the 1969 Annual Meeting and delivering the annual sermon at the 1971 Annual Meeting.[66]

The year 1972 started with a $104,410.90 budget being approved by the church members. The Cooperative Program allocation was $15,661.64, or 15 percent of the total budget. The Pottawatomie-Lincoln Baptist Association allocation was $2,610.26, or 2.5 percent of the total budget. Rev. Lawrence Stewart's salary was $10,395, with an automobile, parsonage utilities, and Southern Baptist Convention Annual Meeting expense allowance of $2,700.

At the February 8, 1972, Deacons' meeting, the Deacons approved Rev. Lawrence Stewart's recommendation that the spring revival be led by Rev. Newman McLarry and Rev. Pete Butler. On Wednesday, July 26, 1972, the Ashland Baptist Church Youth Choir from Ashland, Kentucky, performed a concert for Immanuel Baptist Church. At the August 8, 1972, Deacons' meeting, the Deacons voted to initiate discussions with the city of Shawnee to purchase the old Shawnee Hospital property. At the October 10, 1972, Deacons' meeting, it was announced that the negotiations with the city for the old Shawnee Hospital property had ended. At the November 14, 1972, Deacons' meeting, the Deacons recommended to Reverend

Figure 10.4.
Dr. Dan Holcomb,
interim pastor

Stewart that Wednesday-night services before Thanksgiving be cancelled so that the church membership could support the citywide Thanksgiving celebration.[67]

Immanuel Baptist Church started 1973 as a strong church with a resident membership of 1,326, with 889 enrolled in Sunday School and 198 enrolled in Training Union. Average Sunday School attendance was 390, and average Training Union attendance was 121. The church had a budget of $110,000. The church's contribution to the Cooperative Program was 15 percent of the budget, or $16,500. The church's contribution to the Pottawatomie-Lincoln Baptist Association was 2.5 percent of the budget, or $2,750. Rev. Lawrence Stewart's salary for the year was set at $10,915 plus the use of the parsonage and a $2,400 expense account for his car and utilities and a $700 expense allowance for the annual meeting of the Southern Baptist Convention.

Expansion of the facility continued to be an item of interest for the church. In the March 14, 1973, business meeting, the church members voted to renew negotiations with the city of Shawnee to purchase the property where the Shawnee Hospital was once located. The church members also voted to pave the current unpaved parking lot areas at an estimated cost of $5,863.50. Maintenance problems with the church facility continued to be a concern for the church. At the June 13, 1973, business meeting, the church membership voted to approve a $22,403.00 contract with the Mid-Continental Waterproofing Company of Fort Scott, Kansas, for repairing, sandblasting, and waterproofing the sanctuary, towers, and basement. The value of the contract was twice the pastor's salary and 1/5 of the church budget.

On June 27, 1973, Rev. Lawrence Stewart resigned from the pulpit of Immanuel Baptist Church to become the pastor of First Baptist Church, Sedalia, Missouri. Reverend Stewart's last day in the pulpit was July 8, 1973. Dr. Dan Holcomb, an Oklahoma Baptist University professor of religion, was called as interim pastor at a salary of $125 per week.[68]

Rev. Lawrence Stewart, the Years after Immanuel

After leaving Immanuel Baptist Church, Rev. Lawrence Stewart became pastor of the First Baptist Church, Sedalia, Missouri. He served there from August 1973 until July 1984. During his tenure, a new sanctuary was dedicated on October 3, 1976. On January 10, 1982, a major fire severely damaged the education building and a portion of the fellowship hall of the sanctuary.[69]

Revivals were still a vital part of Rev. Lawrence Stewart's evangelical approach while he was pastor of First Baptist Church, Sedalia, Missouri. Moreover, based on his solid service to Baptist causes within the state of Oklahoma, Reverend Stewart maintained solid relationships with some of the state's Baptist leaders. In June 1974, Rev. Stewart hosted a revival at First Baptist Church, Sedalia. Baptist General Convention of Oklahoma executive secretary and former Immanuel Baptist Church pastor Dr. Joe Ingram served as the evangelist. Loyd Wren, minister of music and recreation of First Southern Baptist Church, Tucson, Arizona, led the music.

There were eleven additions by baptism and one by letter. In a letter printed in the June 27, 1974, issue of *The Baptist Messenger*, Reverend Stewart stated, "Joe was a tremendous blessing to our church, and my people truly fell in love with him. He has the most gracious spirit and is a fine preacher. Oklahoma Baptists are so fortunate to have a man of his spiritual stature to lead them."[70]

After retirement from the pulpit. Rev. Lawrence Stewart and Dennie returned to Edmond, Oklahoma, not far from where he was born. Reverend Stewart continued to serve Oklahoma churches in retirement. He did supply preaching in 1990, and again in 1995, he served as interim pastor at Classen Boulevard Baptist Church, Oklahoma City. He was seventy-six when he completed his second interim pastorate at the church.[71, 72, 73]

The Stewarts eventually joined the First Baptist Church, Edmond. Reverend Stewart died on May 25, 2006, in Oklahoma City. His survivors include his wife, Dennie; his son and daughter-in-law, Larry and Sandy Stewart of Oklahoma City; his two grandchildren, Robyn and Lauryn Stewart; his brother Jack; and many nieces and nephews. He was eighty-six when he died.[74] Dennie Stewart died on July 16, 2010.[75]

CHAPTER 11

The Renovation of Amazing Immanuel

Dr. Larry Adams, March 1974–April 1982

Introduction

Dr. Larry Adams was the thirteenth pastor of Immanuel Baptist Church. He served from 1974 to 1982. His wife was Edwine Adams. Both Dr. and Mrs. Adams hailed from Hopkinsville, Kentucky. Perhaps the most significant event during the pastorate of Dr. Adams was the renovation of "Amazing Immanuel," as Dr. Adams lovingly called the church.[1]

The world scene during the years that Dr. Adams served Immanuel was filled with turmoil and strife. The Soviet Empire loomed as a massive challenge to the United States, and unrest in the Middle East posed economic and diplomatic challenges. The year 1974 saw Richard Nixon and Leonid Brezhnev meet in Moscow to discuss arms limitation agreements. Toward the end of 1974, Emperor Haile Selassie of Ethiopia was deposed. A Communist military dictatorship assumed power, and persecution of Christians and Christian missionaries in Ethiopia began.[2]

The year 1975 saw Communist dictator Pol Pot and his party, the Khmer Rouge, take over Cambodia. Eventually, Pol Pot and the Khmer Rouge would kill 1.5 million Cambodians. The Vietnam War finally ground to an end in 1975.[3]

The year 1976 saw a moment of joy and celebration when Israeli airborne commandos attacked Uganda's Entebbe Airport and freed 103 hostages held by pro-Palestinian Muslim terrorists who had hijacked an Air France plane.[4] In September 1978, Egyptian president Anwar Sadat and Israeli premier Menachem Begin signed the Framework for Peace in the Middle East after a 13-day conference at Camp David.

In November, Jim Jones's followers committed mass suicide in Jonestown, Guyana.[5] The year 1979 saw the beginnings of turmoil in Iran that has continued to this day. The shah was forced to leave Iran after a year of unrest and amid his serious health problems. Jimmy Carter helped return Muslim leader Ayatollah Ruhollah Khomeini from exile in France. Revolutionary forces under the Ayatollah soon took power. In November, Iranian militants seized the United States embassy in Tehran and took hostages.[6]

In October 1981, the Middle East became even less stable when Islamic extremists assassinated Egyptian president Anwar Sadat during a military parade in Cairo.[7] In 1982, Argentina invaded the Falkland Islands, thus starting a brief war between Argentina and the United Kingdom. After a few months, the British military overcame Argentina and freed the Falkland Islands.[8]

As with the world scene, the national scene was filled with turmoil and strife during the years that Dr. Adams served Immanuel. In July 1974, the House Judiciary Committee adopted three articles of impeachment against President Nixon. Nine days later, Richard Nixon announced he would resign.[9] Gerald Ford succeeded Richard Nixon as president.

In 1976, Jimmy Carter was elected president, and the nation celebrated its bicentennial.[10] In 1977, the Supreme Court ruled that states could not be required to spend Medicaid funds on abortions.[11] In 1978, the United States Senate approved the Panama Canal Neutrality Treaty and voted to turn the Canal over to Panama by the year 2000.[12] In 1979, Ronald Reagan was elected president in a Republican sweep.[13] In 1981, John W. Hinckley Jr. wounded President Reagan in an assassination attempt.[14] In 1982, John W. Hinckley Jr. was found not guilty by reason of insanity in the shooting of President Reagan.[15]

Dr. Larry Adams, the Years before Immanuel

Larry Adams was born in the town of Hopkinsville in western Kentucky. He attended the Christian County Public School System through his junior year in high school when he withdrew from school and joined the navy with a high school friend. Dr. Adams served in the navy from 1950 to 1953; after which, he returned to the Hopkinsville area. A few months after returning to Hopkinsville, on December 12, 1953, Larry Adams married his childhood sweetheart, Edwine. Larry and Edwine grew up on adjacent farms and rode the

school bus together. They dated through the first three years of high school. "She waited for me while I went off to the Navy," Larry said.

Larry's call to Christ came on Wednesday, July 14, 1954, when Larry attended a revival at New Palestine Baptist Church in Crofton, Kentucky, with his wife Edwine. At the end of that evening's revival service, Brother Adams felt the call of Christ on his heart and came forward to accept

Figure 11.1. Dr. Larry and Edwine Adams

Christ as his Lord and Savior. The New Palestine Baptist Church was small and did not have a baptismal; so after a few weeks, Larry, his aunt, and his uncle were baptized, along with thirty-two other people, at the Second Baptist Church in Hopkinsville.

According to Dr. Adams, the number of people being baptized overwhelmed the facility. To keep the floor from being damaged by all the water that was dripping off the people after their baptism, the church leaders put several wash tubs just outside the baptismal area. The church leaders asked the newly baptized Christians to stand in the tubs while their wet robes were removed, and they were toweled dry before going into the changing rooms.[16]

In his early years of marriage, Larry Adams worked as a traveling automobile parts salesman, serving several garages in western Kentucky. As he explained. "I have always loved cars, and this was a great job for me at the time." In addition to selling automobile parts, Larry and Edwine Adams raised hogs to help feed the family and bring in some extra money.

As Larry Adams drove his sales route, he would pass area churches and would feel the call of God on his heart to preach the Word of God. He resisted the call until one night when he was feeding his six sows. He was rather tired, and the night was late. He had just brought a bucket of corn from the crib to feed his sows when he again felt the strong call of God to preach.

According to Larry, he sat down on the ground and carefully explained to God how he had picked the wrong man, having never spoken to more than three people in a group in his life. He was twenty-four years old, was married, and had two children. God had simply picked the wrong man. Larry got up and returned his empty bucket to the crib. When he opened the crib door, something hit him square in the head. It was a barn rat, and the rat proceeded to bite his ear. Larry said he immediately changed his mind. "Lord, You have my attention. I will do it. I am ready to preach Your Word."

Larry soon went to the dean of Bethel Baptist College in Hopkinsville and asked to take a General Educational Development (GED) test so that he could enroll in college and learn to be a preacher. The dean agreed, and Larry took the test. A few days later, Larry saw the dean in a local bank and asked if the GED test results were good enough to allow him to become a student. The dean replied, "Son, with your GED scores, you can be anything you wish to be."

As soon as the term began, Larry enrolled in Bethel Baptist College and began studying under J. C. Franks, a Bible professor. Larry enrolled in General Epistles and Preaching through the Prophets. Professor Franks served as a mentor for Brother Larry, not only teaching him the course topics but also teaching him how to outline and prepare a sermon and how to serve the people of a church.

In parallel to this, Brother Larry was given his first pastorate at West Mount Zoar Baptist Church outside of Hopkinsville. "The church members were mostly relatives of Edwine," Larry explained. Dr. Adams was a bivocational pastor at the time, having been given an opportunity to work in the insurance field.

Larry Adams eventually received an associate of arts degree from Bethel Baptist College. In 1961, he enrolled in Austin Peay State University in Clarksville, Tennessee, and received his bachelor of education degree and a teaching certificate in 1963. He majored in history and English.

In the fall of 1963, Rev. Larry Adams enrolled in Southern Baptist Theological Seminary in Louisville, Kentucky. While a student at Southern Baptist Theological Seminary, Reverend Adams served as the pastor of South Fork Baptist Church, Hodgenville, Kentucky. South

Figure 11.2. South Fork Baptist Church, connecting people to Jesus since 1782!

Fork Baptist Church has the distinction of being the oldest continuously serving church west of the Appalachian Mountains. South Fork Baptist Church's motto is "Connecting People to Jesus since 1782!"

As Larry Adams was finishing his degree from Southern Baptist Theological Seminary, he was approached by Southern Baptist minister, humorist, television personality, and author Grady Nutt, who was also the director of alumni affairs and assistant to the president of Southern Seminary at the time. Pastor Nutt told Larry Adams that the seminary had found a rare and wonderful opportunity for him at a church in a resort town on a newly built man-made lake. The opportunity was exciting, but the location was challenging since the opportunity was at First Baptist Church of Eufaula, Oklahoma, and neither Reverend Larry nor Edwine Adams had ever been west of the Mississippi River. A short time later having completed his degree, Reverend Adams had delivered a message to the church and had been called as their pastor.

The church moved Reverend Adams, Edwine, their four children, and all their worldly possessions, including a freezer full of meat, from Hodgenville, Kentucky, to Eufaula, Oklahoma—a journey of over seven hundred miles. Reverend Adams and his wife, Edwine, had just been given a butchered cow and a butchered hog by their church members from South Fork Baptist Church, and the Adams wanted to take full advantage of that good meat and not let any of it go to waste. The ministry at First Baptist Church, Eufaula, was pleasing and successful for the family, and they gained many good friends.[17] However, the Lord had another move in store for Reverend Adams and his family.[18]

Dr. Larry Adams, the Immanuel Years

On March 1, 1974, Rev. Larry Adams was called from First Baptist Church, Eufaula, Oklahoma, to be the next pastor of Immanuel Baptist Church. From March to June of 1974, Pastor Adams camped out by himself in the Immanuel parsonage while his wife, Edwine, and the children stayed in Eufaula for their son Pat to graduate from high school. The day that Reverend Larry arrived in the parsonage, Nona Wright delivered a large pot roast to him. That pot roast lasted him two weeks.[19]

Rev. Larry Adams was a very popular and personable pastor. He had an excellent memory and remembered names and events in people's lives well. One of the first things that he did when he got to Immanuel Baptist Church was to conduct a prayer walk around the neighbor surrounding Immanuel. He prayed a prayer of blessing, specifically for every family in the neighborhood.[20]

Figure 11.3.
Dr. Larry Adams,
the Immanuel years

Within a few months of assuming the leadership of Immanuel, plans were made for several building programs that would take place during Reverend Adams's ministry. As Reverend Adams put it,

> One Wednesday evening, I stepped to the pulpit to deliver the message to a large crowd. Wednesday attendance was always good at Immanuel Baptist Church. The church had been constructed of Arkansas limestone, the blocks of which were delivered from the railroad station to the church with great effort in mule-drawn wagons. The building was beautiful and

magnificent, but the limestone always drew moisture, and the basement leaked massively. As I started my message, there was a crash of plaster at the side of the podium, and then piece-by-piece-by-piece about a pickup load of plaster came crashing to the stage. I looked over the pile of plaster when it had stopped falling and said, "I always thought that God's house should be the nicest house in the town." That's all I said, and I went right into my message. After the services, I went back to the parsonage, took a shower, and got into my pajamas for bed. Then the telephone rang. It was Chuck Thompson, and he asked me to come over to his place. I deferred because I had just got out of the shower and my hair was still wet. He explained that his wife Laverne had just made a pie, and he and Bro. Adams needed to talk. When I got to his house, Chuck told me, "Preacher, you hit us hard tonight. Laverne and I have been praying, and we want to underwrite the remodeling and repairs that are needed for the church." Bro. Chuck proceeded to work on the worship center. He hired a consultant to do the design and staff to do the labor. They turned the Immanuel sanctuary into a true gem, the envy of many churches in the town.[21]

On May 4, 1975, a homecoming and dedication service was held for the newly remodeled auditorium. H. G. Thompson did the invocation for the service, and two messages were brought. The first was by Dr. H. Tom Wiles, retired pastor from First Baptist Church, Lawton. Dr. Wiles was pastor of Immanuel Baptist Church from 1938 to 1945. The second was brought by Dr. Frank Baugh, the pastor of Exchange Avenue Baptist Church, Oklahoma City. Dr. Baugh was pastor of Immanuel Baptist Church from 1950 to 1959. Reverend Adams led the congregation in a special dedication cere-mony, and A. V. Daugherty led the dedication prayer. Cap Gardner gave the benediction.

Several key individuals involved in the remodeling were recognized at the homecoming and dedication service. Kenneth Eyer headed the Building Committee. The members of the Construction Committee were Carl Webb, A. V. Daugherty, Walker Thompson, H. G. Thompson, and Joe Russell. The Finance Committee was chaired by H. G. Thompson, with Ed Case, Thelma Thompson, Preston Adair, John Flegel, and Harold McMillan as members. The architecture firm was Bruce Ervin Associates of Tulsa. The engineering firm was Hal Kallenberger Associates of Tulsa. The decorator was Charles McEntire of Shawnee. The designer was Robert Braswell of Waco, Texas. The contractors were United Builders of Shawnee and Avent and Lakey of Oklahoma City.[22]

The remodeling effort was a major endeavor, and the church services were held in Raley Auditorium at Oklahoma Baptist University for almost five months. Extensive work was done on the walls, woodwork, windows, and pews. New carpeting and new pew cushions were added. The remodeling included a major renovation to the basement also.

The basement area had been plagued with moisture problems and was largely unusable. As part of the renovation, the basement walls were sealed with a moisture-proof sealant. As a result, the basement area became usable for family ministry and Sunday School classes. The remodeled and refurbished basement also included a kitchen and dining area. Part of the remodeling effort was dedicated to opening the balcony area and putting pews in the balcony. The balcony had not been used prior to the remodeling.

A second major construction project took place under Dr. Adams's leadership. It became clear to Dr. Adams that Immanuel needed more space for future ministries and future expansion. One evening, Pastor Adams walked the block of homes and buildings in the block surrounding Immanuel and prayed over each house and building, claiming it for the use of the Kingdom.

After a period of negotiations, the church was able to purchase the old Shawnee Hospital that was located just to the east of Immanuel and had not been fully used for some time. The facility was razed to the ground, and after fourteen months of construction work, the new Family Life Center was completed. Dedication services for the Family Life Center were held in May 1979.4This greatly expanded the ministries that the church could perform.[23]

One of the unique features of the Family Life Center was that the hardwood floor gymnasium was used as both a basketball arena and a skating rink.[24] The Family Life Center was a great asset for the church and the community. All-day Thanksgiving dinners were held there. Exercise classes were also held there. An October 31 celebration was started at the Family Life Center and served many community individuals for many years.

Linn Turner remembers the Family Life Center and a very busy place with someone at the desk all day long to coordinate events. The adult special needs Sunday School class met in the Family Life Center. As many as seventy children were bussed in on Sunday evening meal and Bible study. Several Sunday School classes helped to finance the meals. Pat and Randy Williams were instrumental in establishing and managing this ministry which still exists today.[25]

On January 12, 1976, Immanuel began operating a mission church on North Harrison Street. One year later, the church voted to discontinue participation in this mission. This mission church was known as the Friendship Baptist Church but moved and is now the Riverside Baptist Church of Tecumseh.

The ministries performed by Immanuel during the Adamses' years were many and were led by several strong and gifted individuals. For several years, Ron Chancellor led music and the youth ministry. Reverend Adam's daughter Pam was a student at Oklahoma Baptist University at the time and played organ for Brother Chancellor and the church. Later, Stu Tulley took over as youth director and was also the director of the Family Life Center. Stu Tulley came from First Baptist Church, Moore, and, according to Reverend Adams, "was the best Youth Director in the state."

Stu Tulley and Juanita Allison were instrumental, as with others, in starting the Immanuel Prayer Ministry. That ministry was started in December 1979 and quickly became a worldwide ministry with prayer items being provided from all fifty states and from thirty-five foreign countries. Immanuel members committed to pray in the prayer chapel for one hour each week for requested prayer needs. That ministry has continued up to the time of the printing of this history.[26]

Mrs. Allison had some physical limitations, but those limitations did not keep her from sharing her desire for prayer ministry with other churches around the state. For years, Juanita's husband would drive her to her speaking and training events. After he died, Mrs. Allison purchased a specially modified car that used hand control braking and steering. She learned to drive and drove herself to her speaking and training events.[27]

John Caulfield served as education and youth pastor, and Paul Golay served as education pastor. Tony Ward served as music minister and college minister. Rev. Jim Smith also served as an associate pastor and an education minister. Paul Stutz served as a youth pastor and was also the director of the Family Life Center.

In 1979, Immanuel began two new ministries. A weekday preschool was begun in August under the leadership of Mary Margaret Kasterke. The preschool provided a loving, Christian environment for preschoolers and children. At the same time, a mothers' day out program was started under the leadership of Luise Jenkins. Support all of these programs was provided by Carla Gierhart and Irene Coates, the office staff.

Several members of Immanuel played key roles during the years that Reverend Adams served as pastor. Chuck and Laverne Thompson were especially dear to Reverend and Mrs. Adams. The Thompsons not only did the auditorium renovation but also sent the Adams on a Renaissance and Reformation tour of Europe. The Thompsons also went on this trip as did Oklahoma Baptist University president Dr. Bill Tanner and Baptist General Convention of Oklahoma executive secretary Dr. Joe Ingram.

The tour included many of the sites that were important to the Renaissance and Reformation, including the Wittenberg Cathedral where Luther nailed the *Ninety-five Theses* and the Worms Cathedral where Luther declared "Here I stand, I can do no other." J. W. Kinnett was an important leader who helped raise funds to send the Adamses to Hawaii. However, Rev. Larry and Edwine Adams said they would prefer to go to the Holy Land, and they ended up leading a trip there with thirty-four members of Immanuel joining them.

Other members of Immanuel who were dear to the Adamses were Joe Russell who headed up the maintenance efforts at Immanuel. Brother Russell, a Shawnee businessman, supervised many of the water leak, electrical, and plumbing projects that were needed from time to time. Dr. Adams also spoke highly of Fred Williams, Kenneth Eyer, and A. V. Daugherty for their roles in the Training Union and Sunday School programs. Brother Williams was the Training Union director, and Bro. Eyer was the Sunday School director.

Figure 11.4. Stephanie and Dana Taylor

Speaking of Kenneth Eyer, Dr. Adams said, "Kenneth Eyer was one of the best men I ever knew." Concerning A. V. Daugherty, Reverend Adams explained that his Sunday schedule had him preaching at 8:15 a.m. and 11:00 a.m. and teaching a Sunday School class in the sanctuary at 9:30 a.m. When the workload began to wear him down, Reverend Adams approached A. V. Daugherty and asked him to take over the 9:30 a.m. Sanctuary Sunday School class. Brother Daugherty did this joyously and effectively.

Reverend Adams claimed, "A. V. Daugherty is the best lay Sunday School teacher I have ever known. He would put more time into preparing for his Sunday School class than most pastors would in preparing for their sermon." Reverend Adams also spoke highly of Bob and Miyoko Strong and Paul and Pat Slone. Some of his strongest praise was reserved for Stephanie Taylor. He says of Stephanie, "Stephanie was a real source of joy and encouragement for me. She has a tremendous personality and a brilliant mind. She still calls Edwine and me regularly. I like to tell Stephanie, 'When we get to Heaven, we will run and jump with joy before the throne of Jesus.'"[28]

During the Adams years, Immanuel Baptist Church experienced strong growth in membership. When Reverend Adams came, the church was averaging 300 members in Sunday School and 400 in worship with a budget of $110,000. These numbers soon grew to 450 members in Sunday School and 500 in worship. When Dr. Adams left Immanuel, the church was experiencing 800 members in Sunday School and 1,000 in worship.

During this time of growth, Dr. Adams promoted his "Amazing Immanuel" program. In signs around town and during his pulpit time. Reverend Adams would declare the blessings of "Amazing Immanuel" as the church served the Kingdom of God, the members of the church, and the city of Shawnee.

According to Reverend Adams, the growth in the church coincided with his studies for his doctorate. The program in which Reverend Adams enrolled was through the University of Southern California and Fuller Theological Seminary. Excellent professors and theologians would be brought to Phoenix, Arizona, for seminars; and the students would then write a ten- to fifteen-page paper over the lectures. The lectures were very challenging, and one series dealt with church growth.

Many of the ideas and techniques that Dr. Adams used to grow the membership of Immanuel came directly from this lecture series. According to Dr. Adams, Fred Williams, the Immanuel Training Union director, would say to him, "I can always tell when you go out to one of your seminar lectures. You come back all fired up and full of new ideas."[29]

While the remodeled sanctuary was a magnificent improvement to the Immanuel Baptist Church facility, the cost of remodeling activity put some strain on the Immanuel Baptist Church budget. At the February 10, 1982, business meeting, Dr. Larry Adams proposed a ten-week program beginning on February 21, 1982, whereby each Immanuel family would give a 10 percent increase to their regular offering to help catch up the budget. Although the building had been remodeled, it continued to have problems.

At the April 14, 1982, business meeting, the Building Committee noted that the roof needed to be repaired and that the air-conditioning unit would need to be moved to accommodate the repair. The cost of the roof repair and the air-conditioning unit relocation came to twenty thousand dollars. At that same meeting, Dr. Adams submitted his resignation stating that he had been called to New Orleans Baptist Theological Seminary to serve as the capital campaign director with May 9, 1982, as his final Sunday in the pulpit.

Bro. Jim Smith gave a brief testimony of the growth of Immanuel Baptist Church under Dr. Adams's leadership and his loving shepherding.[30] At the May 11, 1982, Deacons' meeting, Robert Britt moved and Randy Williams seconded that Rev. Jim Smith be called as the interim pastor of Immanuel Baptist church.[31] A week later, on Sunday, May 9, 1982, Tony Ward, who served as music minister and college minister, was ordained to the gospel ministry.[32]

Dr. Larry Adams, the Years After Immanuel

After leaving Immanuel Baptist Church in summer 1982, Dr. Adams went to New Orleans Baptist Theological Seminary to serve as the capital campaign director. After a short stay at the seminary, Dr. Adams became the pastor of First Baptist Church, Piedmont, Oklahoma, from 1983 to 1986. He then became the director of the Baptist Retirement Center (BRC) for ten years. Dr. Adams said, "For me, my years as pastor of Immanuel Baptist Church were great. But being head of the BRC was the best ministry that I ever had. I was everything—pastor, administrator, finance manager, and mayor."

Dr. Adams has always been a strong supporter of Baptist institutions and ministry, both at the state and national level. He served on the board of directors for the Baptist General Convention of Oklahoma from 1976 to 1980.[33] He also served on the board of trustees of Oklahoma Baptist University for several years and was the chairman of the board in 1980. In addition, Dr. Adams served on the board of trustees for Southern Baptist Theological Seminary in Louisville, Kentucky, from 1986 to 1996.

At its February 12, 2012, board meeting, the Baptist Retirement Center awarded Larry and Edwine Adams the 2012 Will and Nora Baskett Legacy of Love Award. The Will and Nora Baskett Legacy of Love Award is the highest recognition given by BRC. The award is named after Will and Nora Baskett, two pioneers in aging services. In its press release announcing the award, the BRC stated,

Larry Adams faithfully served BRC for many years as both the campus director at Baptist Village of Oklahoma City and the BRC's Vice-President of Development. A talented and experienced fundraiser, he led a capital campaign that far exceeded BRC's goals. He also planned and organized an annual fund effort, which is now carried out on a yearly basis. He was instrumental in developing numerous friends of the BRC ministry. For his and Edwine's influence and efforts, the Larry and Edwine Adams Assistance Fund was established by BRC in their honor."[34]

In addition to his service to the Baptist Retirement Center, Dr. Adams has continued to serve the churches of the state of Oklahoma. He has served as the interim pastor at sixteen churches around the state. One year, he was a guest preacher or a supply pastor for forty-three churches. He said,

I served from Woodward to Claremore and from Bartlesville to McAlester. Todd Fisher and I even fulfilled one of my "Bucket List Items" when he allowed me to preach one last time at Immanuel in June of 2011. A few months later, I had a major heart attack. I have also had pancreatitis, which I would wish on no one. But I am well and feeling good now.

Dr. Larry and Edwine Adams have four children—three girls and one boy. The children are Pam, Patrick, Penny, and Polly. Pam and Patrick are graduates of Oklahoma Baptist University. Penny is a graduate of the University of Oklahoma, and Polly is a graduate of Southeast Oklahoma State University. The Adamses have nine grandchildren and five great grandchildren.[35]

Chapter 12

Steady Growth and Service

Rev. Steven Boehning, August 1982–March 1986

Introduction

In 1982, Rev. Steven M. Boehning, was called as pastor. During his years at Immanuel Baptist Church, a new pipe organ was purchased and dedicated.[1]

The world scene when Rev. Steven Boehning was pastor of Immanuel Baptist Church was one of strength and advancement for the United States. In November 1982, Soviet premier Leonid Brezhnev died. He had ruled the Soviet Union for eighteen years.[2]

Yuri Andropov, who would rule the Soviet Union for just over one year, succeeded him.[3] Andropov was succeeded by Konstantin Chernenko, who also ruled for just one year. Mikhail Gorbachev succeeded Chernenko. Premier Gorbachev presided over the final collapse of the Soviet Union.[4]

In 1983, two major tragedies occurred. In August 1983, a South Korean Boeing 747 jetliner bound for Seoul strayed into Soviet airspace and was shot down by a Soviet fighter jet. All 269 passengers were killed. In October, Muslim terrorists killed 237 United States Marines in a Beirut barracks bombing.[5] In 1985, the combination of Communist government mismanagement and drought led to a famine in Ethiopia. Approximately 1 million Ethiopians died. Also in 1985, Muslim terrorists hijacked TWA Flight 847 with 179 passengers onboard.

In a stop in Beirut, an American Navy diver named Robert Stethem was murdered, and seven Americans with Jewish-sounding names were removed from the flight and placed in a Shiite prison. Also in April 1986, just after Dr. Boehning resigned, a Soviet nuclear reactor in Chernobyl, Ukraine, suffered a malfunction, resulting in a major nuclear accident.[6]

The American scene during the years that Rev. Steven Boehning served as pastor of Immanuel Baptist Church was one of strength, prosperity, and advancement under Ronald Reagan. In 1982, the movie *E. T. the Extra Terrestrial* was released. In June 1983, Sally K. Ride became the first American woman in space as a crewmember of the space shuttle *Challenger*. In 1984, President Reagan was reelected over Walter Mondale in a landslide with 59 percent of the vote. In 1985, the Coca-Cola Company experimented with a new, sweeter version of their product known as New Coke. The experiment was a resounding failure. In 1986, the nation was shocked and filled with sorrow when the Space Shuttle *Challenger* exploded, killing all onboard. Also in 1986, Halley's Comet passed by the earth on its seventy-six-year circuit of the solar system.[7]

Dr. Steven Boehning, the Years before Immanuel

Steven Boehning was born July 1, 1949, in Granby, Missouri. He received Christ as his Lord and Savior at an early age in Missouri. He received a bachelor of arts from the University of Arkansas. When he was twenty-one years old in 1970, he received his certificate of license to preach at First Baptist Church, Geyer Springs, Arkansas. Geyer Springs is a neighborhood within the Little Rock city limits.[8]

In 1971, he was ordained at First Baptist Church, Geyer Springs. In 1971, he enrolled in Southwestern Baptist Theological Seminary in

Fort Worth, Texas, where he earned a master of divinity degree. From 1971 to 1975, while a student at Southwestern Baptist Theological Seminary, he was youth pastor of Birchman Avenue Baptist Church, Fort Worth, Texas.[9]

In 1973, while a student at Southwestern Baptist Theological Seminary, Reverend Boehning and his wife, Susan, traveled to Oklahoma City and

Figure 12.1. First Baptist Church, Geyer Springs, Arkansas

Tulsa to give their personal testimonies at the December 27–29 State Youth Evangelism Conference sponsored by the Baptist General Convention of Oklahoma.[10] In 1975, Reverend Boehning received the Stella P. Ross Evangelism Award for scholarship and service in the field of evangelism from Southwestern Baptist Theological Seminary. In 1976, he received a doctorate of divinity degree from the California Graduate School of Theology.

In 1976, Dr. Boehning was minister of evangelism at Central Baptist Church, Jonesboro, Arkansas. In 1977, Dr. Boehning was selected as an Outstanding Young Man of America for his professional achievements, leadership ability, and service to the community.[11] In 1977, Dr. Boehning was called as pastor of Highland Park Baptist Church, Bartlesville, Oklahoma. In November 1977, he attended the Baptist General Convention of Oklahoma Annual Meeting held at First Baptist Church, Tulsa, on November 14–16 as a messenger from Highland Park Baptist Church. He served no role other than a messenger.[12]

However, in November 1978, Dr. Boehning and his wife, Susan, both attended the Baptist General Convention of Oklahoma Annual Meeting held at First Baptist Church, Oklahoma City, on November 14–16, as messengers from Highland Park Baptist Church, Bartlesville. Dr. Boehning served on the Tellers Committee.[13] By 1979, Dr. Boehning had gained sufficient recognition within the body of Oklahoma Baptists to be selected for the board of directors of the Baptist General Convention of Oklahoma at the Annual Meeting. Within the board of directors, he was selected to serve on the Planning and Promotion Committee.[14] At the 1980 BGCO Annual Meeting held at First Southern Baptist Church, Del City, Dr. Boehning continued his seat on the board of directors and was selected for the Child Care Committee.[15]

On February 25–27, 1980, the Baptist General Convention of Oklahoma hosted an Oklahoma preaching conference at First Baptist Church, Norman. The conference featured messages on sermon development by Glenn Brown, BGCO associate director for planning and promotion. The keynote speaker was Frank Pollard, pastor of First Baptist Church, Jackson, Mississippi, and host of *The Baptist Hour* and *At Home with the Bible.*

The conference focused on the practical aspects of providing new input and inspiration for the pastor's weekly task of sermon development. The three-day conference highlighted specific experiences of step-by-step sermon preparation under the leadership of ten Oklahoma pastors, three of whom had Immanuel Baptist Church connections—current pastor Dr. Larry Adams, future pastor Dr. Steve Boehning, and former music minister Rev. Bob Green.[16]

On May 4 to 9, 1980, Dr. Steve Boehning continued his service to the churches of Oklahoma by conducting a revival for First Baptist Church, Pawhuska. There were nineteen additions to the church by baptism. The singer for the revival was Paul Biggs. The pastor of First Baptist Church, Pawhuska, was Rev. R. Fred Selby Jr.[17]

Dr. Boehning's growing respect within the Oklahoma Baptist community was reflected in the August 14, 1980, issue of *The Baptist Messenger* that contained an article entitled "Churches Benefit from Stewardship Program." The article promoted the activities of the planning and promotion department of the BGCO and used Highland Park Baptist Church in Bartlesville and Dr. Steve Boehning to illustrate how the department assists local churches by providing training, resources, and information in areas of stewardship, budgeting, leadership skills, church organization, and long-range planning for support to the church and to the Cooperative Program. The article quoted Dr. Steve Boehning as saying the following:

> My first year in Bartlesville, we planned a stewardship program. I invited Glenn Brown, Associate Director of the Planning and Promotion Department, to meet with our stewardship committee. We put things into practice from the guidelines he shared with us, and as a result we're almost doubling our income. Many of the people who have been joining our church are married young adults. They have been taught some basic principles of stewardship that they had not known prior to our stewardship emphasis. What they've been doing is putting tithing into practice, and we've had several testimonies telling how God has blessed them through their tithing. All along as we have grown, it has been a process of our married young adults, and older people, too, learning about tithing, and at that point they begin to tithe and share testimonies about how God has been blessing them because of it. I had one young man ask me one night, "Preacher, you talk about stewardship and tithing, but exactly what is a tithe? My wife and I give, but we don't know what tithing means." Together they make about $36,000 a year, and they were not giving nearly a tithe. They did not have any problem with giving. It was just that they didn't understand stewardship. Once [stewardship was properly] explained, they have been tithing for two years. We are grateful for everything Glenn Brown shared with us. It is an offspring of everything else that's happened concerning stewardship in our church.[18]

In August 1981, during Dr. Boehning's term on the Child Care Committee, the 37.5-acre property where the Baptist Children's Home located in Oklahoma City sold for $12 million. The property was at 63rd in Pennsylvania in Oklahoma City and was at a very desirable location for commercial and residential development. In 1905, Oklahoma City gave the original property and $2,000 in cash to the Baptist General Convention of Oklahoma as an inducement to the convention to locate the convention's orphanage in Oklahoma City as opposed to Holdenville or El Reno.

The property was appraised for $7.5 million a year before it was sold to the Irish Realty Corporation, a real estate development firm headed by John Kilpatrick, John Kennedy, and Michael Samis. The $12-million purchase price of the Baptist Children's Home property was the highest per-square-foot price paid in Oklahoma City at the time.[19]

In the 1981 Annual Meeting of the Baptist General Convention of Oklahoma held at Eastwood Baptist Church in Tulsa, Dr. Boehning again attended as a messenger from Highland Park Baptist Church. He continued on the BGCO board of directors and was appointed to the Retirement Centers and Chaplaincy Committee.[20]

Reverend Boehning kept active in Oklahoma Baptist life in 1982. The January 14, 1982, issue of *The Baptist Messenger* had a picture of Reverend Boehning in front of a newly purchased travel bus that was part of a special project entitled "82 × 82." The purpose of the project was to promote the ministry projects of Highland Park Baptist Church. Among the projects was a monetary gift to Lampoanga Church in the Philippines as well as remodeling of the Highland Park Baptist Church educational facilities and purchasing new educational equipment.[21]

On March 15, 1982, a tornado hit Virginia Avenue Baptist Church and caused nearly $1 million in damage. In April 1982, Rev. Steve Boehning presented a check for $5,000 from the Washington-Osage Baptist Association Disaster Relief Committee to Rev. Ralph Dershem, pastor of Virginia Avenue Baptist Church, Bartlesville. The disaster relief money came from the state convention's disaster relief fund, financed by the Cooperative Program and the state missions offering. Nine families also received checks ranging from $250 to $500 to assist them in their losses. The Baptist General Convention of Oklahoma distributed a total of $8,300 in disaster relief funds in the Bartlesville area.[22]

One of the initiatives of the Baptist General Convention of Oklahoma in 1982 was the Oklahoma Baptist-Spanish Baptist partnership project. Highland Park Baptist Church under Rev. Steve Boehning's leadership was active in that partnership. On June 23, 1982, Rev. Dan White, a missionary to Spain, told the church members that because of a new constitution in Spain, the doors were now open for effective witnessing there. Dr. Steve Boehning was one of eighteen Oklahoma pastors who went to Spain in fall 1982 to conduct Continuing Witness Training Seminars as a part of the partnership evangelism between Baptist churches in Oklahoma and Baptist churches in Spain.

Reverend White said that when he and his family arrived in Spain twenty years prior, the image most people had of Baptist work there was of a "closed door." Reverend White said,

> After 1963, a greater tolerance of evangelical churches brought new opportunities for Baptists to share the gospel openly. In June of 1967, a new law gave legal recognition to non-Catholic religious groups if they registered with the government. After General Franco's death in 1975, Spain adopted a new constitution that provided religious freedom for all. Based on this new freedom, the Spanish Baptist Convention adopted the five-year Bold Mission Thrust Program.

This program's goals included tripling the number of Spanish Baptists from five thousand to fifteen thousand by 1985, establishing thirty-eight new mission churches by 1985, and starting fifteen new churches in cities with a population of over a hundred thousand. As a follow-up to the fall 1982 Continuing Witness Training Seminars, pastors, musicians, and lay leaders from Oklahoma churches went to Spain in April 1983 for Simultaneous Revivals.

Reverend White also praised the personal witnessing project conducted by a group of twenty-five college students from Oklahoma in Spain during the World Cup soccer games. Dr. Steve Boehning said members of Highland Park Baptist Church had already begun their partnership with churches in Spain as they prayed daily for the Baptist efforts in Spain.[23]

Dr. Steven Boehning, the Immanuel Years

On August 29, 1982, Dr. Steve Boehning became the fourteenth pastor of Immanuel Baptist Church. He was thirty-three years old when he assumed the Immanuel pulpit. At the August 8, 1982, business meeting, Mike Sperry brought a joint recommendation from the Search Committee, the Deacons, and the Finance Committee that Dr. Boehning be called as the new pastor.

Ed Case made a motion that the church accept this recommendation, and Dale Gierhart seconded the motion. The vote was 93 percent in favor and 7 percent opposed. Dr. Boehning's first business meeting was on September 8, 1982.

At that meeting, Kenneth Eyer brought forward a motion to purchase a piece of property at 106 South Center Street for future church expansion. Fred Williams seconded the motion. The motion carried. The church membership was reluctant to borrow funds commercially, so two financing methods were put forward. The first was for the church to issue one-thousand-dollar promissory notes at 6 percent simple annual interest. The second was to issue one-hundred-dollar shares in the purchase, carrying 6 percent simple annual interest.[24]

Within a month of assuming the pulpit at Immanuel Baptist Church, Dr. Boehning held a revival on September 19–26, 1982. Rev. Paul Jackson was the evangelist, and Mike Speck and Curtis Coleman were the singers. The revival resulted in sixty-nine professions of faith and forty-one additions by letter.[25]

Within two months of assuming the pulpit, Dr. Boehning was faced with some of the structural problems of the Immanuel Baptist Church facility. At the October 12, 1982, Deacons' meeting, Steve Weeks of the Building Maintenance Committee recommended that the front of the church towers receive a waterproofing treatment at an estimated cost of $10,930. Carl Webb made a motion that the recommendation be approved. Cap Gardner seconded the motion, which passed.[26]

The first Annual Meeting of the Baptist General Convention of Oklahoma that Reverend Boehning attended as a messenger from Immanuel Baptist Church was the 1982 meeting at First Southern Baptist Church, Del City, on November 15–18. Dr. Boehning continued in his role as a member of the board of directors and was assigned to the Retirement Centers and Chaplaincy Committee.[27] In conjunction with the 1982 BGCO Annual Meeting, Dr. Steve Boehning was elected to be the new president of the pastors' conference that was held at Meadowood Baptist Church, Midwest City.

The transition from the 1982 budget year to the 1983 budget year proved to be a little difficult. At the year end of 1982, the church had overspent its 1982 budget of $655,912.85 by $33,240.25. To compensate for the overspending and to bring expenses back in line with receipts, the 1983 budget called for a curtailing of spending.

The two biggest items that were cut were donations to the Cooperative Program of the Baptist General Convention of Oklahoma and to the Pottawatomie-Lincoln Baptist Association. The Cooperative Program donation budget was cut from $77,490.78 to $44,387.07. The Pottawatomie-Lincoln Baptist Association donation was cut from $15,898.12 to $8,877.41.[28]

At the February 9, 1982, business meeting, membership at Immanuel Baptist Church was listed as 2,255. The church had three outstanding loans at the time—$124,500 for the Family Life Center, $3,840.00 for the property at 102 South Center Street, and $6,760.00 for the property at 106 South Center Street. Payments on these three loans required $9,706.51 per month.

Figure 12.2. LIFEGIVER advertisement, April 12, 1984, Baptist Messenger

In addition, at the February 9, 1982, business meeting, the church voted to borrow ninety-five thousand dollars for roof repair, additional waterproofing, organ and sound system renovation, and other expenses. On April 10, 1983, Rev. Paul Stutz, who had served as a youth pastor and director of the Family Life Center since the Dr. Larry Adams's days, resigned to become the minister of family activities at First Baptist Church, Grand Prairie, Texas.[29]

In March 1983, Rev. Steve Boehning sponsored a ski trip to Glorieta, New Mexico. The ski trip was evidently very remarkable as witnessed by an article entitled, "Ask Steven Boehning about His Ski Trip to Glorieta" that appeared in the April 14, 1983, issue of *The Baptist Messenger*. The article stated the following:

> The 1984 youth activities calendar at Shawnee, Immanuel, will include dates for a ski trip to New Mexico. There will probably be an extra space available next year because it's doubtful that Steven Boehning, Immanuel's pastor, will make the trip. He's probably had all of skiing, snow, ski lifts, and mountains that he wants. Here's the saga of the pastor and the ski trip. He took a tumble on the slopes March 15, but "no big deal," he thinks. The next day he fell again. Only this time, he was taken to a hospital in Albuquerque where X-rays confirmed a broken leg ... and a broken shoulder suffered unknowingly in the first fall. After flying to Oklahoma City [on] March 17 for a stay in the hospital, Boehning made it back home on the 22nd of March. So here's the preacher with his upper body wrapped for the shoulder injury and a cast on his leg. How's he going to preach in that shape? To the rescue comes Chuck and Rick Thompson of Thompson Construction Company. A ramp was built leading to the platform so the motorized wheelchair Boehning uses could maneuver to the pulpit. But how is the congregation going to see the preacher behind the pulpit? The Thompsons rigged up a motorized chair which elevates Boehning to the "proper pulpit

height" and is equipped with an extension on which to rest his leg in its cast. He returned to the pulpit March 27. Boehning faces several weeks in the cast, but he has company. Jan Brown, a high school senior, is also a ski-trip casualty. She twisted her knee, underwent surgery, and will be on crutches for a couple of months. —Bob E. Mathews (with information from church secretaries who asked to remain anonymous)[30]

Figure 12.3. Immanuel advertisement in August 23, 1984, Baptist Messenger

The process of purchasing property adjacent to Immanuel Baptist Church continued when the property at 120 South Center Street became available. On Sunday, September 25, 1983, a recommendation to purchase the property was presented to the attendees at both the 8:15 a.m. service and the 10:50 a.m. service. The price of the property was twenty-eight thousand dollars. The recommendation was approved with only two dissenting votes at the 8:15 a.m. service and one dissenting vote at the 10:50 a.m. service.[31]

At the 1983 Annual Meeting of the Baptist General Convention of Oklahoma, Dr. Boehning had a very active role. He and his wife Susan both attended as messengers from Immanuel Baptist Church. He was again elected to the board of directors and was placed on the

Executive Committee and the Planning and Promotion Committee, where he was chairman. Dr. Boehning was also the chairman of the Resolutions Committee. He was also selected as one of the morning assembly directors for the Falls Creek Youth Assembly.[32]

As president of the Oklahoma Baptist Pastors' Conference, Dr. Steve Boehning was very active in the program and conduct of the 1983 Pastors' Conference. A special session on ministerial burnout and spirit-anointed preaching were the highlights of the conference. The Monday afternoon session featured a discussion on ministerial burnout by Brooks Faulkner, career guidance supervisor in the church training department of the Baptist Sunday School Board in Nashville. The Monday evening session was combined with the Woman's Missionary Union session. Rev. Tony Ward and the forty-voice TNT Senior Adult Choir of Immanuel Baptist Church were the featured music for the pastors' conference.[33]

On Sunday, January 1, 1984, Immanuel Baptist Church started the year in a very momentous way. Youth minister Scott Neighbors was ordained to the gospel ministry. Steve Bowlan served as secretary for the ordination, and Fred Williams brought the motion that Brother Scott be ordained. The second to the motion was by J. W. Kinnett.

Rev. Tony Ward brought special music through "I Am a Servant" and "Upon This Rock." Membership was reported at 2,532 by the end of the year 1983. At the March 5, 1984, business

Figure 12.4. Steve Boehning, the Immanuel days

meeting, Rev. Scott Neighbors was moved to the position of minister of education and administration, and Kevin Price was hired as youth minister at an annual salary of $16,500.00. Cooperative Program giving was again reduced from $44,387.07 to $42,246.40. Pottawatomie-Lincoln Baptist Association giving was also reduced from $8,877.41 to $8,449.28.[34]

At Easter 1984, Immanuel Baptist Church continued its presentation of the musical and drama event known as *LIFEGIVER*. The presentation involved a cast of approximately 200 church members. Also in summer 1984, Dr. Steve Boehning continued his involvement in the Falls Creek youth assemblies. He was selected to be a morning assembly teacher for the third week of the assemblies.[35] In September 1984, the property at 116 South Center Street that was owned by church member and deacon J. W. Kinnett became available for purchase for $36,000. Brother Kinnett pledged a tithe of $3,600 if the church purchased the property. The trustees and Deacons recommended the property be purchased.[36]

Dr. Steve Boehning continued to be active in the Baptist General Convention of Oklahoma Annual Meetings. At the 1984 Annual Meeting held in Bethany, he and his wife Susan headed a team of ten messengers from Immanuel Baptist Church. The delegation also included Jeff Anderson, Nat Bettis, A. V. and Lucille Daugherty, Dale and Carla Gierhart, Scott Neighbors, and Rev. Tony Ward.

Dr. Boehning was again appointed to the board of directors and served on the Business Management Committee where he was the chairman. At the Tuesday evening service, Dr. Boehning read the opening scripture. A state Planned Growth in Giving task force was named to help guide the Cooperative Program efforts in the state and to assist in conducting twelve two-day training events for pastors and church leaders in February, March, and April 1985.

Dr. Boehning was included in the task force along with other dignitaries with Shawnee connections such as Dr. Joe Ingram, former Immanuel pastor and currently the executive secretary-treasurer of the BGCO; Dr. Bob Agee, Oklahoma Baptist University president; and Dr. Mack Roark, an Oklahoma Baptist University religion professor. Also at the annual meeting, Dr. Steve Boehning was nominated to be the president of the Baptist General Convention of Oklahoma for the 1985 convention year. Also nominated were Rev. Wendell Estep of Council Road Baptist Church, Bethany, and Rev. Paul Box of First Baptist Church, Moore. Two rounds of voting were required to select the president. In the first round, Reverend Box was eliminated. In the runoff between Dr. Boehning and Rev. Estep, Rev. Estep won.[37]

In January 1985, church membership was listed at 2,652. The pastor's salary and benefits were listed in the budget at $47,500. Other salaries and benefits were listed as $31,000 for the music minister's, $29,000 for the education minister, and $13,750 for the youth minister.

Cooperative Program giving was again reduced from $42,246.40 to $41,463.00. Pottawatomie-Lincoln Baptist Association giving was also reduced from $8,449.28 to $7,211.00.[38] In May 1985, Rev. Tracy Morgan was called as minister of evangelism and singles at Immanuel Church, Shawnee. Reverend Morgan had just graduated from Southwestern Baptist Theological Seminary.[39]

In the fall of 1985, Dr. Steve Boehning attended the Annual Meeting of the Baptist General Convention of Oklahoma, which was held again in Bethany. He and his wife Susan led the Immanuel Baptist Church delegations of seven messengers, including Nat Bettis, George and Cleo McDow, Henry Wall, and Rev. Tony Ward. Dr. Boehning was again appointed to the board of directors. Within the Board, he served on the Special Care Ministries Committee. However, his level of activity within the convention itself decreased significantly. He did participate in the Planned Growth in Giving Training Seminars on March 4–5 at the Quartz State Lodge and on March 7–8 at Texhoma State Lodge.[40]

The year 1986 started strongly for Immanuel Baptist Church. The January 31, 1986, church roster listed 2,891 members. On March 16, 1986, Rev. Steve Boehning resigned as pastor of Immanuel Baptist Church to accept the pulpit at Northway Baptist Church, Dallas, Texas. He was thirty-seven years old when he resigned from the Immanuel pulpit. On May 25, 1986, the church membership voted to call Dr. Mack Roark of the Oklahoma Baptist University School of Religion as interim pastor.

Dr. Boehning's resignation seemed to have had a small, cascading impact upon the staff of Immanuel Baptist Church. On June 8, 1986, Dr. Bob Dawson resigned his position as acting administrator but retained his position as minister of education. On June 17, 1986, Rev. Tracy Morgan resigned his position as minister of evangelism and singles to become minister of education and evangelism at Northway Baptist Church in Dallas, Texas, reporting to Rev. Steve Boehning. On June 27, 1986, Greg Jones resigned his position as minister of activities to become minister of youth and recreation at Highland Hills in Oklahoma City.

At the October 25, 1986, business meeting, by a vote of 356 for and 7 against, the church voted to call Dr. Mike Taylor as pastor of Immanuel Baptist Church. His hiring agreement called for an annual salary and benefits of $45,000 plus two weeks for vacation, two weeks for revivals, and two weeks for conventions and assemblies. Dr. Taylor was also offered one day per week off as compensation for his Sunday services. Dr. Taylor's first duty day was November 7, 1986.[41]

Dr. Steven Boehning, the Years after Immanuel

After leaving Immanuel Baptist Church in March 1986, Dr. Boehning became pastor of Northway Baptist Church, Dallas, Texas. He also served as minister of single adults at Second Baptist Church, Houston, and associate pastor of the First Baptist Church, Pearland, Texas. In 1992, he became founder and chief executive officer of Boehning Home Health Care. In 1999, he served as a senior executive consultant to Resource Services, Inc.

Dr. Steven M. Boehning died on Thursday, December 2, 2004, in Shreveport, Louisiana. He was fifty-five at the time of his death. Dr. Boehning was preceded in death by his daughter, Autumn Lynn Boehning. His survivors include his wife, Susan; two daughters, Jennifer and Paige; two sons, Larry and Steven; his parents, Marshall and Flossie Boehning; and five grandchildren.[42]

CHAPTER 13

A Biblical Scholar
with a Heart for Evangelism

Dr. Mike Taylor, November 1986–January 1992

Introduction

Dr. Mike Taylor was the fifteenth pastor of Immanuel Baptist Church. He served from November 1986 to January 1992. Dr. Taylor was born and raised in the Oklahoma City area. Dr. Taylor was known for his strong biblical preaching. During his ministry, the North Campus satellite was begun.[1]

The world scene during the years that Dr. Mike Taylor served Immanuel was one of prosperity and growth. Unfortunately, Islamic terrorists continued to commit atrocities, causing horror and sadness for millions. The United States was respected on the world scene, the Soviet Empire was crumbling, and dictators were being replaced with democracies.

In January 1987, Muslim terrorists in Lebanon executed William Buckley, an American hostage held and tortured for over fifteen months. In May, Iraqi missiles killed thirty-seven sailors in an attack on the United States frigate *Stark* in the Persian Gulf.[2] In December 1988, a bomb planted by Libyan terrorists exploded aboard a Pan American 747 passenger airliner over Lockerbie, Scotland, killing all

259 aboard and 11 on the ground.[3] In April 1989, tens of thousands of Chinese students took over Beijing's Tiananmen Square in a rally for democracy. In May, the Communist regime named Mikhail Gorbachev as president of the Soviet Union. Shortly thereafter, the Soviet Empire began to fall apart.[4]

In August 1990, Iraqi troops invaded Kuwait, setting off the Persian Gulf War.[5] In April 1991, after swift action by Pres. George H. W. Bush, a United States-led coalition of thirty-four nations under Gen. Norman Schwarzkopf soundly defeated the Iraqi forces occupying Kuwait. In July, Boris Yeltsin became the first freely elected president of the Russian Republic. In August, Lithuania, Estonia, and Latvia declared independence from the Soviet Union. In December, Soviet president Gorbachev resigned, thus completing the dissolution of the Soviet Union.[6] The year 1992 closed out with the North American Free Trade Agreement (NAFTA) being signed in December.[7]

As with the world scene, the years that Dr. Mike Taylor served Immanuel saw a period of growth and prosperity in the United States. In July 1987, the Democrats nominated Michael Dukakis for president, and the Republican convention nominated George H. W. Bush for president. The Republicans swept forty states in the election, and Bush soundly defeated Dukakis.[8]

The year 1989 saw two disasters, one man-made and one natural. In March, the oil tanker *Exxon Valdez* struck a reef in Prince William Sound, Alaska, and ruptured, spilling 11 million gallons of crude oil. In October, a San Francisco Bay area earthquake measuring 7.1 on the Richter scale in magnitude killed 67 people and injured over 3,000 people.[9]

In July 1991, Pres. George W. H. Bush nominated Judge Clarence Thomas to the United States Supreme Court. By a vote of 52–48, the Senate confirmed Thomas.[10] In 1992, Bill Clinton was nominated as the presidential candidate in the July Democratic convention. The Republicans renominated George H. W. Bush in their August convention. In November, Bill Clinton was elected President, and the Democrats kept control of Congress.[11]

Dr. Mike Taylor, the Years before Immanuel

Mike Taylor was born in Oklahoma City and raised in Del City. His parents were Christian parents and were members of First Southern Baptist Church, Del City. First Southern Baptist Church, Del City, was a mission church founded by First Baptist Church, Oklahoma City. During his childhood and adolescent years, Dr. Taylor saw First Southern Baptist Church, Del City, grow from a small mission church into one of the strongest churches in Oklahoma, with some of the strongest pastors in Oklahoma.

He first became aware of his need for Jesus Christ as his Lord and Savior when he was eight years old. Although as an eight-year-old child, he had knowledge of sin, of the sacrifice of Jesus for him, and of his need to accept Christ, Mike Taylor did not make a public profession of faith until 1961 when he was twelve years old. First Southern Baptist Church, Del City, held a revival meeting in the spring of that year.

On the final Sunday morning, Mike Taylor's heart was strongly stirred, and he came forward during the closing invitation, along with several other people. Mike Taylor's pubic profession of faith was accepted that morning, and he was baptized that night. His parents were very supportive of his decision to accept Jesus Christ as Lord and Savior.

During his teenage years, Mike Taylor continued to grow spiritually at First Southern Baptist Church, Del City. Both Mike Taylor and his brother David Taylor were active in the church. Especially influential on Mike Taylor's spiritual development was the preaching and pastoral leadership of Rev. John Bisagno who came to First Southern Baptist Church, Del City, in 1965. Dr. Taylor said, "I grew greatly under the leadership of Rev. John Bisagno."

Mike Taylor's postsecondary education began at the University of Oklahoma in 1966 where he enrolled in the prelaw program and the Air Force Reserve Officer Training Corps (ROTC). He excelled in his studies and ROTC activities. God used an event in spring 1967 to turn Mike Taylor's heart in a different direction.

The University of Oklahoma had a new, young, and wildly popular head football coach named Jim Mackenzie. Coach Mackenzie had completely turned around what had been a losing program in a single season, but he died of a heart attack in April 1967. Eulogies heralded Jim Mackenzie's contributions to the University of Oklahoma, the state of Oklahoma, and the world of sports; but the Holy Spirit began to lead Mike Taylor to see that the only contributions that are truly lasting are those made in obedient service to the Lord Jesus Christ.

After completing two years of study at the University of Oklahoma, Mike Taylor took the Air Force Officer Qualification Test in May 1968 and scored exceptionally well. He was awarded the air force scholarship with all college expenses paid along with a monthly stipend to begin that fall and continue through graduation and commission in the United States Air Force. However, in June 1968, Mike Taylor attended a starlight crusade at First Southern Baptist Church, Del City, led by Rev. John Bisagno.

During that crusade, Mike Taylor received and publicly announced his call to the preaching ministry. Upon hearing the news, his father encouraged him to withdraw from the University of Oklahoma and enroll at Oklahoma Baptist University. However, Mike Taylor had a commitment to the air force, which he felt he needed to honor. Consequently, his father visited Colonel Bates, the commander of the ROTC unit at the University of Oklahoma, and petitioned for his son's release from his commitment. Because Mike Taylor had not yet begun receiving funds from the air force, Colonel Bates did indeed release him from his commitment.

In fall 1968, Mike Taylor began classes at Oklahoma Baptist University in the School of Religion. He was especially influenced in his studies by Dr. Rowena Strickland, associate professor of New Testament and Greek. "Her gracious teaching deepened my love for the Bible," Mike Taylor said about Professor Strickland.

After graduating from Oklahoma Baptist University in 1970, Mike Taylor went on to Southwestern Baptist Theological Seminary in Fort Worth, Texas. He graduated with a Master of Divinity degree in 1973. While at Southwestern Baptist Theological Seminary, Rev. Mike Taylor served at Ridglea West Baptist Church in Fort Worth, Texas, where he was called as minister of evangelism and youth. He led the youth, outreach, and bus Ministries there. Reverend Taylor had always believed his ministry was to be that of an evangelist. When he left Southwestern Baptist Theological Seminary, he purchased an Airstream trailer and led revivals for two years in Oklahoma, Texas, Arkansas, Arizona, California, and Idaho.

Figure 13.1. Mike Taylor, the OBU days

One of his Oklahoma revivals was at Akins Baptist Church, just outside of Sallisaw. The church was without a pastor and asked him to be their interim pastor during summer 1975 on weeks when he was not preaching a revival meeting elsewhere. While at Akins Baptist Church, Reverend Taylor met Dr. Eldridge Miller of First Baptist Church, Sallisaw.[12] Dr. Miller was a key moral and spiritual leader of Oklahoma Baptists and Southern Baptist at the time.

He served on the Southern Baptist Convention Executive Committee and was a prolific writer. Dr. Miller's articles were frequently published by *The Oklahoma Baptist Messenger* and other state Baptist convention papers.[13] He also preached the annual sermon at the Baptist General Convention of Oklahoma Annual Meeting on November 15, 1995.[14] A strong friendship grew between Dr. Miller and Reverend Taylor. When the opportunity arose, Dr. Miller asked Mike Taylor to serve as his evangelism minister. As a condition of employment, Reverend Taylor was given the privilege of being able to continue to do revivals around the country.[15]

While serving at First Baptist, Sallisaw, Mike Taylor began a doctor of ministry degree from Luther Rice Theological Seminary of Jacksonville, Florida. Dr. Eldridge Miller began his doctor of ministry degree at the same time, and the two men encouraged one another in their studies and degree requirements. The degree work consisted of four components:

1. Bible-based communications,
2. Time management,
3. Church organization and administration, and
4. Creative writing.

All aspects of the program stressed the practical aspects of the ministry.

Figure 13.2. First Baptist Church, Sallisaw

During the time Reverend Taylor served the First Baptist Church, Sallisaw, he came to understand his ministry was to be conducted, not as an itinerant evangelist but as a pastor serving a local church. In 1980, Reverend Taylor left First Baptist Church, Sallisaw, to become the senior pastor of First Baptist Church, Stigler. His years at First Baptist Church, Stigler, were years of growth and development for both Reverend Taylor and the church.

While he was at the Stigler church, Reverend Taylor finished his degree work with Luther Rice Theological Seminary. The church steadily grew in Sunday School enrollment and attendance, and additional educational space became greatly needed. A planning committee proposed the construction of a new Christian life education center that would house preschool, children, and youth educational space; senior adult activities space; a racquetball court' and a basketball court, which would also be used as a larger fellowship hall.

Dr. Taylor challenged the church to build the new building without borrowing money but paying for it with quarterly sacrificial offerings for building construction. A plan was adopted to build the building in three phases. Each phase would be started only when the funds were on hand

Figure 13.3. First Baptist Church, Stigler

to complete it. The building was constructed with no delays between phases, for God provided all the funds needed to build the building without construction pauses through the faithful, sacrificial giving of His people. When the building was completed, the church moved into the facility totally debt free.[16]

In spring 1986, Dr. Taylor was asked to preach a revival at First Baptist Church, Bowlegs. A few weeks afterward, he was contacted by the chairman of the Pulpit Committee of Immanuel Baptist Church who asked Dr. Taylor to send his résumé to the committee. Jeff Anderson, a CPA in Shawnee and faithful member of Immanuel, was also a member of the pulpit committee.

Jeff's mother, a member of First Baptist Church, Bowlegs, had heard Dr. Taylor preach in the spring revival meeting and suggested to her son that the Pulpit Committee should consider him. Dr. Taylor had never prepared or sent a résumé to a church before but felt he should fulfill the request to determine if God might be in it. The résumé was prepared and mailed to Immanuel's Pulpit Committee.

As summer 1986 was coming to an end, Dr. Taylor drove to Tulsa one Saturday afternoon to visit a Stigler church member who was in the hospital there in critical condition. The visit lasted late into the evening hours, and as Mike was driving home to Stigler the thought came unexpectedly into his heart that the Immanuel Pulpit Committee would be in the worship service the next morning. Dr. Taylor believed the Holy Spirit had spoken that word to him.

When he arrived home in Stigler, he was told that the Immanuel Pulpit Committee had called earlier that evening to notify him they would be in the morning worship service on Sunday. The committee was in the morning worship service the next morning and asked the Taylor family to have lunch with them following the service. Dr. Taylor and his family sensed God's hand in the events that led up to the invitation to come to Immanuel Baptist Church in view of a call as pastor.[17]

Dr. Mike Taylor, the Immanuel Years

Dr. Mike Taylor was called to Immanuel Baptist Church as pastor in October 1986. His pastorate began November 9, 1986. Dr. Taylor was known for his strong biblical preaching. During his ministry, the north campus satellite church was begun. This satellite church was seen as an extension of Immanuel Baptist Church—one church body, two different locations.[18]

Dr. Taylor's years at Immanuel saw much growth for the church and much personal growth for him. During his interview for this history, Dr. Taylor said, "Serving Immanuel Baptist Church was the most joyful and fulfilling ministry experience that I ever had. The members of Immanuel were always loving and supportive." Dr. Taylor takes no credit for any good thing that happened

Figure 13.4. Mike Taylor, the Immanuel days

at Immanuel during his pastorate. He said, "I am nothing; I did nothing. Jesus is everything; He did it all." Dr. Taylor considers the reduction and elimination of the church debt to be one of the more important accomplishments at Immanuel during his pastorate.

In 1987, more than $123,000 of the church budget—18.7 percent of the entire budget—was required to service the debt the church incurred to construct the Family Life Center. Dr. Taylor encouraged the church to schedule three "Sacrificial Sundays" in May, August, and November on which to receive special offerings to reduce the debt on the Family Life Center. The three special offerings were received, and the note on the Family Life Center was paid off in January of 1988. A fourth offering for debt reduction was received in February, and on March 7, 1988, the church's only remaining debt—a consolidation loan—was paid off.

Note burnings were conducted in both morning worship services on March 20, and 981 people attended Sunday School. God's people rejoiced and gave Him the glory. Immanuel was debt free, and the freed-up funds for debt service were used to increase mission giving, to provide increased funding for church's ministries, and to begin an expansion fund for providing additional parking. The first purchase of additional property for parking was authorized in April 1988, additional properties were purchased later that year, and new parking areas were paved in summer 1989. Mission giving increased so that Immanuel, which was ranked 86th in Cooperative Program giving among Oklahoma Southern Baptist churches in 1986, rose to be ranked 36th in Cooperative Program giving in 1989.

Dr. Taylor also fondly remembered the Easter Pageant Ministry and Living Christmas Tree Ministry that were strong at Immanuel during his years with us. He spoke especially highly of Rev. Tony Ward who led these efforts and the college ministry. Dr. Taylor said of Tony Ward,

> Tony Ward had an outstanding personality and provided strong and joyful leadership to our Music and College Ministries. He held up his pastor's hands and helped me extend my ministry. He was especially helpful with my transition from First Baptist Church, Stigler, to Immanuel Baptist Church.[19]

Evangelism was always a central part of Dr. Taylor's life, and evangelism was a strong part of Dr. Taylor's ministry at Immanuel. During the 1986–87 church year, Immanuel baptized 96 people and was recognized by the state convention as an "evangelism pacesetter" for leading the churches of the Pottawatomie-Lincoln Baptist Association and ranking 12th in total baptisms among all Southern Baptist churches in the state of Oklahoma. Over the years of his pastorate, Immanuel Baptist Church hosted revival meetings with evangelists Kelly Green, Paul Burleson, Tim Williams, Freddie Gage, and Rick Scarborough which resulted in more than 260 professions of faith.

A life action crusade led by Life Action Ministries under the leadership of Evang. Del Fehsenfeld, Jr., was a major event in January and February of 1989. Evangelist Fehsenfeld and his team of specialized ministry teams arrived in several buses and other vehicles. The teams led unified worship services for the entire church and group seminars for parents, youth, women, and men. The crusade was scheduled to last for two weeks but was extended a third week. God visited Immanuel with the blessings of revival among His people, drew fresh commitments from the lives of many members, and sent a fresh breath of heaven blowing through the congregation.

One of the key ministries for Immanuel Baptist Church during the Mike Taylor years was the creation of the Immanuel Baptist Church North Campus satellite church. An existing independent Baptist church known as the Bryan Road Baptist Church had been established before Dr. Taylor's arrival at Immanuel. The church was under the leadership of Rev. Lonnie Gee and had been struggling for a few years, to the point of being in fear of foreclosure by the bank holding its mortgage.

Immanuel Baptist Church members Dean Hudlow and Chuck Thompson were aware of the church's frail financial situation and approached Dr. Taylor about assuming the mortgage and acquiring the facility. The basic concept was saving a failing sister Baptist church and having an extension of Immanuel Baptist Church on the north side of Shawnee. The concept was "One Church Body, Two Different Locations."

With the aid of Reverend Gee, the acquisition of the property went smoothly. Dr. Taylor would preach at 8:00 at the Main Street facility. He would then go to the Bryan Road satellite facility and preach at 9:30, while the Main Street facility had Sunday School. He would then return to the Main Street facility to preach at 10:50, while the Bryan Road satellite facility had Sunday School. According to Dr. Taylor, the staff at both facilities were extra diligent and the whole schedule worked amazingly well.[20]

Other ministries that were significant while Dr. Taylor was at Immanuel included the college ministry under Rev. Tony Ward, the use of the old Immanuel Baptist Church parsonage as a visiting missionary home, an expansion of the Vacation Bible School program, and the Falls Creek Youth Ministry. The prayer ministry was also very vital and active during Dr. Taylor's years.

While Dr. Taylor served at Immanuel, several improvements were made to the facilities. Some significant maintenance that had been deferred was initiated and completed. Waterproofing was done to the exterior walls, and Plexiglas was placed over the stained-glass windows. These projects involved significant expenditures.

Several key staff members were involved in all of these ministries and activities. They included Rev. Tony Ward doing music and college ministry; Dr. Bob Dawson who was the interim education minister until Rev. Sam Hendry from First Baptist Church, Ardmore, became the Education Minister; Mary Margaret Kasterke who headed the children's ministry; and Kevin Price and Butch Booth who headed the youth ministry. According to Dr. Taylor, Kevin Price was an outstanding youth leader and gifted singer. He eventually went to First Baptist Church, Henderson, Texas, to serve the Lord Jesus there. Butch Booth was the youth minister at First Baptist Church, Stigler, and had worked with Dr. Taylor there, so he was a natural fit as youth minister for Immanuel.

Butch Booth had done youth camps for the Kiamichi Baptist Association and helped initiate the ministry of summit camps there, so he brought a wealth of knowledge for the Immanuel Baptist Church Youth Program at Falls Creek. One of the best additions to the Immanuel Baptist Church staff while Dr. Taylor was at Immanuel may have been Jeff Anderson who joined the staff as business administrator/recreation minister. Brother Anderson was a certified public accountant who served on the Pulpit Committee that aided in the call of Dr. Taylor to Immanuel Baptist Church. Dr. Taylor and Jeff Anderson established a strong relationship then, and Dr. Taylor rejoiced when Jeff Anderson sensed the call of the Lord into vocational ministry. Brother Anderson became Immanuel's recreation minister and business administrator and enjoyed a long, fruitful ministry at Immanuel Baptist Church until Calvary Baptist Church, Hannibal, Missouri, called Reverend Anderson to be their senior pastor. Reverend Anderson serves Calvary to this day.[21]

Several lay members of Immanuel were blessings in the regular functioning and growth of the church. These included, to name only a few, A. V. Daugherty, who taught the auditorium Bible class and served as deacon chairman; G. C. Blakemore, who was a source of strength and wisdom and a prayer warrior and also deacon chairman; Fred Williams, who headed up the Discipleship Training Program; Juanita Allison, who led Immanuel's powerful prayer ministry; and Rick Thompson (who faithfully served as Treasurer of the church). Dr. Taylor also noted Kenneth and Nell Eyer, Cap and Wanda Gardner, Wilbur and Fran Patterson, Thelma Thompson, Lloyd Wilkins, David Jett, Jim and Debbie Wilsie, Stan and Diane Blakemore, Gary and Linda Hathcock, Steve and Kathy Bowlan, J. D. and Pat McQuerry, Ed and Donna Guthrie, John and Cheryl Wright, Carl Webb, Bob Strong, Woodrow Whitely, Randy and Pat Williams, and Harold and Rowena Britt as members of distinction. He added that he knew he was failing to recall many others, for so many of Immanuel's people were committed and faithful to the Lord and His church.[22]

Dr. Mike Taylor, the Years after Immanuel

After leaving Immanuel Baptist Church, Dr. Taylor moved back to the Del City area and renewed his membership at First Southern Baptist Church, Del City. He was very active in the church, teaching a Sunday School class and conducting a Bible study. An Immanuel member named Frank Whitney invited Mike to begin working with him as a health insurance agent and helped Mike study for and pass the exam to receive an insurance license.

Mike and Frank worked together for Scotsman Insurance Group of Dallas for several months until Scotsman proved itself to be an unethical employer. At that time, another Immanuel member—Jimmy Trotter, who was also a health insurance agent—invited Mike to work with him for Combined Insurance Company. Mike and Jimmy worked together for several months until Combined made changes in its Oklahoma operations.

At that time a third Immanuel member—David Thompson, who owned his own independent health insurance agency in Shawnee—invited Mike to work with him. God blessed their work together for several years until David decided to move to Marble

Falls, Texas, and begin a related business there. At that time, Mike and his daughter, Teresa Gardner, purchased the health insurance business from David and have continued to work together for the past twenty years.

Also after leaving Immanuel Baptist Church, Mike Taylor married his wife, Paula. Paula had been a member of Immanuel while Dr. Taylor was pastor. Paula and her son Chad were baptized together by Dr. Taylor following a revival meeting in which they both professed faith in Christ. She then became a very active member, being strongly involved in the singles' ministry and the ladies' Bible study. After leaving Immanuel and with the encouragement of some who knew them both, Mike and Paula renewed their acquaintance and began a relationship that led to love and marriage in 1994.[23]

Dr. Taylor reentered the pulpit through his friendship with Rev. Larry Sparks, a Shawnee and central Oklahoma pastor who has touched many lives over the years. Reverend Sparks had left the Shawnee area and pastored First Southern Baptist Church, Pearl Harbor, Hawaii. In November 1999, Reverend Sparks returned to the Shawnee area and started an independent church named New Beginnings Church in January 2000. He called Dr. Taylor to determine his interest in serving at New Beginnings Church. Dr. Taylor agreed to support the church by conducting a Wednesday-evening Bible study, beginning in early 2000.

A Wednesday-evening Bible study fit into Dr. Taylor's schedule very well, since he was still a member of First Southern Baptist Church, Del City, and was very active with his insurance business. His relationship with Reverend Sparks and New Beginnings Church grew, and he joined the church in January 2002. In 2014, Dr. Taylor became the senior pastor at New Beginnings Church and continues in this capacity.

Mike Taylor and his wife, Paula, have five children. Teresa lives in Shawnee and works with her father in the health insurance industry. Teresa is married to David Gardner and has a son and a daughter. Stephanie lives in Edmond, is married to Steve Vernon, and has four sons. Both Stephanie and Steve work in the oil and gas leasing industry. Jason lives in Edmond with his wife, Amanda, and has three daughters and one son. He works in construction management. Brad and his wife, Shannon, live near Macomb and have one daughter. Brad is an electrician at Oklahoma Baptist University. Chad and his wife, Janna, live in Moore and have one son and one daughter. Chad is a firefighter for the city of Norman. Mike and Paula have thirteen grandchildren and two great grandchildren.[24]

CHAPTER 14

The First Relocation Attempt

Dr. Joe Dan Fowler, June 1993 to October 1995

Introduction

In June 1993, Immanuel Baptist Church called Dr. Joe Dan Fowler as pastor. Dr. Fowler led the church to adopt a mission statement and begin work on a new constitution and bylaws. Immanuel joined into a missions partnership with the Rosario Baptist Association of Rosario, Argentina. The church's first trip to Argentina was in January 1997. Dr. Joe Dan Fowler was the sixteenth pastor of Immanuel Baptist Church. He served from June 1993 to October 1995.[1]

The world scene during the years that Dr. Fowler served Immanuel was a scene of relative calm, but turmoil and strife lurked on the horizon. The year 1993 saw hopes of peace with a few scatterings of concern. The Soviet Empire had fallen apart, and the Middle East was enjoying a period of relative calm following the defeat of Iraq by a coalition of nations led by the United States after Iraq's invasion of Kuwait. In August, an Israeli-Palestinian peace accord was reached. In October, Communist China broke the international nuclear test moratorium with an underground nuclear test.[2]

The year 1994 began on two negative notes as Serbian forces pounded the city of Sarajevo with heavy weapons in January; and thousands of people, mostly Tutsis, were killed in Rwanda in an intertribal massacre that began in April. The death toll of the intertribal warfare in Rwanda reached between five hundred thousand and one million people by the one-year anniversary of the Tutsi-Hutu warfare. On the other hand, the Catholic Irish Republican Army declared a ceasefire in Northern Ireland in August, and the Ulster Protestants declared a ceasefire in October. Israel signed a peace accord with the Palestinians in May and a peace treaty with Jordan in October.[3] In March 1995, cosmonauts on the Russian Space Station *Mir* greeted their first American visitors who arrived on a Russian rocket. Later in June, a United States space shuttle docked with *Mir*.[4]

As with the world scene, the national scene was mostly filled with a mixture of troubling events and encouraging events during the time that Dr. Fowler served Immanuel. In January 1993, Pres. Bill Clinton agreed to lift the military's ban on homosexuals with his "Don't ask, don't tell" policy. In February, Muslim terrorists exploded a truck bomb in the World Trade Center, killing five and injuring thousands. In March, federal agents began a siege of the Branch Davidian religious compound outside Waco, Texas. When the siege ended in April, eighty-seven people, including twenty children, were killed.[5]

In May, President Bill Clinton was accused of sexual harassment while governor of Arkansas. He later settled the case out of court for $850,000. In June, former football star and actor O. J. Simpson was arrested for the murders of his wife Nicole Brown Simpson and Ron Goldman, a family friend. In June, the United States Supreme Court placed limits on abortion protests.[6] In April 1995, 168 people were killed when domestic terrorist Timothy McVeigh exploded a truck bomb outside the Murrah Building in Oklahoma City. In October, a Los Angeles jury found O. J. Simpson not guilty of murder.[7]

Dr. Joe Dan Fowler, the Years before Immanuel

Joe Dan Fowler was born in 1948 in Athens, Texas, and grew up in Murchison, Texas, a small town of approximately 250 people in Henderson County about 80 miles southeast of Dallas. His wife, Patsy, was also born in Athens and grew up in Brownsboro, another small town about 15 miles east of Athens. Joe Dan Fowler's father worked for the Lone Star Gas Company and was an appliance repairman. Eventually, his father decided to go into public service and was elected to the post of County Clerk for Henderson County. His father had a solid reputation for being honest and reliable and was reelected several times, always running without opposition.

His mother was a homemaker. Joe Dan Fowler had three sisters and was the eldest child in the family. He was raised in a Christian home, with his parents being active members of First Baptist Church, Murchison, Texas. His parents usually attended church three times a week, taking the four children with them. Joe Dan Fowler said, "Murchison was a wonderful place to grow up. I felt love and peace throughout my childhood. My childhood was filled with hunting, fishing, and baseball."[8]

When Joe Dan Fowler was about twelve years old, he trusted Jesus Christ as his Lord and Savior. He knew the Gospel message quite well because he and his family regularly attended church. He knew that he was spiritually lost and needed to be saved, but he couldn't quite grasp how that could happen for him. His mother, father, and even his pastor tried to explain it to him; but he just couldn't understand it. But what his mother, father, and pastor couldn't do, his maternal grandmother could! In his telephone interview, he said it happened like this:

> One day at school, I told my teacher I was sick and needed to go home. I really was sick. I was worried sick about being spiritually lost and on my way to an eternity without God. My mother was called. She picked me up and took me to my maternal grandmother's house. My maternal grandmother was the godliest woman I have ever known. As she talked with me, she pointed outside to Highway 31 that ran past her house. She told me to imagine that instead of a highway, it was a dusty old dirt road. She said to imagine further that I was walking along that dirt road and had come to a suspension bridge that stretched across a deep chasm. The bridge was old,

and its ropes and planks were rotten. It was obvious that if I stepped out on the bridge, it would collapse, and I would fall to my death. However, the bridge was the only way across to the other side. She then said, "What if you were about to turn around and go back, and Jesus suddenly appeared at the other end of the bridge, extended his hand, called you by name, and told you to come on across because He wouldn't let the bridge fall? Could you trust Him enough to step out on that bridge, believing that He wouldn't let it fall?" I remember thinking for a few moments before finally answering with a confident, "Yes!" She asked, "Well, in the same way, can you simply trust in Jesus to forgive you of your sin, come into your heart, and save you?" I again thought seriously before finally answering with another confident, "Yes!" For the first time in my life, I truly TRUSTED Jesus to forgive and save me. I suddenly felt a burden of sin and guilt lifted from me, and my heart was flooded with joy. In a crescendo fashion, I repeated, "Yes, Yes, Yes," as I trusted only in Jesus for my salvation. In that moment, I experienced that we are "saved by grace through faith, and not of ourselves. It is the gift of God." That moment was the beginning of my Christian walk. The next Sunday, I went forward in the First Baptist Church, Murchison, to make my profession of faith public and was baptized a Sunday or two after that.[9]

Joe Dan Fowler had sensed for as long as he can remember that he was supposed to be involved in pastoral ministry. Soon after accepting Christ as his Lord and Savior, that sense began to intensify into a strong calling into special service. However, there was a problem. He really didn't object to becoming a pastor. He did object, however, to what he believed he had to become in order to be a pastor.

His only mentors for ministry were the men who had been his pastors at the little Baptist church in Murchison. They were all wonderful men of dignity and grace who loved the Lord and were all faithful pastors. However, they were all older men who were meek and mild. To him, they seemed to be "otherworldly" and disconnected from life— almost lifeless! While they seemed to him to be quiet, passive, and pious, Joe Dan Fowler, on the other hand, was outgoing, loved sports, and was passionate about life. He wanted to live life to the fullest. To become like them would be to miss out on life. And to him, if that was what he had to do to be a pastor, he just couldn't do it.

Figure 14.1. Gober Baptist Church historical marker

When Joe Dan Fowler graduated from high school, he decided to go to Henderson County Junior College in Athens, Texas. There, having rejected the idea of becoming a pastor, he decided to become a dentist and began working on a double major in biology and chemistry. After finishing the two-year program at Henderson County Junior College, he transferred to East Texas State University in Commerce, Texas, now Texas Agricultural and Mechanical University–Commerce. By then, he had married his wife, Patsy, and together they moved to nearby Sulphur Springs. There they joined the First Baptist Church, Sulphur Springs, which was led by Dr. Charles Killough. It was through his new pastor, Dr. Killough, that Joe Dan Fowler made a life-changing discovery. Not all pastors are alike! He related,

> Dr. Killough was outgoing and actually had fun. He laughed out loud with enthusiasm. He came to our Sunday School class parties and was the life of the party! He played golf and played it extremely well. He liked the Dallas Cowboys! He was a wonderful preacher and pastor, and he clearly loved living life! I soon decided that if I could *be myself, keep my own*

personality [editor's italics], then I could be a pastor if
that was what God wanted for my life.[10]

Therefore, Joe Dan Fowler had some decisions to make. He
continued to pursue a predental degree at East Texas State University,
but he was out of God's will and he knew it. He had no peace about
the direction of his life and his studies. He also knew something had
to change. Three semesters before graduation, he was sitting in the
American Chemical Society study room and noticed the nuclear
magnetic resonance (NMR) instrument across the hall. In one of his
classes, he would soon begin to learn about the instrument. He suddenly felt a rush of questions as he relates here:

Figure 14.2. Gober Baptist Church

OK, if I master that NMR, if I become a dentist, have
a successful professional career, make lots of money,
and gain a reputation and respect... when I am 65
years old and look back at my life, will I be able to
say it was worth it? The answer was an immediate and
resounding "No!" I knew my life had to count for
eternity. Everything on earth ... success, money, reputation ... everything earthly is temporary. Ultimately,
only eternity matters. I knew that while dentistry is
a wonderful and honorable profession, it was not for
me. I felt the presence of a Holy God calling me to
change my life to make an impact for eternity. Within

a week, I was in Dr. Killough's office. I related my story to him and asked, 'Is God calling me to preach?" Dr. Killough said, 'I can't tell you that. But, if you can do anything else with your life and *be content*, do whatever that is. God is not calling you to preach, because if He is, He *will not let you be content* [editor's italics].

The next Sunday at the end of worship, Dr. Killough gave the invitation. In his own words, Joe Dan Fowler said,

I felt the need to go forward and "surrender to preach." But I wanted to be sure I was right. So I said a prayer, "God, don't let me make a mistake! If this is not your will, stop me." Nothing happened. I prayed, "Lord, I'm about to go forward. If I'm out of your will, do something. Render me unconscious, do whatever you need to do, but don't let me make a mistake." Again, nothing. So, I said, "OK Lord, here I go," and I went. I surrendered to God's will for my life, and I have never regretted it. Afterwards, Dr. Killough encouraged me and said, "You need to go to seminary." To show you how naive I was, I actually asked him, "What's a seminary?" I obviously had a lot to learn! I still do! Dr. Killough took me under his wing, modeled for me how to be a "soul winner," how to visit folks in the hospital and how to prepare a sermon. He made a terrific impact on my life. I owe him more than I could ever repay.

Joe Dan Fowler went on to finish his degree in biology and with a minor in chemistry. He then enrolled at Southwest Baptist Theological Seminary in Fort Worth, Texas. Reverend Fowler was able, with the support of Dr. Killough, to secure a pastorate at Gober Baptist Church in Gober, Texas. Reverend Fowler and his wife, Patsy, moved there shortly after graduation and began serving the church.[11]

Gober Baptist Church is a small and historic church in Fannin County. The Rev. S. P. Clement and twelve charter members founded the church in 1889. Early worship services were first held in the one-room Gober schoolhouse and then in a brush arbor. In 1893, a sanctuary—the first church structure built in Gober—was completed. That sanctuary was replaced by a two-story frame building in 1924. This building was in turn replaced by a new structure in 1953. The 1953 facility was the one where Rev. Joe Dan Fowler served his first pastorate.[12]

Gober is 108 miles northeast of Fort Worth, and Joe Dan would commute daily from Gober to Fort Worth to take classes. In his first semester in seminary, he took a brutal schedule of 21 course hours and made a 2.5-hour commute 4 days a week. In the subsequent semester, he took a more reasonable class load. Serving Gober Baptist Church was a wonderful first experience for Reverend Fowler as a pastor. The congregation was appreciative and supportive. Reverend Joe Dan and Patsy started their family in Gober. They first had a daughter whom they named Christy and then 18 months later, a son whom they named Bart.

After serving Gober Baptist Church for two and a half years, Reverend Fowler was called to First Baptist Church, Blue Ridge, which was a larger church with a better salary and was a few minutes closer to Fort Worth. Reverend Fowler finished his master of divinity degree from Southwestern Baptist Theological Seminary while serving at First Baptist Church, Blue Ridge. Reverend Fowler served at First Baptist Church, Blue Ridge, for two and a half years.

Reverend Fowler was then called to become the pastor of the Springlake Baptist Church in Paris, Texas. But after receiving the call, he was uncertain about God's will in the matter. Dr. Fowler's point of contact on the Springlake Baptist Church Pulpit Committee was a Deacon named Ken Brown. When Brother Ken called to see if he had made a decision on the call to come to Springlake, Reverend Fowler said he was still uncertain.

After two weeks of praying and waiting, he was still unsure. Brother Ken indicated that the church could wait another week, but if he still could not make up his mind, they would have to take that as a no. Near the end of that week, Reverend Fowler prayed, "Lord, not to decide is to decide. It will in effect be no. I'm 60 percent certain you want me to go. I'll go, believing that if I'm making a mistake, you'll work it out somehow!" And so, he went.

After a month at Springlake Baptist Church, Reverend Fowler sat down with pencil and paper and within a few minutes had a list of twenty-five specific items of confirmation that he was indeed following God's will. What a relief! Reverend Fowler served Springlake Baptist Church for five and a half years. While there, he helped the church build and relocate to a new facility.

Reverend Fowler was then called to the pulpit of First Baptist Church, Whitewright, Texas.[13] Whitewright is located in north central Texas, just south of Durant, Oklahoma. First Baptist Church, Whitewright, is another historic church in Texas and is famous for being the church where the twenty-three-year-old Sunday School director and teacher George Truett was approached by one of the Deacons in 1890 and asked to consider ordination as a minister. Truett went on to become financial secretary of Baylor University; pastor of the First Baptist Church, Dallas, from 1897 to 1944; president of the Southern Baptist Convention from 1927 to 1929; and president of the Baptist World Alliance.

During his 47-year pastorate at First Baptist Church, Dallas, membership increased from 715 to 7,804, and 19,531 new members were received.[14] One of the unique things about Reverend Fowler's call to serve God at First Baptist Church, Whitewright, was that Reverend Fowler did not apply for the position. First Baptist Church, Whitewright, Pulpit Committee member Bro. Leonard Robinson told Reverend Fowler that they had received five letters recommending him to the church, but none from him indicating any interest in the church. Reverend Fowler was the only pastor that the Pulpit Committee went to hear, and the committee decided that very day that they had the man who God wanted for their church. Reverend Fowler said that First Baptist Church, Whitewright, was a wonderful and loving church and he and his, wife, Patsy truly loved the people there.

Reverend Fowler was then called to the pulpit of First Southern Baptist Church, Guthrie, Oklahoma. This was his first pulpit outside the state of Texas, and he and his family truly enjoyed living in Guthrie. The church was filled with wonderful people, and the town had beautiful buildings and tremendous historical roots. In 1993, while at First Southern Baptist Church, Guthrie, Joe Dan Fowler completed his doctor of ministry degree from Midwestern Baptist Theological Seminary Kansas City, Missouri. Dr. Fowler served in First Southern Baptist Church, Guthrie, for eight and a half years.[15]

Dr. Joe Dan Fowler, the Immanuel Years

In June 1993, Dr. Joe Dan Fowler was called to the pulpit of Immanuel Baptist Church. The Pulpit Committee that called him included Rick Thompson and Robert Kellogg. Dr. Fowler expressed great confidence in and affection for these two men, being sources of great strength and support, and greatly helping with the smooth transition of his family from Guthrie to Shawnee.

Figure 14.3. Rev. Joe Dan Fowler, the Immanuel year

When Dr. Fowler got to Immanuel Baptist Church, it did not take him long to understand the desperate need for a new facility and a new location. The facilities were all full, and young couples with children were driving into the parking lot and leaving either because they could not find a convenient parking place or because after parking and entering the sanctuary, they could not find places to sit as a family. In addition, the main building was old and needed continual repairs. Many of the repairs would be quite expensive if done properly.

The main building was built before modern heating and cooling systems existed and was not designed for efficient heating and cooling. As a result, the main building was difficult to keep at a proper temperature, and keeping it at a proper temperature was very expensive. Dr. Fowler approached the facility problems from two directions.

First, to expand the number of people that could be served in the existing facility, Dr. Fowler held three worship services and had two Sunday School hours. Second, he challenged the Relocation Committee with creating a plan and finding a suitable property in the Shawnee area that could serve as the new home for Immanuel Baptist Church. One of Dr. Fowler's great concerns was the possibility of the creation of disharmony and a potential split within the church over a move to a new location. Fortunately, because of his pleasing personality and charm and his setting a high threshold for approval, there was no disharmony or even a threat of a split.

He expressed to the Relocation Committee and the Deacons that he wanted an extremely strong commitment for relocation from the congregation. Thus, he wanted to set a very high threshold for the approval of the church for the relocation. Consequently, Dr. Fowler set an approval rate of 85 percent before the relocation proposal would be approved. When the Relocation Committee presented its plan and proposal to the church, the plan received an 83.7 percent approval, not the 85 percent approval that was set as the approval threshold. Dr. Fowler told the church and committee that the committee would disband and reform later and submit a new proposal.[16]

Immanuel Baptist Church had several mission and ministry endeavors while Dr. Fowler served. One mission effort was the missions partnership with the Rosario Baptist Association of Rosario, Argentina. The first trip to Argentina was in January 1997, after Dr. Fowler had left Immanuel. Oklahoma Baptist University professor and Immanuel Baptist Church member Dr. Bob Dawson and education minister Rev. Sam Hendry were the driving forces behind this ministry. These two did most of the coordination and communication between the Rosario Baptist Association and Immanuel and within Immanuel Baptist Church.[17]

One of the things that impressed Dr. Fowler when he began serving at Immanuel Baptist Church was how well managed the church was. Several pastors, the church staff, and church leaders had put together smooth and well-functioning processes. The church team knew what to do and how to do it. As Dr. Fowler said, "Immanuel exercised 'Good Churchmanship.'"

Despite the fact that the church functioned well, Dr. Fowler felt that the mission, processes, and procedures of the church were not documented very well. Therefore, he set out to have a team of church leaders to write a mission statement and a new constitution and bylaws.[18] It should be noted that the constitution and bylaws have been reviewed regularly and updated as needed. The last update was in 2014. The next review will occur in 2019.[19]

During the years that Dr. Fowler served Immanuel Baptist Church, the church began experiencing new vitality and growth, but physical space for new members continued to be a problem for Immanuel. In order to provide additional Sunday School space and to promote Sunday School growth, Dr. Fowler began a second Sunday School hour in September 1996.[20]

There were several key staff members whom Dr. Fowler remembers fondly. Rev. Tony Ward served as both music minister and college minister. Dr. Fowler remembers his sweet and cooperative spirit.

The college ministry under Rev. Tony Ward was especially strong and vital. Each Sunday during the Oklahoma Baptist University academic year, scores of students would participate in Immanuel services and activities. Rev. Tony Ward also supervised an annual Easter drama called *The Lifegiver* and the annual Living Christmas Tree. Both events were extremely well received by not only the members of Immanuel Baptist Church but also by residents of Shawnee and the surrounding area.

Also part of the music ministry, Reba Dawson was a wonderful organist. Jeff Anderson served effectively as church recreation minister and business administrator, but Dr. Fowler sensed that Jeff had not really found his true calling. As time would later prove, Jeff's true calling was the pastoral ministry. Jeff continues to serve in that capacity to this day.

Mary Margaret Kasterke headed the children's ministry. Dr. Fowler remembers her sweet and loving approach to her work and to the children. The youth ministry under Rev. Ron Haye was also strong, with annual trips to Falls Creek. One of the most impressive individuals for Dr. Fowler at Immanuel Baptist Church was Juanita Allison who did prayer ministry. She was fully dedicated to the prayer ministry and helped explain the ministry to other churches and help them to start their own prayer ministries.

"Juanita Allison was the greatest prayer warrior that I have ever known," said Dr. Fowler. "At first she didn't drive, and her husband would take her to all corners of the state to talk to church groups about Prayer Ministry. Later, after the death of her husband, she learned to drive and then there was nothing stopping her." Dr. Fowler also had words of praise for Carla Gierhart and Fran Lancaster. "Both ladies and our entire administrative staff were very capable and kept the office functioning effectively and efficiently. They lovingly corrected many of my errors without having to be told to do so," Dr. Fowler commented.

Several church members were also dear to Dr. Fowler while he served at Immanuel Baptist Church. Robert Kellogg was on the Pulpit Committee who called Dr. Fowler and was always a source of knowledge, encouragement, and support. Dr. Fowler and his wife Patsy formed an especially strong bond with Dr. Tom and Jackie Wilks. Dr. Fowler also had great praise for Frank Whitney who taught the young adult Sunday School class. "Frank was a big key to our growth in those years and was a real spark plug. He is now a pastor in Missouri," Dr. Fowler said.

Also receiving praise from Dr. Fowler were Dr. Bill Mullins, a history professor from Oklahoma Baptist University, and J. D. McQuerry, a Shawnee automobile businessman. "Bill was always a wise and stable factor in Deacon Meetings. I could look to him for knowledge about what was done in the past and what is the proper way to do a project. J.D. was a good man of God. He was reliable and competent," Dr. Fowler recalls. Two special church members that impressed Dr. Fowler with their warm Christian spirit and love for missions were John and Cheryl Wright.

After being at Immanuel for two years, Dr. Joe Dan Fowler received a telephone call from the chairman of the Pulpit Committee of First Baptist Church, Bartlesville, Oklahoma, asking if the committee could come and hear Dr. Fowler preach. Dr. Fowler responded that it is a free country but that he had no plans to leave Immanuel. He felt his ministry was just beginning here.

The committee came, and a dialogue began. Dr. Fowler steadfastly maintained that God called him to Immanuel and he had no indication he was supposed to leave. After six months of discussions and prayer, Dr. Fowler gave what he thought was a final no. Soon afterward, he received a phone call from the First Baptist Church, Bartlesville, Pulpit Committee chairman, asking if he would pray about it one more time. Reluctantly, Dr. Fowler said yes.

Days later, after "praying it through," he was preparing to make the telephone call and give the Bartlesville committee his absolutely final no. He would make the call the following Monday. However, on that Sunday morning, as Dr. Fowler was sitting on the platform at Immanuel while Tony Ward was singing his special before the message, he looked out over the congregation and suddenly and unexplainably felt like a stranger in his own church. In the church he dearly loved, he simply did not feel at home. The experience was deeply unsettling.

After church that evening, Dr. Fowler and Patsy asked Tom and Jackie Wilks to go with them to a local restaurant. While there, Dr. Fowler told them about his contact and conversations with First Baptist Church, Bartlesville. He also related his experience on the platform at church that morning. Jackie began to cry. Dr. Fowler asked what was wrong. She said, "You have to go!" "I do?" he asked, somewhat startled. Still weeping, she said, "Yes, God is in it. I don't want you to, but you have to go." Reluctantly, Dr. Fowler finally concluded that God was truly calling him to First Baptist Church, Bartlesville, and because God called, he had to go.[21]

Dr. Joe Dan Fowler, the Years after Immanuel

After leaving Immanuel Baptist Church in 1995, Dr. Fowler went to be the senior pastor of First Baptist Church, Bartlesville. He served there for seventeen years. The church needed to make some transitions to be able to move effectively into the future. Dr.

Figure 14.4. First Baptist Church, Bartlesville

Fowler soon felt the calling to help the church to begin making those transitions. Dr. Fowler said that First Baptist Church, Bartlesville, was a wonderful place to serve and while there, he was able to make many of those transitions that would pave the way for the future life and growth of the church.

One of the significant accomplishments of Dr. Fowler's service at First Baptist Church, Bartlesville, and one that will have a lasting legacy, was the creation of the Basil and Arlene Toland Memorial Scholarship. The Tolands were longtime members of First Baptist Church, Bartlesville, and strong supporters of Oklahoma Baptist University. The scholarship was established by the church under the direction of George Meese, chairman of the Deacons at the time, and Henry Powell. It was first awarded in the 2004–2005 academic year and averages five recipients each year. The primary recipients of this scholarship are active members of First Baptist Church, Bartlesville. However, if funding is available, active members of other Southern Baptist churches located in Washington County, Oklahoma, are also eligible to receive scholarships.

After serving at First Baptist Church, Bartlesville, for seventeen years, Dr. Fowler took early retirement, knowing that his pastoral ministry was not yet quite complete. He and Patsy spent their first six months of retirement visiting other churches in the Tulsa area, all the while praying and exploring ministry possibilities for the future. Then, a telephone call from Jim Dawson, a Deacon from First Baptist Church, Webb City, Missouri, opened the door Dr. Fowler was waiting for.

Brother Dawson explained that First Baptist Church, Webb City, needed a healing hand and asked Dr. Fowler if he would preach as a fill-in for a couple of Sundays. Dr. Fowler agreed, but a fill-in for a couple of Sundays turned into a full call to be the pastor of the church. Dr. Fowler was at First Baptist Church, Webb City, for three years.

During that time, the church experienced much healing and growth. A new pastor was found to permanently take the leadership of First Baptist Church, Webb City, and Dr. Fowler fully retired from full-time vocational ministry. He and Patsy now live in Temple,

Texas, about an hour north of Austin where their son, Bart, a law-yer, lives with his wife, Heather, and their two-year-old daughter, Mallory.

Dr. Fowler's daughter Christy lives in Conway, Arkansas, and is married to Rev. Paul Hudson, the pastor of One-Church. Paul and Christy have an eighteen-year-old son PJ and two daughters—Savannah, seventeen; and Aubrey, twelve. Dr. Fowler is currently working with retired Oklahoma Baptist University Religion Professor Dr. Mack Roark, deepening his knowledge of the Greek language and translating books of the New Testament.

Looking back on his life, Dr. Fowler said,

> I have passed the 65-year-old mark. When I think about being back in college and on my life since sur-rendering to God's will for me in the pastoral min-istry, with the deepest gratitude to God, I affirm, it was worth it! I couldn't have done anything else. I wouldn't have done anything else. I found content-ment in life. And I found it the only place it can truly be found—within the will of God for my life.[22]

CHAPTER 15

Land Purchased for a New Home

Dr. Jeff Moore, October 1996–March 2002

Introduction

Dr. Jeff Moore was the seventeenth pastor of Immanuel Baptist Church. He served from October 1996 to March 2002. Both Jeff and his wife Sharla hailed from Duncan, Oklahoma. During his tenure as pastor of Immanuel Baptist Church, overcrowding and structural problems with the main church building continued. As the first major step in solving these problems, land was purchased on Forty-Fifth Street for a new home for the church.[1]

The world scene during the years that Dr. Moore served Immanuel was a period of global turmoil due largely to continued Islamic terrorism. The Soviet Empire had fallen, but the world was still a dangerous place. In 1996, when Dr. Moore arrived at Immanuel, Muslim extremists in Chechnya took 1,500 Russians hostages at the Budyonnovsk hospital. Over 100 Russian civilians died before the terrorists withdrew.

Figure 15.1. USS Cole

In the Middle East, Iraq launched air and ground strikes at a Kurdish enclave. The attack included the use of chemical weapons on civilians.[2] The year 1997 saw Hong Kong returned to Chinese rule from the United Kingdom as a separate autonomous region but under control of the Chinese Communist government.[3] In 1998, Muslim terrorists bombed the United States embassies in Kenya and Tanzania, killing several hundred people.[4] In 1999, the predominately Christian East Timor population voted for independence from predominately Muslim Indonesia in August 1999. Pro-Indonesian forces then massacred and uprooted thousands of East Timorese Christians.[5]

In October 2000, seventeen United States sailors aboard the Navy destroyer USS *Cole* were killed in the port of Aden in Yemen when Muslim terrorists attacked the ship.[6] On September 11, 2001, Moslem terrorists attacked the World Trade Center and the Pentagon using hijacked passenger airplanes. In addition, a third airplane was hijacked and was en route to Washington, DC, when its passengers attempted to regain control of the airplane, causing it to crash in Pennsylvania.[7] The United States and Great Britain then launched bombing campaigns on the Taliban government and al-Qaeda terrorist camps in Afghanistan. In 2002, the United States launched Operation Anaconda against the al-Qaeda and Taliban fighters in Afghanistan.[8]

As with the world scene, the national scene was filled with turmoil and strife during the years that Dr. Moore served Immanuel. In April 1996, the Federal Bureau of Investigation arrested the Unabomber, a domestic terrorist who killed three people and injured twenty-three others. In a major disappointment for the prolife community, Pres. Bill Clinton vetoed a bill that would block late-term abortions. The Republican

Figure 15.2. Elian Gonzales seized

convention nominated Bob Dole as its candidate for president. The Democratic convention nominated incumbent Bill Clinton who went on to win the national election.[9]

In 1997, O. J. Simpson was found liable in a civil suit for the wrongful deaths of ex-wife Nicole Brown Simpson and her friend Ron Goldman.[10] The biggest news item for the year 1998 occurred when President Clinton was accused of perjury, witness tampering, conspiracy, obstruction of justice, and abuse of power. The House of Representatives impeached President Clinton in December of 1998.[11] In 1999, the Senate went on to acquit President Clinton. Also in 1999, students Eric Harris and Dylan Klebold stormed the Columbine High School in Littleton, Colorado, and killed twelve other students and a teacher and then themselves.[12]

The year 2000 began with a touching story about a six-year-old Cuban boy named Elián González who was at the center of an international custody dispute. A federal court ruled that Elián must be taken from his maternal relatives in Miami and returned to his father in Cuba. Federal agents raided the Miami relatives' home and forcibly removed the boy.

In November 2000, George W. Bush defeated Al Gore in the closest presidential election in decades.[13] The biggest story of 2001 was the Muslim terrorist attack on the World Trade Center and the Pentagon on September 11.[14] In his 2002 State of the Union Address, Pres. George Bush vowed to expand the fight on terrorism and labeled Iran, Iraq, and North Korea as "an axis of evil."[15]

Dr. Jeff Moore, the Years before Immanuel

In 1996, Dr. Jeff Moore came to be the pastor of Immanuel Baptist Church. Dr. Moore was born and raised in Duncan, Oklahoma. He was raised in a Christian home. His home church was Immanuel Baptist Church, Duncan, Oklahoma.

At the age of nine, he realized that the story about Jesus and his death and resurrection applied to his life as much as it did anyone else's life. He went to his father on a Saturday night in 1973 and told him that he wanted to ask Jesus to come into his heart. Jeff's father wanted to make sure that Jeff understood his decision, so he made an appointment with the pastor for the next morning.

Between Sunday School and worship, the pastor met with Jeff and his father. The pastor shared the plan of salvation from the Bible and invited Jeff to pray to trust Christ. They knelt together in the pastor's office, and Jeff invited Jesus Christ into his life to be his Lord and Savior. After accepting Christ, Jeff was baptized in April 1973 at Immanuel Baptist Church, Duncan, during a Sunday evening service.

In summer 1980, Jeff was sixteen years old when he felt that God was calling him to "special service." Jeff did not know what that meant, but he knew God was placing a calling on his life. Later that year, in December 1980, he attended the Youth Evangelism Conference in Norman, Oklahoma, at the Lloyd Noble Arena with his church group from Immanuel Baptist Church, Duncan.

Figure 15.3. Jeff Moore, the OBU days

During the invitation time of the first night of the conference, he felt God's overwhelming call to preach. He did not go forward at the conference, but he did tell his youth minister about the calling. The following Sunday, he went forward and publicly surrendered to God's call to preach to the joy of the congregation.

Upon graduation from Duncan High School, Jeff Moore attended Oklahoma Baptist University in Shawnee, Oklahoma. While attending OBU, he attended Immanuel Baptist Church. He graduated from Oklahoma Baptist University in 1986 with a bachelor of arts degree in pas-

Figure 15.4. Martha Road Baptist Church

toral ministry with a minor in history. His interest in history is evident in his rich use of history in his sermons.

After graduating from OBU, he attended Southwestern Baptist Theological Seminary in Fort Worth, Texas, where he received a master of divinity in 1989. While attending Southwestern Baptist Theological Seminary, Jeff served as senior pastor at Mount Carmel Baptist Church, Cleburne, Texas. He was called to the Mount Carmel pulpit in 1988. He left a year later when he completed his master of divinity degree work.

He then attended Midwestern Baptist Theological Seminary in Kansas City, Missouri, where he received a doctor of ministry degree in 1995. In parallel with working on his doctorate at Midwestern Baptist Theological Seminary, Dr. Moore served as senior pastor for several churches—Martha Road Baptist Church, Martha, Oklahoma, 1989–1990; Calvary Baptist Church, Lindsay, Oklahoma, 1990–1993; and Regency Park Baptist Church, Moore, Oklahoma, 1993–1996.[16]

Dr. Jeff Moore, the Immanuel Years

Dr. Jeff Moore came to Immanuel Baptist Church in October 1996 from Regency Park Baptist Church, Moore. One of the first projects for Dr. Moore was initiating the eightieth anniversary celebration that occurred in October 1997. The congregation was very excited about having an enthusiastic, new young pastor with a recently awarded doctor of ministry degree. Speaking of Dr. Moore, the Eightieth Anniversary History Committee wrote, "In October, 1996, Dr. Jeff Moore became pastor of Immanuel. The enthusiasm and leadership of a young pastor brings continued growth." Rev. J. D. Dowdell chaired the History Committee, with the support of Manoi Adair and A. V. Daugherty.[17]

While under the leadership of Dr. Moore, Immanuel Baptist Church became involved in several significant missions and ministries. The church continued the partnership that had begun during the Dr. Joe Dan Fowler years with the churches in and surrounding Rosario, Argentina. The ministry was called Harvest 2000. Immanuel

Baptist Church sent mission teams there every six months for three years. During this partnership, the Immanuel Baptist Church missions team planted several new churches in Argentina and started several preaching points.

While Dr. Moore was at Immanuel, the church used the FAITH Evangelism Program.[18] FAITH Evangelism Program is a Lifeway Christian Resources discipleship program that creates a culture of evangelism in a local church by equipping and mobilizing believers in lifestyle evangelism, disciple making, and ministry.[19] At one point, Immanuel Baptist Church had ninety people trained in FAITH Evangelism techniques. These members were going out on two different nights of the week, every week.

One of the fun and rewarding ministries that Dr. Moore initiated while he was at Immanuel was the Block Party Ministry. The Block Party Ministry was designed to provide outreach to the community surrounding Immanuel. The ministry was a true blessing to the community that surrounded the church facilities at its East Main location at the time.

Perhaps the most significant and long-reaching activities that occurred during Dr. Moore's years at Immanuel was the purchase of the property on Forty-Fifth Street, the property that would eventually become the site of the current Immanuel Baptist Church facilities. When Dr. Moore came to Immanuel, it became clear to him that the facilities that Immanuel Baptist Church occupied had several structural problems. Moreover, the facilities would not support the growth that Immanuel was experiencing and would continue to experience in the future.

Within the congregation, there was a great deal of discussion over the idea of relocating the church and thus being able to support the growth that was being seen. Through time, prayer,

Figure 15.5. Dr. Jeff Moore, the Immanuel days

and patience, Dr. Moore, the church staff, and the church lay leadership were able to help formulate a vision of relocating the church to a strategic location on the north side of Shawnee. The conversation and planning that went into the discussions about the relocation were continually bathed in prayers for wisdom and an understanding of God's will. When the vision for a relocation was presented to the church, the members voted to relocate. A great deal of excitement began to grow in the hearts and lives of the members.

The leadership team looked at several locations around Shawnee and discovered that the price of land was very expensive in the prime locations that were considered. Some very desirable pieces of property were priced as high as ten thousand dollars an acre at this time. Linda Sperry, a member of the Building Committee and local real estate agent, became aware that a developer named Frank Bryant had purchased an old farm on Forty-Fifth street and was going to develop part of it into a new residential area.

Mr. Bryant had expressed interest in selling a portion of the property to Immanuel Baptist Church. Dr. Moore made contact with him and shared with him Immanuel's vision for a new and dynamic facility. Mr. Bryant said he liked the idea of a church being close to the homes he planned to build. He shared with Dr. Moore that he had paid $3,500 per acre, but he was willing to sell 31 acres to Immanuel Baptist Church at $4,500 an acre (less than half the going rate at the time).

Dr. Moore presented his discussion with Mr. Bryant to the Building Committee. The Building Committee approved and agreed to present the arrangements to the congregation. The congregation approved the terms, and a victory day was set in June to raise funds for the purchase. The goal was to raise $170,000 to purchase the land. The Lord blessed Immanuel as $193,000 was raised that day in actual money, not pledges. The land was purchased the very next day. While everyone on the Building Committee was supportive, Dr. Moore recalled that the work done by Linda Sperry, Robert Kellogg, and Steve Bowlan were especially vital to the success of the project. Dr. Moore noted, "It was an exciting time as we watched God bless us over and over again."[20]

Because of the growth of the membership during Dr. Jeff Moore's years at Immanuel and because of shortage of seating space, Dr. Moore took the bold step of holding the Immanuel Baptist Church Easter services at Raley Chapel on the Oklahoma Baptist University campus. Raley Chapel has a seating capacity of two thousand and could easily hold all Immanuel's members. Overcrowding within Immanuel's Main Street facility made Easter a very crowded event, and many people went to other churches for Easter Sunday services because they could not find a place to sit.[21]

During his tenure at Immanuel Baptist Church, Dr. Jeff Moore was supported by several wonderful staff members. He commented,

> Juanita Allison was a precious lady on the staff when I came to be pastor at Immanuel. She had started the Intercessory Prayer Ministry at Immanuel in 1981, under the leadership of Dr. Larry Adams. She was bent over by disease and had difficulty moving around, but she was mighty in prayer. She was perhaps the greatest prayer warrior that I have known. In a meeting at Oklahoma Baptist University, Henry Blackaby stated that he had taken his proverbial shoes off in the presence of a woman in Shawnee named Juanita Allison. She was a powerful prayer warrior.

Under Dr. Moore's leadership, the Immanuel Baptist Church added Rev. Scott Schooler to the staff as the student minister during his time at Immanuel. Dr. Moore said, "Scott did a great job with the students and was a true friend." The church also called Rev. Mark Wright from First Baptist Church, Durant, as minister of music during that timeframe. Dr. Moore said, "Mark was an excellent worship leader and a hard worker."

While Dr. Moore was at Immanuel, several building and renovation projects occurred on the Main Street facility. The main building had to be refurbished while he was there. The rocks on the façade had to be tuck-pointed and sealed. This process involved masonry workers carefully going around each and every rock with tools to remove damaged mortar and resealing each stone by hand with fresh mortar.

This process should have been repeated every five years like clockwork since the time the building was first built in 1929, but the repairs were not always made. The repairs were a very time-consuming and expensive process. As with the tenure of other pastors, large sections of plaster and lathe fell off inside the sanctuary during Dr. Moore's tenure. The falling plaster and lathes served as the indicator that it was time to have the outside of the building repaired. The ongoing maintenance and expense of the building weighed heavily in the discussion to relocate and build new buildings.

One of Dr. Jeff Moore's favorite memories of his time at Immanuel was time spent making visits to homebound and shut-in members of our church with G. C. Blakemore. G. C. was such a good friend and godly man who inspired Dr. Moore deeply. G. C. was faithful to go with Dr. Moore every Thursday morning to make visits to homebound and shut-in members. Dr. Moore said,

> We had the privilege of hearing so many rich and powerful stories from some of the oldest members of the congregation. I always remember the joy G.C. had every day. I do not remember a single time that I ever saw him angry or upset about anything.[22]

Figure 15.6.
Dr. Jeff Moore,
the Altus years

Concerning his years at Immanuel, Dr. Jeff Moore noted the following:

> Another great blessing for me was to see some of the members go from being adamantly opposed to relocating the church to being enthusiastically in favor of the move. God gave a clear vision to all of us and the unity of the church body was truly a blessing. I am still humbled by the power of the Lord in that whole

process. When I see the beautiful building on 45th Street and hear wonderful stories about what the Lord is doing at Immanuel, it brings a smile to my face.[23]

Dr. Jeff Moore, the Years after Immanuel

Since leaving Immanuel Baptist Church, Dr. Moore has been the senior pastor at First Baptist Church in Altus, Oklahoma. Through First Baptist Church, Altus, he has participated in mission trips to Africa, China, and Mexico. Dr. Moore is also strong in his service to Southern Baptist and Oklahoma Baptist institutions. He served the Southern Baptist Convention as a member of the Executive Committee from 2004 to 2012. He has also served three times on the board of trustees for Oklahoma Baptist University, once while at Immanuel and twice since leaving Immanuel.

Besides pastoring the congregation of First Baptist Church, Altus, Dr. Moore enjoys hunting, golfing, and fishing. He is the author of 'Til Death Do Us Part: A Minister's Guide to Officiating at Funeral Services. The book was published in 2011.[24]

Jeff Moore is married to the former Sharla Clary. He met Sharla in 1983 in Duncan at Immanuel Baptist Church, Duncan, where they were both attending. Dr. Moore relates that he was sitting in a pickup with one of his best friends when he saw Sharla walk by for the first time. He was immediately interested in finding out who she was. Through mutual friends, he was able to meet her.

A little later that year, the church sponsored a trip to the movies in Lawton, Oklahoma, and they sat by each other. The movie was the just-released Return of the Jedi. The next week, their church youth group attended the Falls Creek Baptist Assembly. There, Sharla and Jeff had their first "date"—a trip to the Icee Stand after worship service. He asked Sharla to marry him on December 24, 1983. They were married at the Immanuel Baptist Church of Duncan, Oklahoma, on August 4, 1984.

Dr. Moore and Sharla have two daughters, Whitney and Allison. Whitney was born May 24, 1990, and Allison was born May 31, 1992. Whitney is married to Trey Graham, who is the pastor of the First Baptist Church, Cache, Oklahoma. They have one son, Hudson, born January 14, 2016. Allison is married to Lee Gregg. They live in Burkburnett, Texas, and both of them work in Wichita Falls, Texas. Allison and Lee have one daughter, Landree, born April 16, 2016. Dr. Moore stated, "Having grandchildren is better than I was told."[25]

CHAPTER 16

The Final Days on Main Street

Dr. Todd Fisher, the Main Street Years, July 2003–March 2008

Introduction

Dr. Todd Fisher is the eighteenth pastor of Immanuel Baptist Church. He was the final pastor to serve at the Main Street Campus. Dr. Fisher served from July 2003 to March 2008 on the Main Street Campus and is presently serving at the Forty-Fifth Street Campus. His wife is Jamy King Fisher. Todd hails from the Fort Worth area of Texas, and Jamy hails from Ponca City, Oklahoma.[1]

The world scene during the years that Dr. Fisher served Immanuel Baptist Church on Main Street was one of years of strife and turmoil. War with Iraq was the most significant story of 2003. Having failed to get Iraq to adhere to numerous United Nations sanctions, a forty-nation coalition led by the United States and Great Britain invaded Iraq in March 2003. Baghdad fell to coalition forces in early April. In December, American troops captured Saddam Hussein.[2]

The year 2004 started poorly. In March 2004, Muslim terrorist bombings rocked Spain, killing more than two hundred people. In September 2004, Muslim Chechen terrorists took about 1,200 schoolchildren and others hostage in Beslan, Russia. Over 325 people, many of them children, died. In July 2005, Muslim terrorist bombings hit London, killing fifty-two and wounding about seven hundred.[3] The greatest tragedy of the year 2006 occurred in December when an enormous tsunami devastated eleven Asian nations, killing over two hundred thousand people.[4]

The year 2006 also had several events of concern. In February, a Danish newspaper printed cartoons of Muhammad. Angry demonstrators throughout the Muslim world smashed windows, set fires, and burned Danish flags. In July 2006, North Korea test-fired ballistic missiles over the Sea of Japan and, in October, it exploded a nuclear device.[5] In February 2008, Cuban president Fidel Castro stepped down after forty-nine years in power.[6]

As with the world scene, the national scene was filled with turmoil and strife during the years that Dr. Fisher served Immanuel on Main Street. The year 2003 began with a major disaster for NASA and the United States when the Space Shuttle *Columbia* exploded in February, killing all seven astronauts aboard.[7] In July 2004, the Democrats nominated John Kerry for president, and in August, the Republicans renominated George W. Bush for president. Surprising the major news media, George W. Bush was reelected president in November.[8]

In August 2005, Hurricane Katrina brought catastrophic damage on the Gulf coast. More than one thousand people died, and many tens of thousands were left homeless.[9] The year 2007 began with California Democrat Nancy Pelosi becoming the first female Speaker of the United States House of Representatives.[10] The year 2008 was an election year. The presidential candidates included Democrats Hillary Clinton and Barack Obama and Republicans Ron Paul, Mitt Romney, Mike Huckabee, and John McCain. By March 2008, when Immanuel Baptist Church moved to Forty-Fifth Street, John McCain had enough delegates to secure the Republican presidential nomination.[11]

Dr. Todd Fisher, the Years before Immanuel

Todd Fisher was born in Arlington, Texas in 1969. He was raised in the North Richland Hills area of Fort Worth. Todd Fisher's parents were both public school teachers. His father was a high school speech and drama teacher, and his mother taught first and third grades.

His mother taught for thirty-five years before retiring. Todd Fisher's parents divorced when he was eleven years old, and there was a void for a father figure in his adolescent and teenage years. That void was filled when Todd Fisher was sixteen years old, and he went to work for Jack Renfro of Renfro Foods.

Jack Renfro was a godly man who became not only his employer but also his friend and mentor. Jack Renfro

Figure 16.1. Todd Fisher and Jack Renfro

served as a Deacon in North Fort Worth Baptist Church where Todd Fisher was a member and was a great positive influence on the teenage Todd Fisher. That positive influence continues even to this day. Todd Fisher would continue to work for Jack Renfro off and on from that summer until he married Jamy.[12]

When Todd Fisher was fourteen years old, he accepted Christ as his Lord and Savior. Todd Fisher had a friend who was the son of a pastor. The son would invite him to church, especially to the church's youth activities. Usually, Todd Fisher would decline the invitation, but from time to time, he would attend. Doing so, he was able to hear the Gospel message.

That message was a seed in Todd Fisher's heart that needed only to be watered by the proper vessel for it to bloom into eternal life. That watering came through Todd Fisher's intense interest in sports when a popular Christian athlete appeared on a television program about his life in sports. He watched the show with eager interest. As part of the show, the athlete presented the Gospel message in his own words. That message stirred the fourteen-year-old Todd Fisher's heart, and at that moment, he understood who Jesus Christ really was and his own personal need to be relieved of his sin burden.

Todd Fisher began regularly attending North Fort Worth Baptist Church in Fort Worth, Texas, where his friend's father was the pastor. There at North Fort Worth Baptist Church, Todd Fisher went forward and made a public profession of faith. He was baptized the next Sunday. As it turned out, North Fort Worth Baptist Church was in the midst of changing locations. Todd Fisher made his profession of faith during the last Sunday service in their former facility and was one of the first to be baptized in their new facility.

Todd Fisher continued to grow in his knowledge of the Living God while at North Fort Worth Baptist Church. He was consistent in his attendance for worship services and active in the youth program. He especially enjoyed the Centrifuge Youth events at the Glorieta, New Mexico, Baptist Conference Center. When he was sixteen years old, Todd participated in a Disciple Now event at North Fort Worth Baptist Church.

During that event, Todd Fisher felt the call of God upon his life to go into special service. However, at the time, he was uncertain how he would answer that call. Possibilities were youth ministry, serving as a foreign or domestic missionary, or being a pastor. However, at his next Centrifuge Youth event at Glorieta, he felt a clear call of God to be a pastor.

The leadership and membership of North Fort Worth Baptist Church greatly supported and encouraged him. In fact, while at North Fort Worth Baptist Church, Bro. Todd Fisher completed the first step to becoming a pastor—that is, being licensed to preach. As he expressed it,

Figure 16.2.
Mrs. Renfro's
Habanero Salsa

> I was blessed with an almost universal
> affirmation and loving support of my church family. When I needed loving friends to guide me and
> encourage me, the North Fort Worth Baptist Church

family was there. The strong support that I received from both the adults and the youth at North Fort Worth Baptist Church greatly encouraged me on my path.

One of the key individuals for Todd Fisher at North Fort Worth Baptist Church was the youth pastor, Rev. Gary Gramling. Reverend Gramling has had a very successful career after leaving youth ministry at North Fort Worth Baptist Church. He has a doctorate in biblical studies from Golden Gate Baptist Theological Seminary and is now the director of the graduate program in Christian studies at Howard Payne University.[13]

Figure 16.3.
Dr. Gary Gramling

When Todd Fisher finished high school in the spring of 1988, he decided to go to Baylor University in Waco, Texas. His family had a tradition of attending Baylor, and Baylor was the premiere Baptist institution of higher education in Texas. Several adults, knowing that Todd Fisher had stated a calling by God to preach, gave him what they thought was sound advice. Todd Fisher was advised that he should *not* major in religion at Baylor University but rather in a different subject "in case this preacher thing doesn't work out."

Consequently, as he graduated from high school, Todd fully intended to enroll in Baylor and major in English as a fallback position. He had even made all of the preliminary deposits and had a schedule, a dormitory room, and a roommate assigned to him. However, Brother Todd claims God had other plans for him.

Out of Todd Fisher's high school graduating class of 650 students, 26 went to Oklahoma Baptist University, including Todd's good high school friend Clint Paschall, brother of Paula Paschall Compton. Paula and Clint were children of Rev. Paul Paschall who was the music minister of North Richland Hills Baptist Church.

Reverend Paschall was also a passionate graduate of Oklahoma Baptist University.

One day late in the spring of his senior year, Todd Fisher went over to the Paschall home to take Clint to breakfast. Clint was not ready to go, and Reverend Paschall asked Todd to sit and chat with him while Clint got ready. Reverend Paschall then proceeded to give Todd the "you really ought to go to OBU" speech.

Todd Fisher respectfully received the talk, but he knew he was going to Baylor. It turned out, however, that some of Todd's friends had a scheduled trip to Oklahoma Baptist University. Doug Melton, the Oklahoma Baptist University Texas admissions coordinator, planned the trip. Todd went on that trip merely to be with his friends.

While on that trip, however, Todd felt the hand of God upon him and heard the soft voice of God saying, "Have I not called you to preach My Word? Why then are you enrolling in a place that does not strongly affirm My will for your life? Why are you majoring in English—'in case this preacher thing doesn't work out?' You need no fallback position for My will." Todd knew immediately that it was the will of God for him to come to Oklahoma Baptist University and to major in pastoral ministry.[14]

Todd Fisher began his pastoral ministry studies at Oklahoma Baptist University in fall 1988. While a student at Oklahoma Baptist University, Todd attended Immanuel Baptist Church unless he was delivering a message at an Oklahoma church. As part of his academic work, Todd fell under the positive influences of Dr. Tom Wilks and Dr. Bob Evans, two professors whom he respected greatly.

Figure 16.4.
Rev. Paul Paschall

Dr. Wilks, who was also a member of Immanuel with his wife Jackie, sponsored a program called the Ministerial Practical Experience (MPE) program whereby several Oklahoma Baptist University ministerial students would be sent into a Baptist Association on a given Sunday to preach in the churches of the association. Typically, the students would preach the Sunday sermon; have lunch with the pastor and his family or with church members; and spend the afternoon with the pastor learning more about the operations of a church, associational polity, and Baptist General Convention of Oklahoma polity. That evening, the student might or might not lead the evening church service, depending on the student's schedule and the pastor's schedule.

Overall, it was a great method to give the Oklahoma Baptist University students some experience in the pulpit and some working knowledge of church and Baptist operations. Whenever possible, Todd took advantage of these opportunities. As a result, he got to preach in churches all over the state of Oklahoma and got a strong confirmation of God's calling on his life and his decision to come to Oklahoma Baptist University.

Todd Fisher did say, however, that his conviction to preach was challenged at his first ministerial alliance meeting of his freshman year. About two hundred ministerial students, many of them freshmen, attended that first meeting. The speaker opened his talk with, "Freshmen, look around the room. By your senior year, half of you won't be here." That statement challenged Todd Fisher as an unusual way to address students who felt they were called by God to join the ministry. Unfortunately, the statement proved to be true, but in his case, it only deepened his desire to be true to his calling.

In Todd Fisher's freshman year, Tom Wilks and his secretary, Rhonda Whittington, kept him busy preaching in churches through the Ministerial Practical Experience (MPE) program. In his sophomore year, however, a unique opportunity presented itself to Todd Fisher. First Baptist Church, Weleetka, asked him to be their youth pastor.

After three months of working with the youth group, Todd Fisher was informed that the pastor had resigned for a larger church in Tulsa and was asked to preach that Sunday morning. He did well, and the church asked him to preach the next Sunday. The church then asked him to be their interim pastor until they filled the pulpit. The adult leadership graciously took over his youth pastor duties while he served as interim pastor.

He served the church for six months as interim pastor while the church located a new pastor. He then returned to being the youth pastor. However, as he sat in the pews under the preaching of the new pastor, he deeply missed being in the pulpit and knew that pastoral ministry was indeed his calling. Todd Fisher said, "The church was filled with wonderful, affirming people such as Chuck and Donna Simmons who helped me to grow and supported me and loved me through my first full ministry experience."

In 1991, during his junior year, Dr. Wilks and Rhonda Whittington again kept Reverend Todd Fisher busy doing MPE events all over the state of Oklahoma and in a variety of settings. On one pair of Sundays, Reverend Fisher spoke in a small, rural church in the Salt Fork Baptist Association and then at First Baptist Church, Elk City, in the Beckham-Mills Baptist Association. The first church had eight people in Sunday School and twelve people in the worship service. The second had 850 people in its worship service.[15]

Figure 16.5.
Dr. Todd Fisher,
the OBU days

In fall 1992, at the start of his senior year at Oklahoma Baptist University, Rev. Todd Fisher received a unique opportunity. Hopewell Baptist Church, a few miles southwest of Shawnee, asked him to preach one Sunday for a pastor who had recently left their congregation. The Pulpit Committee was sufficiently pleased with Reverend Fisher's message that they asked him to preach the next Sunday also. Eventually, the Pulpit Committee asked him to be their interim pastor while they searched for a full-time pastor.

By May 1992, the Pulpit Committee was sufficiently pleased that the leadership asked Rev. Todd Fisher to be their pastor. Knowing that he had a serious obligation to finish his Oklahoma Baptist University degree that year as well, the church leadership took over much of the mechanics of the church's business and ministry and allowed Reverend Fisher to concentrate on the preaching and his studies.

"The church provided me a tremendous opportunity to develop my preaching skills and to understand the functioning of a church. The church showered me with unconditional love and support. Hopewell Baptist Church and the people there will always have a special place in my heart," Reverend Fisher said. While at Hopewell Baptist Church, Reverend Fisher completed his second great step in becoming a pastor—that is, being ordained as a preacher.

Rev. Todd Fisher continued to serve Hopewell Baptist Church after his graduation at Oklahoma Baptist University in spring 1993 and through his first two years of seminary at Southwest Baptist Theological Seminary in Fort Worth. His schedule as both a seminary student and preacher was quite hectic. He would preach on Sunday, take seminary classes at their Southwest Baptist Theological Seminary extension facility on the Oklahoma Baptist University campus from 9:00 a.m. until 9:00 p.m. on Monday, and then drive to Fort Worth late on Monday night. He would then work at Renfro Foods on Tuesday through Friday and then drive back to Shawnee to preach at Hopewell Baptist Church. In total, Reverend Fisher spent two and a half years at Hopewell Baptist Church.

Part of the reason why Reverend Fisher continued his relationship with Hopewell Baptist Church past his Oklahoma Baptist University graduation date was that during the 1992–93 academic year, he met Jamy King through mutual friends. Jamy King was an Oklahoma Baptist University family psychology major from Ponca City. A romance blossomed, and Todd Fisher proposed to Jamy King in September 1993. Jamy King graduated from Oklahoma Baptist University in May 1994. Rev. Todd Fisher and Jamy King were married in July 1994.[16]

One month before their marriage, Rev. Todd Fisher was called to be the pastor of First Baptist Church, Wellston. The pastorate at First Baptist Church, Wellston, was again a time of

Figure 16.6. Todd and Jamy Fisher, wedding day

growth and development for Reverend Fisher. During his time there, he finished his master of divinity degree in biblical languages from Southwest Baptist Theological Seminary. His degree was granted in 1996.

Having finished his master of divinity degree, Reverend Fisher began to think about a doctoral degree. He learned that Midwestern Theological Seminary in Kansas City had an extension program that operated through classes taught at the Baptist General Convention of Oklahoma facility in Oklahoma City. The program featured having a cohort of five students who would work together, study together, and support each other.

When he contacted Midwestern Theological Seminary, Reverend Fisher learned that the school was trying to create an Oklahoma cohort but had just three students committed to the program and needed two more. Reverend Fisher contacted Rev. Andy Taylor, a close friend of his, who had been the youth minister at Regency Park Baptist Church in Moore, serving under Dr. Jeff Moore. Reverend Taylor also performed the marriage ceremony for Todd Fisher and Jamy King in Ponca City. After Reverend Fisher explained the situation to him, Reverend Taylor cheerfully agreed to join the program. The program was very successful for Reverend Fisher, and he completed his doctor of ministry degree in 2001.

In November 1997, Highland Hills Baptist Church in north-west Oklahoma City called Rev. Todd Fisher to be their pastor. "Highland Hills was a sweet church with a gentle, older congregation. It was an easy place to be a pastor," Dr. Fisher said.

In 2002, Dr. Fisher and his congregation at Highland Hills Baptist Church jointly read through and studied *The Purpose Driven Life* by Dr. Rick Warren. Dr. Fisher preached a sermon series in connection with the book while the joint reading occurred. The book was enjoyable and challenging to both the congregation and Dr. Fisher. One of the statements from the book that especially challenged Dr. Fisher was the statement "God's will might not be the Easy Path." Dr. Fisher had served at Highland Hills Baptist Church for just over five years and suddenly had the conviction that God may have a more challenging pastoral assignment for him.[17]

Dr. Todd Fisher, the Years on Main Street

In 2002, the Immanuel Baptist Church Pulpit Committee contacted Dr. Fisher concerning their opening. The committee asked him to provide a résumé, and Dr. Fisher did so but he had no further contact from the committee. However, ten months later, Dr. Fisher received a telephone call from Robert Douglas who was on the Pulpit Committee.

Robert's son, Kent, was the youth pastor for Dr. Fisher at Highland Hills Baptist Church and felt moved to encourage his father to make contact with Dr. Fisher. At that time, Dr. Fisher was under the conviction that God may have a challenge ahead for him. Robert Douglas asked Dr. Fisher to provide his résumé, at which Dr. Fisher replied he had already done so. At which, Robert Douglas replied, "The committee never received it." A second résumé for Dr. Fisher and first résumé for the committee was soon provided.

As part of his decision process for considering the position at Immanuel, Dr. Fisher called several older pastors whom he considered friends and mentors and asked them about the position at Immanuel Baptist Church. Dr. Fisher recalled, "To a man, they all told me not to go. They said the church was in the middle of a relocation and building program that was not feasible, and I would be eaten alive."[18]

Figure 16.7. Dr. Todd Fisher, the Immanuel days

The Immanuel Pulpit Committee proceeded to call Dr. Fisher in for an interview that went very well for both Dr. Fisher and the Pulpit Committee. At one point in the interview, one of the committee members asked for the first instance in the Old Testament foreshadowing the sacrifice of Jesus for the sins of and salvation of mankind. Dr. Fisher quickly answered the slaying of the animals to provide coverings for Adam and Eve following their sin in the Garden, that a blood sacrifice was needed to wash away man's sins.

The questioner expressed great joy that at last they had a candidate who understood the Old Testament and the sacrifice of Christ well enough to give a correct answer. The interview proceeded extremely well after that. Also, as part of the interview process, the Pulpit Committee and the Fisher family shared a meal at Todd Tate's house. Robert Douglas and Zachary Fisher, age six, were part of a side table away from the main table. Robert and Zachary formed a strong bond and had a great discussion of sports.

Zachary asked Todd Tate why he and his family had been invited to Shawnee to share a meal with all these people. Todd Tate replied that Immanuel Baptist Church was looking for a pastor. Zachary then proceeded to walk over to his father and quietly get his attention and telling him in secret, "Daddy, you need to know, these people are looking for a pastor." Dr. Todd Fisher joined Immanuel Baptist Church as its senior pastor in July 2003.

Several significant ministries and missions occurred while Dr. Todd Fisher served at the Main Street campus, and one ministry ended. The ministry that ended was the ministry with a collection of the churches in and around Rosario, Argentina. The ministry had fulfilled its purpose for a great part, and the interests of the key participants had transitioned to a new ministry called Mission Shawnee. Dr. Bob Dawson was the driving force behind Mission Shawnee, an effort to provide services to poor families in Shawnee.[19]

During Dr. Fisher's years on Main Street, Immanuel Baptist Church also increased its level of participation in Pottawatomie-Lincoln Baptist Association Partnership ministry efforts. In 2006–2008, Immanuel sent a mission team to support director of missions Tim Pruitt of the Gila Valley Baptist Association. The team conducted vacation Bible Schools for the churches in the area and did cleanup and construction work on a youth campground. Often, two trips to the Gila Valley area were made in a given year, one for Immanuel families and one for Immanuel youth.[20]

A major mission effort that was initiated by Dr. Fisher was the Quito, Ecuador, Ministry which began in 2006. The ministry's origins trace back to a Hispanic church affiliated with Immanuel Baptist Church that was founded by International Mission Board missionaries Mark and Mary Fuller. The Fullers were on leave at Immanuel Baptist Church from Ecuador. The Fullers brought Gallo Barreiro from Quito to Shawnee to be the pastor of the Hispanic church. Based on those relationships, the deep needs of the Baptist churches and the poor people of Quito became clear to Dr. Fisher and the Immanuel staff. In addition, Dr. Fisher had a burden on his heart to expand the mission outreach of Immanuel Baptist Church and to increase greatly the frequency of mission trips and the number of people involved in those trips.

In the eleven years since the Quito mission trips started, Immanuel Baptist Church has indeed increased the number of mission trips, both domestic and international, and has greatly increased the number of church members involved. For Quito, in particular, a firm relationship was established with several local churches and individuals in Quito. In the early years, Immanuel Baptist Church worked directly with Frank and Julie Lamca, two international mission board missionaries serving in Quito, and Eduardo Andrade, a local Christian evangelical leader who provided housing, meals, and coordination for the Immanuel mission teams. Also, important in the relationship was *el presidente de la asociación* (the Quito Baptist association director of missions). Annual trips have been made to Quito since the ministry started in 2006. Often, multiple trips are made to Quito in a given year.

Dr. Fisher fondly remembers G. C. Blackmore participating in 2007 Quito mission trip at eighty years of age and walking up to the edge of the observation platform of the Pichincha Volcano in the Avenue of the Volcanos at an elevation of fourteen thousand feet. "G. C.'s wife, Francis, had just died, and he was 80 years old, but he kept up with everyone and surpassed many in our activities. G. C. got such joy from working with the Vacation Bible School Team and the children from some of Quito's poorest areas," Dr. Fisher said.

Another major ministry effort was the relationship that Immanuel Baptist Church had with Stephen and Nicole Hall who served in a very difficult area overseas and did work in water development and agriculture. That relationship began while Dr. Fisher served as senior pastor on the Main Street campus. In addition, under

Dr. Fisher's leadership, several missionaries on leave from the international mission board resided at the Immanuel Missions House, and several members of Immanuel Baptist Church have gone out as missionaries in very difficult areas of the world. These members receive regular support and visits from the church.[21]

During Dr. Fisher's years of leadership at the Main Street campus, several ministry efforts took place toward the members of Immanuel and the Shawnee community. These included The Living Christmas Tree, the Sportsman Banquets, block parties, and the I'll Be Home for Christmas dinner theater. The Living Christmas Tree was a significant effort by the Immanuel Baptist Church family.

When the idea of The Living Christmas Tree was first developed by the Immanuel staff, Paul Kelley went to a church in Oklahoma City that had an existing living Christmas Tree and took pictures of their tree. He then designed and constructed the tree in the Family Life Center. Each part of the tree was numbered and the even bolts to hold the tree together were numbered.

The tree had five tiers and was very heavy. Several strong workers were required to put it together, but the construction was easy, thanks to Paul Kelley's design and numbering. The Living Christmas Tree included an elaborate light show. Mark Bowlan often controlled the lights. The singers entered and climbed the structure from both sides. The last year for The Living Christmas Tree program was 2005.

In 2006, the church did a dinner theater called *I'll be Home for Christmas*. The dinner theater was held on three nights and included a standup bass jazz band. All three dinner theater showings were well attended. Dr. Todd Fisher served as the radio station disk jockey for the program, and his son Zach was the little boy in the play. According to Rev. Mark Wright, Mark Cannon superbly played an older gentleman.

The disposal of the framework for The Living Christmas Tree was also a significant event for the church. Rev. Mark Wright, through his connections with pastors in the Durant, Oklahoma, area, learned that the music minister of Calvary Baptist Church in Durant wanted to have a living Christmas Tree at his church. Contact was made with Calvary Baptist Church, and the music minister sent a pair of flatbed trailers to retrieve the tree. The Living Christmas Tree was used by Calvary Baptist Church in Durant for several years.[22]

One of the first challenges for Dr. Todd Fisher at the Main Street facility was in the area of education ministry. Within a week of starting his ministry at Immanuel Baptist Church, Rev. Ray Griffin, the education minister, came into Dr. Fisher's office to inform him that God had called him to go to Quail Springs Baptist Church in Oklahoma City. Thus, God had called a key member of the Immanuel pastoral team to another church.

Dr. Fisher's solution was to elevate Rev. Scott Schooler from youth minister to be an associate pastor and the education minister and then to hire a new youth minister. This would allow Reverend Schooler to assume a role of greater responsibility and to use his natural talents in a more challenging area. Dr. Fisher took this proposal to the board of Deacons. The meeting happened to be only the second meeting that he had ever had with the Deacons. Dr. Fisher requested the Deacons place the decision before the Immanuel membership for a vote. The Deacons were enthusiastically supportive of the idea, and the plan was presented to the congregation and was approved. The result has been extremely positive.

During his years of leadership at the Main Street campus, several key staff members served with Dr. Fisher. Rev. Mark Wright served as Music Ministers. "Our Music Ministry has always been second to none across the state of Oklahoma," Dr. Fisher said. Scott Schooler, Mick Hoggart, and Brian Burchfield have served as youth ministers. Mary Margaret Kasterke, Kay Hawkins, and Chris Jones have served as children ministry directors. Sam Hendry served as a seniors' minister. The office staff has had several wonderful workers, including Kathy Bowlan, Ronda Perryman, and Fran Lancaster.[23]

Because of the shortage of seating space at the Main Street campus, Dr. Fisher continued the practice started by Dr. Jeff Moore of having Easter Sunday services at Raley Chapel on the Oklahoma Baptist University campus. Dr. Fisher added one feature to the Easter Sunday weekend, that being an Easter egg hunt on the Saturday morning before Easter on the south lawn in front of Raley Chapel. Dr. Fisher recalled with joy the process of having senior church members stuffing upward to two thousand plastic eggs with candy, scattering those eggs on the Raley front lawn and then having roughly five hundred to one thousand youngsters and adult supervisors run off searching for the eggs and putting them in Easter baskets.[24]

The single most intensive effort that Dr. Fisher was involved in was the building of the new facility on Forty-Fifth Street and the relocation from Main Street to Forty-Fifth Street. Dr. Fisher said,

> When I arrived, we had a set of blue prints for a massive and beautiful building. The facility, when the blue prints were drawn, was estimated to cost between $10 million and $12 million. By the end of construction, however, the actual cost would have been up to $15 million. I could see that raising the funds needed to just start the building would take several years. We were facility bound where we were and could not grow. We needed to get out to 45th Street as soon as possible, so I proposed to the Building Committee that we build in two or three phases. The Committee was wonderful to work with and very supportive. We would meet every week and for long hours. Rick Thompson was the head of the committee, David Walkingstick headed up the construction portion of the committee, and Robert Kellogg headed up the finance portion of the committee. They were and continue to be great men with whom to work. They are capable and caring. One of the things that we did was to bring Dr. Alton Fannin of First Baptist Church, Ardmore, in for a "Vision to Victory' Banquet at Oklahoma Baptist University. Our goal was to bring in one of the pillars of the Baptist General Convention of Oklahoma, a man well-known for his leadership, vision, integrity, and humor, to serve a great meal, and to challenge the membership to step forward financially to bring that vision to victory.

The Vision to Victory Banquet was a great success with over five hundred people in attendance. The membership of Immanuel eventually pledged half of the seven million dollars needed for construction.

Construction of the facility began shortly thereafter and proceeded more or less on schedule, with a rainy building season slowing the construction somewhat. One day, in the midst of the construction, Shawnee experienced ten inches of rain. Groundbreaking occurred on January 29, 2006, with the members of the congregation standing on an outline that formed the shape of the church building to give an understanding of the size of the facility. One of the special events during the construction was a gathering of the congregation at the partially completed structure on Sunday afternoon to bathe the girders in scripture. Hundreds of verses were written on the beams that would eventually support the structure and God's blessings were invoked for the structure.[25]

One of the key events of the move from the Main Street campus to the Forty-Fifth Street campus was the disposal of the Main Street facility. Church member and local attorney Kermit Milburn updated the deed and split the facility into two pieces of property. Because the heating and air conditioning system for the main building and the education building were joined together as one unit, the main building and the education building needed to stay together as one property unit.

That property unit was sold to the Fresh Fire Outreach Center under the leadership of Rev. Joe Wilkes for one dollar. Reverend Wilkes had been renting a building for his church family, and the transfer of the main building and the education building to him allowed him to be freed of a monthly rent payment. The other piece of property contained the family life center and was sold to Mission Shawnee for one dollar with the understanding that Good Shepherd Chapel would be allowed to meet in the building.

Once the disposition of the Main Street facility had occurred, the move to the forty-fifth Street campus could take place. The first Sunday service in the Forty-Fifth Street facility was held on March 30, 2008.[26]

CHAPTER 17

The Forty-Fifth Street Years

Dr. Todd Fisher, March 2008–Present

Introduction

Dr. Todd Fisher is the eighteenth pastor of Immanuel Baptist Church and is our current pastor. Dr. Fisher oversaw the move from the Main Street campus to the Forty-Fifth Street campus. He held the first Forty-Fifth Street campus service on March 30, 2008.[1]

The world scene during the years that Dr. Fisher has served Immanuel on Forty-Fifth Street have been years of continued strife and turmoil. In June 2008, Iranian president Mahmoud Ahmadinejad won reelection. Widescale and deadly protests began shortly thereafter in Tehran. At least Seventeen people died.[2] In December 2009, Pres. Barack Obama announced that the United States, China, India, Brazil, and South Africa had reached an agreement to combat man-made global warming.[3]

The year 2010 began with a devastating 7.0-magnitude earthquake in Haiti.[4] In January 2011, a series of demonstrations and unrest known as the Arab Spring began in Tunisia. Protests then broke out in Egypt, Bahrain, Libya, and Syria. Several dictators fell from power, only to be replaced by Muslim militants. In May, United States Special Forces killed Osama bin Laden in Abbottabad, Pakistan.[5] In September 2012, Muslim terrorists stormed the

American consulate in Benghazi, Libya, and killed the United States ambassador Christopher Stevens and three others. Despite knowing that the attack was a terrorist attack, the Obama administration blamed the event on an Internet satirical video about Muhammad.[6]

In February 2013, North Korea detonated a third nuclear bomb. In April, despite warnings by Pres. Barack Obama, the Syrian government used chemical weapons against its rebels.[7] In April 2014, the Muslim terrorist group Boko Haram kidnapped approximately 280 girls, mostly Christians, as sex slaves. In summer 2014, the Islamic State in Iraq and Syria (ISIS) released videos showing the beheading of Americans James Foley and Steven Sotloff.[8] In January 2015, Muslim terrorists killed 12 people at the offices of the satirical magazine *Charlie Hebdo* in Paris. The magazine had printed cartoons of Muhammad.[9]

As with the world scene, the national scene has been also filled with turmoil and strife during the years that Dr. Fisher has served Immanuel on 45th Street. In November 2008, Barack Obama defeated John McCain to become the first African American President of the United States.[10] The year 2009 began with US Airways Flight 1549 making a forced landing in the Hudson River after it struck a flock of geese. All 150 passengers and five crew members survived. In November 2009, Maj. Nidal Malik Hasan killed 13 and injured 29 at Fort Hood, Texas.[11] In 2010, the Apple Corporation introduced the iPad. In April 2010, an explosion on a British Petroleum oilrig off the coast of Louisiana killed 11 people and injured 17. Pollution into the Gulf of Mexico was extensive.[12]

The year 2011 began with violence and ended with violence. In January, Arizona representative Gabrielle Giffords was among seventeen people shot by a gunman who opened fire on the congresswoman's constituent meeting outside a local grocery store. Six people were killed. In February, the Obama administration declared that the Defense of Marriage Act is unconstitutional and ordered the Justice Department to stop defending the law in court. In May, President Obama declared that the borders before the 1967 Arab-Israeli war should be the basis of a Mideast peace deal between Israel and Palestine, thus overturning forty-four years of precedence.[13]

The year 2012 was an election year. Pres. Barack Obama was uncontested in the Democratic nomination, and Mitt Romney won the Republican nomination. In November, President Obama was reelected.[14] In January 2013, the Senate increased the top tax rates from 35 to 39.9 percent. In April, two bombs exploded near the finish line of the Boston Marathon, killing three people. In June, the Supreme Court ruled that the 1996 Defense of Marriage Act (DOMA) is unconstitutional.[15]

In June 2014, the Supreme Court ruled that Hobby Lobby cannot be forced to pay for insurance that covers contraception. In August, in Ferguson, Missouri, police officer Darren Wilson shot and killed Michael Brown, an accused robber who was trying to take the officer's gun. Many businesses were looted and burned in the violent protests that followed.[16] In June 2015, the Supreme Court ruled that homosexual marriage was legal in all fifty states,[17]

Dr. Todd Fisher, the Years on Forty-Fifth Street

The Dr. Todd Fisher years on Forty-Fifth Street began with the move from Main Street. The move was very elementary. Almost all material property (chairs, table, pews, desks, etc.) was left on Main Street for Good Shepherd Chapel and Fresh Fire Outreach Ministry. For the most part, the only items moved were files, records, kitchen items, and personal items. Church staff members and volunteers moved these items.

The first service on the Forty-Fifth Street campus was on March 30, 2008. As had occurred at the Main Street facility, the Sunday morning services on Forty-Fifth Street began with an 8:15 a.m. worship service with traditional music. The 8:15 a.m. service was followed by a 9:30 a.m. Sunday School period. At 10:50 a.m., a worship service was held with a blend of contemporary music and traditional music. Following that first set of services on March 30, 2008, Immanuel Baptist Church experienced a very rapid increase in attendance.

The church staff had assumed an increase in attendance at the new facility, but the increase was much greater and much more rapid than they had anticipated. The original prediction and planning by Dr. Fisher and the pastoral staff was that church membership and attendance would be sure and steady, but the growth in attendance greatly exceeded expectations. After just two months in the new facility, attendance reached the level that the staff had anticipated would take two years. At that point, Dr. Fisher and the staff decided a third service had become a necessity.

Dr. Fisher and the staff decided to move the first service to 8:00 a.m. to add a second service at 9:30 a.m. and keep the third service at 11:00 a.m. The first service would have traditional music. The third service would continue to have blended music, but the music for the second service would be entirely contemporary music with a praise-and-worship team. Dr. Fisher and the staff decided to have Sunday School classes at 9:30 and 11:00, opposite the second two worship services.[18]

Figure 17.1. Immanuel Baptist Church, bird's-eye view

There was some uncertainty that the new format would work. Dr. Fisher recalled,

> I went into that first 9:30 a.m. service with a bit of uncertainty. Would anyone come? Will the creation of the third service cause the other services to shrink, especially the first service since we were asking the church members to get up fifteen minutes earlier. On the day we went to three services, the 8:00 a.m. service's attendance was about the same as it had always been, and the people did not seem grumpy because they had to come in a bit earlier. I went into the second service between 9:20 a.m. and 9:25 a.m., and my heart sank. There were fewer than 75 people there. The sanctuary was ominously empty. I thought we

had a disaster on our hands. I went and sat down on the front row and prayed for my message and for attendance and didn't really look back as the praise and worship music started. About the third song, I saw Scott Schooler out of the corner of my eye opening up the side overflow wing. This surprised me, so when Scott came over to sit beside me, I asked him, 'Scott, why did you open up the overflow wing?' He chuckled and said, 'Turn around and look.' I did so and was overwhelmed. We were full to near capacity. I estimated we had 350 people there. I was overjoyed, but a new fear hit me. These are all 11:00 a.m. people, and the third service will be empty. However, the third service was also full. When I saw the size of the 11:00 a.m. service that came on top of a normal 8:00 service and an overwhelming 9:30 a.m. service, I was moved to tears. God had blessed. After moving to 45th Street and going to three services, we added several hundred new members to the church. Our staff meetings soon became filled with discussions on how to solve the many logistical problems that sudden rapid growth creates. How will we handle parking? How will we handle all of the new Sunday School classes? And so on. In some ways, for those first few years of rapid growth, we were barely keeping our heads above water. None of us had experience in such a dynamic growth situation. But we tried to learn quickly and well and did our best to handle everything that came our way.

One of the things that is unique about the three services is the difference in the dynamics of the attendees. The attendees at 8:00 a.m. service average about sixty-two years of age and are seasoned in Baptist life and Baptist worship. The 9:30 a.m. service tends to be a younger group with many college and high school students. These students are often joined by their parents. The 9:30 a.m. worshippers tend to be more interactive with the praise-and-worship music but less interactive during the sermon. However, Dr. Fisher has observed that the 9:30 a.m. worshippers tend to be much more interactive in their use of social media after the service, sending him e-mail messages, tweets, and Facebook posts. The 11:00 a.m. service is a mixture of both with many families with young children.

The new rapid growth of Immanuel Baptist Church meant that space for the youth ministry and for Sunday School classes became a primary concern. Sunday School classes were meeting in every possible area, including the pastor's office. The youth ministry was also growing rapidly and filling its allocated area to overflowing. In June 2012, the church voted to expand the youth ministry facilities. A new ten-thousand-square-foot addition for youth ministry was added to the original sixty-thousand-square-foot facility. The addition was funded through the Baptist foundation and was quickly completed.

With the addition of the youth wing, a new aspect of ministry growth became possible—that is, a Saturday evening worship service. Since the three worship services were tending to fill to capacity, especially the 9:30 a.m. service, the church staff decided to add a Saturday night worship service in the youth worship center. Attendance started with about seventy-five people. The attendees tended to be people who couldn't attend on Sunday due to work obligations or people who wanted to free up their Sundays. The Saturday evening worship service continued for two years, but instead of growing, the number of attendees began shrinking. When the attendance shrank to around forty people, the pastoral staff decided the small number of attendees was not worth the strain that the fourth service was placing on the pastoral staff.[19]

With the move to Forty-Fifth Street and the expansion of the membership came an increase in mission and ministry activities. In many ways, the heart of the Immanuel Baptist Church mission efforts were the Quito and North Africa mission trips that began on Main Street. These mission efforts continued with the move to Forty-Fifth Street. These mission efforts expanded with more trips, different types of trips, and more people being involved. In addition, Immanuel Baptist Church expanded its Gila Valley Baptist Association partnership with director of missions Tim Pruitt.

Trips were made to Casa Grande for vacation Bible school and prayer walking and to the Mt. Lemmon Campgrounds for cleanup and construction. In 2008, Immanuel Baptist Church sent a family mission team first and then a youth mission team to Casa Grande area. In 2010–2012, we sent mission teams to Utah to work with Rev. Donnie Smith and his wife, Dawn, in St. George, Utah. The Immanuel mission teams did prayer walking, vacation Bible school coordination and support, block party coordination and support, and construction. We also formed a partnership with director of missions Bill Lighty of the Pike's Peak Baptist Association in Colorado Springs and sent several mission teams there. Beginning in 2013, Immanuel Baptist Church has regularly sent a men's construction team to Colorado to do construction on a youth camp there. Rev. Scott Schooler coordinated much of this mission work.[20]

In addition to these mission activities, Rev. Mark Wright has been active in motorcycle ministries. Starting in 2009, Reverend Wright and his wife Pat have led motorcycle evangelism efforts in Sturgis, South Dakota; Daytona Beach, Florida; and Fayetteville, Arkansas; either by themselves or with church ministry teams. One key feature of these mission trips is indeed evangelism. Several Oklahoma churches often send teams on these trips, and the Baptist General Convention of Oklahoma provides evangelism training. Mission team members are taught how to share their testimony in three minutes. The Immanuel Baptist Church trip to Sturgis requires two days of travel to get from Shawnee to Sturgis. As the team spends its first night at a motel along the way, Reverend Wright has the team members practice giving their testimony.[21]

One of Immanuel Baptist Church's ongoing ministry projects reflects back to Immanuel Baptist Church's roots as a mission church from First Baptist Church, Shawnee, and to Immanuel's efforts to start Temple Baptist Church and Sharon Baptist Church as mission churches from Immanuel. That project is our partnership with Covenant Hope Fellowship in McLoud. In 2014, Son Rise Baptist Church in McLoud became unviable and disbanded as a church. The property reverted to the Pottawatomie-Lincoln Baptist Association. Director of missions Dr. Russell Cook began to look for ways to reopen the facility as a Baptist church.

Dr. Todd Fisher became involved in the discussions, and a plan developed. Rev. Shawn Crawley, a member of Immanuel, would serve as the pastor of a new church called Covenant Hope Fellowship. Several members of Immanuel would join Covenant Hope Fellowship as the core members to provide stability and serve as a platform for growth. The Baptist General Convention of Oklahoma, the Pottawatomie-Lincoln Baptist Association, Immanuel Baptist Church, and a few other local churches would provide monthly funding to help the church get started and grow. Dr. Fisher and the Immanuel Baptist Church pastoral staff would provide spiritual guidance and assistance to Reverend Crawley as needed. Given this framework of support and aid, Covenant Hope Fellowship was established in 2015.[22]

Perhaps the greatest ministry event for Immanuel Baptist Church once it moved to Forty-Fifth Street has been the Great Day of Service event. For the Great Day of Service, all worship and Sunday School activities at the Forty-Fifth Street facility are cancelled, including evening activities; and the congregation, under the leadership of the pastoral staff, does what Christ did during His ministry on earth—the church serves and is a servant to a neighborhood in Shawnee.[23]

The first Great Day of Service was held in 2015. The concept for the Great Day of Service came from a pastoral staff retreat that took place for several days at First Baptist Church, Ponca City. Dr. Fisher's longtime friend, Rev. Andy Taylor, hosted that retreat.

As part of the retreat, Reverend Taylor and his staff explained their Great Day of Service in Ponca City and the positive impact that the event had on their membership. Dr. Fisher and the pastoral staff took the concept back to Shawnee and put the concept into action. Rev. Scott Schooler created five ministry zones around the former Immanuel Baptist Church facility on Main Street. A team was then sent into these five zones to survey the residents about their service needs.

At first, the team was met with skepticism. The residents were wary that there might be a cost involved. When assured that the effort was purely a ministry effort for the church and there would be no charges for the services, the residents opened up and made requests for services. Based on the success of the survey, the five zones were expanded to twelve, and a new survey was taken.

The second survey was greeted with much more favorable results. The residents of the twelve zones were enthusiastic and excited about receiving some free help. Overall, 110 projects were defined, and 600 members of Immanuel Baptist Church participated in the first Great Day of Service. Many of the projects were lawn cleanup projects.

The Great Day of Service generated a tremendous amount of debris. The church originally ordered five dumpsters, each with a forty-cubic-yard capacity. The debris generated on the Sunday of the ministry event greatly exceeded the capacity of these five dumpsters. The excess was placed in a rather large pile lovingly called "Mount Garbage." Eventually, sixteen dumpsters, each with a forty-cubic-yard capacity, were ordered.

One of the more touching projects was for a retired pastor whose wife had cancer. He requested that his house be painted. Reverend Schooler contacted an Oklahoma Baptist University male social club to assist with the painting. As part of the Great Day of Service, a hot dog cookout was held for the residents of the twelve zones.

A second Great Day of Service occurred in 2016. For this Great Day of Service, the project leaders were asked to specifically enter into discussions with the members of the homes where the service projects occurred and to determine their spiritual needs. If appropriate, the project leaders were to pray for and with the household members. Sack lunches were provided to the workers and the zone residents.

One of the projects was to tear down a small building for a lady and to clear out a drainage ditch. Shortly after the Great Day of Service, the lady came by the church with a thank-you note and a supply of handmade bookmarks. She said the Great Day of Service project probably saved her home. A significant rainstorm took place a few days after the Great Day of Service, and the rainwaters almost rose to the back door of her house. Fortunately, the removal of the building and the clearing of the drainage ditch allowed the water to flow away and stay out of her house. Reverend Schooler observed,

> We get a wide variety of ages involved in the Great Day of Service, from youngster to senior citizens. One of the benefits of having some of our older members involved is that, while they may not be able to do some of the vigorous projects, they can provide a great service by engaging the residents in conversations and determining their spiritual needs.[24]

For the 2017 Great Day of Service, Immanuel Baptist Church collaborated with Calvary Baptist Church under the leadership of Rev. David Henry. Calvary Baptist Church provided helpers for the Immanuel Great Day of Service including a cookout at their facility. Immanuel Baptist Church provided assistance for Calvary Baptist Church to organize its Great Day of Service in its area.[25]

Dr. Todd Fisher, Plans for the Future

As Immanuel Baptist Church continued to expand in the number of members and in the number and scope of its missions, the need to reconsider the overall building plan arose. The original building plan was a several-phase plan. First, the current main facility and worship center were to be completed, and then the youth wing was to be added. Eventually, a large facility containing a much larger sanctuary was to be built. However, the cost associated with that large sanctuary was significant, thus necessitating the church leadership to reassess its plans.[26]

At the Sunday night, January 22, 2017, members' meeting, the church approved recommendations that brought about some exciting changes in the weeks ahead. Construction began on raising and expanding the stage in the worship center, which will include a baptistery. Due to growing attendance and the enlarging of the stage, a fourth worship service was added. The new schedule for worship and Sunday School began on Sunday, February 12, with 8:00 a.m.

worship, 9:15 a.m. worship and Sunday School, 10:30 a.m. worship and Sunday School, and 11:45 a.m. worship.

The additional worship service enabled Immanuel Baptist Church to increase the number of people who attend our worship services. The additional worship service also enabled the church to close the overflow seating for most services. Church members who currently attended the 9:30 a.m. or 11:00 a.m. service and who could make participating in the new 11:45 a.m. service work for their family were encouraged to help us by doing so.

A second recommendation that was approved that Sunday night was to make substantial upgrades to the audio-visual equipment at the church. The new equipment would greatly improve the quality of the livestreaming of services on the Internet and the archiving of worship services on the church's website. Hundreds of people regularly view the livestream broadcast of Immanuel's Sunday services. Many of the viewers had difficulty seeing or hearing the service due to the outdated equipment. In addition, many people today watch a church's worship service online before making a decision to visit for the first time. For these reasons, it was important to upgrade the equipment and provide high quality streaming online.

Finally, at the January 22, 2017, business meeting, the church approved upgrading the signage outside and inside of the church building. The upgrades included a new sign on Forty-Fifth Street to replace the one that was aging and signage inside to help visitors and members navigate their way through the building. These new changes were the fruit of God's blessing and the members' faithful commitment to His church through the years. Dr. Fisher stated,

> Thank you to all who have selflessly served and given. I am excited for the future at IBC and pray that these changes will help us reach more people to hear the teaching of the gospel and the Word of God. I look forward to the days ahead as we grow in making disciples, engaging members in service, and enriching our fellowship for the glory of Christ and his kingdom.[27]

INDEX

NOTES

Dedication

1. Ruby Sands, handwritten notes provided by Teresa Gardner, May 23, 2017.

Chapter 1: The Early Years

1. Ruby Sands, handwritten notes provided by Teresa Gardner, May 23, 2017.
2. Seventy-Fifth-Year Anniversary Program, Immanuel Baptist Church.
3. www.infoplease.com/year/1917.html#world.
4. www.infoplease.com/year/1919.html#world.
5. *The American Republic*, Richard Hofstadter, et al, Prentice-Hall, 1959.
6. *Yahnseh*, 1923 Edition, Oklahoma Baptist University.
7. Proceedings of the Baptist General Convention of Oklahoma, 1912, ds.bgco.org/docushare/dsweb/Get/Document-16418/1912.pdf (hereafter cited as Proceedings).
8. www.bgco.org/bgco-annuals.
9. Proceedings, 1913, ds.bgco.org/docushare/dsweb/Get/Document-16419/1913.pdf.
10. Proceedings, 1914, ds.bgco.org/docushare/dsweb/Get/Document-16420/1914.pdf.
11. Proceedings, 1916, ds.bgco.org/docushare/dsweb/Get/Document-16488/1916.pdf.
12. *Yahnseh*.
13. Proceedings, 1917, ds.bgco.org/docushare/dsweb/Get/Document-16422/1917.pdf.
14. Slayden A. Yarbrough, *The Lengthening Shadow*, (First Baptist Church, 1992).
15. 1975 Dedication Program, Immanuel Baptist Church.
16. Minutes of the Business Meeting, September 1917–September 1924, Immanuel Baptist Church (hereafter cited as Minutes, Immanuel Baptist Church).

17. Uncle Jimmy Owens, *Annuals of O.B.U. (Oklahoma Baptist University)*, (Shawnee: Bison Press, 1956).

18. Proceedings, 1916.

19. Minutes, September 1917–September 1924, Immanuel Baptist Church.

20. Proceedings, 1915, ds.bgco.org/docushare/dsweb/Get/Document-16421/1915. pdf.

21. Minutes, Immanuel Baptist Church.

22. Proceedings, 1918, ds.bgco.org/docushare/dsweb/Get/Document-16493/1918. pdf.

23. Minutes, Immanuel Baptist Church.

24. 1975 Dedication Program, Immanuel Baptist Church.

25. Minutes, Immanuel Baptist Church.

26. Marlin Hawkins, ed., *Oklahoma Baptist Hall of Fam.*

27. Proceedings, November 1925, ds.bgco.org/docushare/dsweb/Get/Document-8048/November%204%2c%201925.pdf.

28. Proceedings, June 1926, ds.bgco.org/docushare/dsweb/Get/Document-8031/June%2030%2c%201926.pdf.

29. Proceedings, February 1926, ds.bgco.org/docushare/dsweb/Get/Document-8102/February%2017%2c%201926.pdf.

30. Proceedings, November 1926, ds.bgco.org/docushare/dsweb/Get/Document-8051/November%2024%2c%201926.pdf.

31. www.okbu.edu/alumni/honorary-doctorates.html.

32. www.obhc.org/assets/Generosity_Fall08.pdf.

33. Seventy-Fifth-Year Anniversary Program, Immanuel Baptist Church.

34. *Yahnseh, 1923 Ed.*, Oklahoma Baptist University.

35. Minutes, Immanuel Baptist Church.

36. Sands, handwritten notes, May 23, 2017.

37. Proceedings, October 1923, ds.bgco.org/docushare/dsweb/Get/Document-7960/October%2017%2c%201923.pdf.

38. Minutes, Immanuel Baptist Church.

39. Proceedings, 1920, ds.bgco.org/docushare/dsweb/Get/Document-16424/1920. pdf.

40. Owens, *Annals of O.B.U.*, 1956.

41. *Yahnseh, 1922 Ed.*, Oklahoma Baptist University.

42. Proceedings, 1930, ds.bgco.org/docushare/dsweb/Get/Document-16434/1930. pdf.

43. Proceedings, 1934, ds.bgco.org/docushare/dsweb/Get/Document-16438/1934.pdf.

44. Proceedings, February 1935, ds.bgco.org/docushare/dsweb/Get/Document-8439/February%2021%2c%201935.pdf.

45. Proceedings, September 1967, ds.bgco.org/docushare/dsweb/Get/Document-10323/September%2028%2c%201967.pdf.

46. www.okcemeteries.net/pott/fairviewshawnee/fairviewshawnee.htm.

47. Proceedings, 1916.

48. Proceedings, September 1921, ds.bgco.org/docushare/dsweb/Get/Document-7862/September%207%2c%201921.pdf

49. Proceedings, 1923, ds.bgco.org/docushare/dsweb/Get/Document-16427/1923.pdf.

50. Proceedings, August 2022, ds.bgco.org/docushare/dsweb/Get/Document-7988/August%2022%2c%201923.pdf.

51. Proceedings, 1929, ds.bgco.org/docushare/dsweb/Get/Document-16433/1929.pdf.

52. "Pond Creek, Oklahoma," Wikipedia, en.wikipedia.org/wiki/Pond_Creek,_Oklahoma.

53. *86th Annual Sessions Report*, October 18, 2016, Pottawatomie-Lincoln Baptist Association.

54. Proceedings, June 1937, ds.bgco.org/docushare/dsweb/Get/Document-8583/June%2010%2c%201937.pdf.

55. Proceedings, July 1938, ds.bgco.org/docushare/dsweb/Get/Document-8674/July%2028%2c%201938.pdf.

56. Proceedings, 1940, ds.bgco.org/docushare/dsweb/Get/Document-16444/1940.pdf.

57. Proceedings, 1944, ds.bgco.org/docushare/dsweb/Get/Document-16448/1944.pdf

58. Minutes, October 1924–September 1934, Immanuel Baptist Church.

59. Proceedings, 1927, ds.bgco.org/docushare/dsweb/Get/Document-16431/1927.pdf.

60. Proceedings, 1934.

61. *86th Annual Sessions Report*, October 18, 2016, Pottawatomie-Lincoln Baptist Association.

62. Proceedings, February 1936, ds.bgco.org/docushare/dsweb/Get/Document-8561/February%2027%2c%201936.pdf.

63. Proceedings, August 1935, ds.bgco.org/docushare/dsweb/Get/Document-8412/August%201%2c%201935.pdf.

64. Proceedings, February 1936, ds.bgco.org/docushare/dsweb/Get/Document-8561/February%2027%2c%201936.pdf.

65. www.okcemeteries.net/pott/fairviewshawnee/fairviewshawnee.htm.

Chapter 2: The Move to Main Street

1. Seventy-Fifth-Year Anniversary Program, Immanuel Baptist Church.

2. Sands, handwritten notes.

3. www.infoplease.com/year/1926.html#world.

4. www.infoplease.com/year/1927.html#world.

5. www.infoplease.com/year/1928.html#world.

6. www.infoplease.com/year/1929.html#world.

7. "1929 Palestine Riots," Wikipedia, en.wikipedia.org/wiki/1929_Palestine_riots.

8. www.thoughtco.com/1920s-timeline-1779949.

9. www.infoplease.com/year/1928.html#world.

10. www.infoplease.com/year/1929.html#world.

11. Proceedings, 1916.

12. Proceedings, November 1916.

13. "Custer City, Oklahoma," Wikipedia, en.wikipedia.org/wiki/Custer_City,_Oklahoma.

14. Proceedings, 1917.

15. Proceedings, October 1918, ds.bgco.org/docushare/dsweb/Get/Document-12203/October%209%2c%201918.pdf.

16. Proceedings, November 1917, ds.bgco.org/docushare/dsweb/Get/Document-7604/November%2014%2c%201917.pdf.

17. Proceedings, April 1918, ds.bgco.org/docushare/dsweb/Get/Document-12077/April%203%2c%201918.pdf.

18. Proceedings, June 1919, ds.bgco.org/docushare/dsweb/Get/Document-12149/June%204%2c%201919.pdf.

19. Proceedings, 1919, ds.bgco.org/docushare/dsweb/Get/Document-16423/1919.pdf.

20. H. Leon McBeth, *The Baptist Heritage*, (Broadman Press, January 29, 1987).

21. Proceedings, October 1919, ds.bgco.org/docushare/dsweb/Get/Document-12202/October%208%2c%201919.pdf.

22. Proceedings, September 1919, ds.bgco.org/docushare/dsweb/Get/Document-12205/September%2010%2c%201919.pdf.

23. Proceedings, 1919.

24. Proceedings, 1921, ds.bgco.org/docushare/dsweb/Get/Document-16425/1921.pdf.

25. Proceedings, February 1920, ds.bgco.org/docushare/dsweb/Get/Document-12102/February%2011%2c%201920.pdf.

26. Minutes, Immanuel Baptist Church.

27. Seventy-Fifth-Year Anniversary Program.

28. Proceedings, June 1926, ds.bgco.org/docushare/dsweb/Get/Document-8027/June%2016%2c%201926.pdf.

29. Minutes, Immanuel Baptist Church.

30. Proceedings, June 1927, ds.bgco.org/docushare/dsweb/Get/Document-8191/June%2022%2c%201927.pdf.

31. 1975 Dedication Program.

32. Proceedings, October 1929, ds.bgco.org/docushare/dsweb/Get/Document-8304/October%2031%2c%201929.pdf.

33. 1975 Dedication Program.

34. Proceedings, September 1929, ds.bgco.org/docushare/dsweb/Get/Document-8305/September%205%2c%201929.pdf.

35. Minutes, Immanuel Baptist Church.

36. Proceedings, April 1931, ds.bgco.org/docushare/dsweb/Get/Document-8319/April%2023%2c%201931.pdf.

37. Proceedings, June 1930, ds.bgco.org/docushare/dsweb/Get/Document-8267/June%2012%2c%201930.pdf.

38. Proceedings, February 1933, ds.bgco.org/docushare/dsweb/Get/Document-8432/February%202%2c%201933.pdf.

39. "Picher, Oklahoma," Wikipedia, en.wikipedia.org/wiki/Picher,_Oklahoma.

Chapter 3: Into the Heart of the Depression

1. Seventy-Fifth-Year Anniversary Program, Immanuel Baptist Church.

2. Sands, handwritten notes.

3. www.infoplease.com/year/1930.html#world.

4. www.infoplease.com/year/1932.html#world.

5. www.infoplease.com/year/1933.html#world.

6. www.infoplease.com/year/1930.html#world.

7. www.infoplease.com/year/1931.html#world.
8. www.infoplease.com/year/1932.html#world.
9. www.infoplease.com/year/1932.html#world.
10. "Altus, Oklahoma," Wikipedia, en.wikipedia.org/wiki/Altus,_Oklahoma.
11. Proceedings, September 1959, ds.bgco.org/docushare/dsweb/Get/Document-9919/September%203%2c%201959.pdf
12. Proceedings, 1913, ds.bgco.org/docushare/dsweb/Get/Document-16419/1913.pdf.
13. Proceedings, 1914, ds.bgco.org/docushare/dsweb/Get/Document-16420/1914.pdf.
14. Proceedings, 1915, ds.bgco.org/docushare/dsweb/Get/Document-16421/1915.pdf.
15. Proceedings, 1916, ds.bgco.org/docushare/dsweb/Get/Document-16488/1916.pdf.
16. Proceedings, 1917, ds.bgco.org/docushare/dsweb/Get/Document-16422/1917.pdf.
17. Proceedings, 1918, ds.bgco.org/docushare/dsweb/Get/Document-16493/1918.pdf.
18. Proceedings, May 1920, ds.bgco.org/docushare/dsweb/Get/Document-12172/May%2026%2c%201920.pdf.
19. Proceedings, October 1930, ds.bgco.org/docushare/dsweb/Get/Document-8297/October%209%2c%201930.pdf.
20. Proceedings, 1923, ds.bgco.org/docushare/dsweb/Get/Document-16427/1923.pdf.
21. Proceedings, April 1924, ds.bgco.org/docushare/dsweb/Get/Document-7974/April%202%2c%201924.pdf.
22. Proceedings, 1925, ds.bgco.org/docushare/dsweb/Get/Document-16429/1925.pdf.
23. Proceedings, 1926, ds.bgco.org/docushare/dsweb/Get/Document-16430/1926.pdf.
24. Proceedings, 1927, ds.bgco.org/docushare/dsweb/Get/Document-16431/1927.pdf.
25. Proceedings, September 1926, ds.bgco.org/docushare/dsweb/Get/Document-8061/September%201%2c%201926.pdf.
26. Proceedings, August 1927, ds.bgco.org/docushare/dsweb/Get/Document-8151/August%2024%2c%201927.pdf.

27. Proceedings, September 1915, ds.bgco.org/docushare/dsweb/Get/Document-7628/September%208%2c%201915.pdf.

28. Proceedings, May 1916, ds.bgco.org/docushare/dsweb/Get/Document-7595/May%2024%2c%201916.pdf.

29. Proceedings, September 1927, ds.bgco.org/docushare/dsweb/Get/Document-8130/September%2014%2c%201927.pdf.

30. Proceedings, 1928, ds.bgco.org/docushare/dsweb/Get/Document-16432/1928.pdf.

31. Proceedings, June 1928, ds.bgco.org/docushare/dsweb/Get/Document-8192/June%2028%2c%201928.pdf.

32. Proceedings, October 1930, ds.bgco.org/docushare/dsweb/Get/Document-|8297/October%209%2c%201930.pdf.

33. Proceedings, 1929.

34. Minutes, Immanuel Baptist Church.

35. Proceedings, 1930.

36. Proceedings, 1930, ds.bgco.org/docushare/dsweb/Get/Document-8285/May%2022%2c%201930.pdf.

37. Proceedings, 1931, ds.bgco.org/docushare/dsweb/Get/Document-16435/1931.pdf.

38. Proceedings, 1932, ds.bgco.org/docushare/dsweb/Get/Document-16436/1932.pdf.

39. Proceedings, 1933, ds.bgco.org/docushare/dsweb/Get/Document-16437/1933.pdf.

40. Minutes, Immanuel Baptist Church.

41. Proceedings, May 1934, ds.bgco.org/docushare/dsweb/Get/Document-8487/May%203%2c%201934.pdf.

42. Proceedings, 1935, ds.bgco.org/docushare/dsweb/Get/Document-16439/1935.pdf.

43. Proceedings, 1936, ds.bgco.org/docushare/dsweb/Get/Document-16440/1936.pdf.

44. Proceedings, June 1935, ds.bgco.org/docushare/dsweb/Get/Document-8472/June%2027%2c%201935.pdf.

45. Proceedings, July 1935, ds.bgco.org/docushare/dsweb/Get/Document-8455/July%204%2c%201935.pdf.

46. Proceedings, March 1935, ds.bgco.org/docushare/dsweb/Get/Document-8476/March%207%2c%201935.pdf.

47. Proceedings, June 1937, ds.bgco.org/docushare/dsweb/Get/Document-8583/June%2010%2c%201937.pdf.

48. Proceedings, 1937, ds.bgco.org/docushare/dsweb/Get/Document-16441/1937.pdf.

49. "Martha, Oklahoma," Wikipedia, en.wikipedia.org/wiki/Martha,_Oklahoma.

50. Proceedings, 1938, ds.bgco.org/docushare/dsweb/Get/Document-16442/1938.pdf.

51. Proceedings, 1939, ds.bgco.org/docushare/dsweb/Get/Document-16443/1939.pdf.

52. Proceedings, October 1939, ds.bgco.org/docushare/dsweb/Get/Document-8713/October%2012%2c%201939.pdf.

53. Proceedings, 1941, ds.bgco.org/docushare/dsweb/Get/Document-16445/1941.pdf.

54. www.fbctah.org/history.htm.

55. Proceedings, April 1945, ds.bgco.org/docushare/dsweb/Get/Document-9044/April%2019%2c%201945.pdf.

56. Proceedings, November 1952, ds.bgco.org/docushare/dsweb/Get/Document-9537/November%2013%2c%201952.pdf.

57. Proceedings, November 1947, ds.bgco.org/docushare/dsweb/Get/Document-9227/November%2020%2c%201947.pdf.

58. Proceedings, September 1959, ds.bgco.org/docushare/dsweb/Get/Document-9919/September%203%2c%201959.pdf.

Chapter 4: A Light Shines through the Depths of the Depression

1. Richard Hofstadter, *The American Republic*, (Prentice-Hall, 1959).

2. Seventy-Fifth-Year Anniversary, Immanuel Baptist Church.

3. Sands, handwritten notes.

4. www.infoplease.com/year/1934.html#world.

5. www.infoplease.com/year/1935.html#world.

6. www.infoplease.com/year/1936.html#world.

7. www.infoplease.com/year/1937.html#world.

8. www.infoplease.com/year/1934.html#world.

9. www.infoplease.com/year/1935.html#world.

10. www.infoplease.com/year/1936.html#world.

11. www.infoplease.com/year/1937.html#world.

12. "Thomas Jefferson 'Tom' Doss," Find a Grave, last modified March 18, 2010, www.findagrave.com/cgi-bin/fg.cgi?page=gr&GRid=49876046.

13. Proceedings, 1923, ds.bgco.org/docushare/dsweb/Get/Document-16427/1923. pdf.

14. Proceedings, October 1923, ds.bgco.org/docushare/dsweb/Get/Document-7964/October%2031%2c%201923.pdf.

15. www.reformedreader.org/sbac.htm.

16. Proceedings, December 1923, ds.bgco.org/docushare/dsweb/Get/Document-7992/December%205%2c%201923.pdf.

17. Proceedings, December 1923.

18. Proceedings, March 1926, ds.bgco.org/docushare/dsweb/Get/Document-8032/March%203%2c%201926.pdf.

19. Proceedings, December 1925, ds.bgco.org/docushare/dsweb/Get/Document-8090/December%202%2c%201925.pdf.

20. Proceedings, May 1925, ds.bgco.org/docushare/dsweb/Get/Document-8042/May%206%2c%201925.pdf.

21. Proceedings, July 1925, ds.bgco.org/docushare/dsweb/Get/Document-8022/July%2029%2c%201925.pdf.

22. Proceedings, June 1926, ds.bgco.org/docushare/dsweb/Get/Document-8023/June%202%2c%201926.pdf.

23. *86th Annual Sessions Report*, October 18, 2016, Pottawatomie-Lincoln Baptist Association.

24. Minutes, Immanuel Baptist Church.

25. Proceedings, 1935.

26. Proceedings, 1936.

27. Proceedings, 1937.

28. Proceedings, February 1936, ds.bgco.org/docushare/dsweb/Get/Document-8561/February%2027%2c%201936.pdf.

29. Seventy-Fifth-Year Anniversary Program, Immanuel Baptist Church

30. Proceedings, May 1939, ds.bgco.org/docushare/dsweb/Get/Document-8699/May%2018%2c%201939.pdf.

31. Proceedings, September 1939, ds.bgco.org/docushare/dsweb/Get/Document-8724/September%2021%2c%201939.pdf.

32. Proceedings, November 1956, ds.bgco.org/docushare/dsweb/Get/Document-9746/November%2029%2c%201956.pdf.

33. Proceedings, September 1960, ds.bgco.org/docushare/dsweb/Get/Document-9967/September%2015%2c%201960.pdf.

34. Proceedings, January 1961, ds.bgco.org/docushare/dsweb/Get/Document-9985/January%2012%2c%201961.pdf.

35. Proceedings, November 1975, ds.bgco.org/docushare/dsweb/Get/Document-10723/November%2013%2c%201975.pdf.

36. "Thomas Jefferson 'Tom' Doss," Find a Grave.

37. "Lula Alice Shirley Doss," Find a Grave, last modified February 1, 2015, www.findagrave.com/cgi-bin/fg.cgi?page=gr&GRid=142082503.

Chapter 5: Out of the Depression and through the War

1. Seventy-Fifth-Year Anniversary, Immanuel Baptist Church.

2. Sands, handwritten notes.

3. Hofstadter, *The American Republic*.

4. Ibid.

5. www.newspapers.com/newspage/38797790.

6. "Ralston, Oklahoma," Wikipedia, en.wikipedia.org/wiki/Ralston, Oklahoma.

7. Proceedings, September 21, 1944, ds.bgco.org/docushare/dsweb/Get/Document-9141/September 21 1944.pdf.

8. *Yahnseh, 1923 Ed.*, Oklahoma Baptist University.

9. Proceedings, September 21, 1944.

10. Proceedings, December 1923.

11. Proceedings, September 1921.

12. Proceedings, August 1923, ds.bgco.org/docushare/dsweb/Get/Document-7988/August%2022%2c%201923.pdf.

13. Proceedings, 1932.

14. Proceedings, 1933.

15. www.newspapers.com/newspage/38797790.

16. Minutes, 1937–1941, Immanuel Baptist Church.

17. Proceedings, October 1938, ds.bgco.org/docushare/dsweb/Get/Document-8718/October%2027%2c%201938.pdf.

18. Minutes, Immanuel Baptist Church.

19. 1975 Dedication Program.

20. Minutes, Immanuel Baptist Church.

21. Deacon Minutes, 1942.

22. Proceedings, September 21, 1944.

23. Proceedings, September 1983, ds.bgco.org/docushare/dsweb/Get/Document-11139/September%201%2c%201983.pdf.

24. Minutes, 1937–1943, Immanuel Baptist Church.

25. Proceedings, 1938.

26. Proceedings, 1940.

27. Proceedings, 1944.

28. Deacon Minutes, 1944–1949.

29. Manoi Adair, handwritten notes sent to author, April 2, 2017.

30. Ruby Sands, handwritten notes.

31. Proceedings, 1945, ds.bgco.org/docushare/dsweb/Get/Document-16449/1945.pdf.

32. www.newspapers.com/newspage/38797790.

33. Proceedings, January 1981, ds.bgco.org/docushare/dsweb/Get/Document-11011/January%2022%2c%201981.pdf.

34. www.newspapers.com/newspage/38797790.

35. Manoi Adair, handwritten notes.

36. www.newspapers.com/newspage/38797790.

Chapter 6: Recovery and Growth after World War II

1. Seventy-Fifth-Year Anniversary, Immanuel Baptist Church.

2. Proceedings, January 1947, ds.bgco.org/docushare/dsweb/Get/Document-9182/January%202%2c%201947.pdf.

3. Seventy-Fifth-Year Anniversary, Immanuel Baptist Church.

4. www.thoughtco.com/1940s-timeline-1779951.

5. Hofstadter, *The American Republic.*

6. www.geni.com/people/Claybron-Deering/6000000022770518356.

7. Proceedings, November 1949, ds.bgco.org/docushare/dsweb/Get/Document-9330/November%2024%2c%201949.pdf.

8. Proceedings, 1929.

9. Proceedings, May 1929, ds.bgco.org/docushare/dsweb/Get/Document-8284/May%209%2c%201929.pdf.

10. Proceedings, 1930.

11. "Alfalfa, Oklahoma," Wikipedia, en.wikipedia.org/wiki/Alfalfa,_Oklahoma.

12. Proceedings, March 1930.

13. Proceedings, 1931.

14. *Yahnseh, 1935 Ed.*, Oklahoma Baptist University.

15. Janice Maynard, e-mail to John Nichols, March 6, 2017.

16. Proceedings, June 1933, ds.bgco.org/docushare/dsweb/Get/Document-8471/June%2022%2c%201933.pdf.

17. Proceedings, July 1935.

18. Proceedings, March 1954, ds.bgco.org/docushare/dsweb/Get/Document-9626/March%2025%2c%201954.pdf.

19. *Yahnseh, 1935 Ed.*, Oklahoma Baptist University.

20. Proceedings, August 1935.

21. Proceedings, October 1935, ds.bgco.org/docushare/dsweb/Get/Document-8507/October%203%2c%201935.pdf.

22. Manoi Adair, handwritten note.

23. "Graham, Oklahoma," Wikipedia, en.wikipedia.org/wiki/Graham,_Oklahoma.

24. Proceedings, September 1938, ds.bgco.org/docushare/dsweb/Get/Document-8729/September%208%2c%201938.pdf.

25. Proceedings, 1941.

26. Proceedings, 1942, ds.bgco.org/docushare/dsweb/Get/Document-16446/1942.pdf.

27. Proceedings, 1943, ds.bgco.org/docushare/dsweb/Get/Document-16447/1943.pdf.

28. Proceedings, March 1944, ds.bgco.org/docushare/dsweb/Get/Document-9104/March%202%2c%201944.pdf.

29. Proceedings, 1944.

30. Proceedings, December 1944, ds.bgco.org/docushare/dsweb/Get/Document-9067/December%207%2c%201944.pdf.

31. Proceedings, November 1945, ds.bgco.org/docushare/dsweb/Get/Document-9121/November%2015%2c%201945.pdf.

32. Deacon Minutes, 1944–1949.

33. Seventy-Fifth-Year Anniversary, Immanuel Baptist Church.

34. Deacon Minutes.

35. Manoi Adair, hallway conversation with author, April 9, 2017.

36. Proceedings, March 1946, ds.bgco.org/docushare/dsweb/Get/Document-9209/March%2021%2c%201946.pdf.

37. Deacon Minutes.

38. Proceedings, August 1947, ds.bgco.org/docushare/dsweb/Get/Document-9156/August%2014%2c%201947.pdf.

39. Deacon Minutes.

40. Proceedings, May 1947, ds.bgco.org/docushare/dsweb/Get/Document-9215/May%2015%2c%201947.pdf.

41. Proceedings, May 1946, ds.bgco.org/docushare/dsweb/Get/Document-9216/May%2016%2c%201946.pdf.

42. Proceedings, May 1946, ds.bgco.org/docushare/dsweb/Get/Document-9224/May%209%2c%201946.pdf.

43. Proceedings, May 1946.

44. *86th Annual Sessions Report*, October 18, 2016, Pottawatomie-Lincoln Baptist Association.

45. Proceedings, March 1948, ds.bgco.org/docushare/dsweb/Get/Document-9314/March%2025%2c%201948.pdf.

46. Sands, handwritten notes.

47. Proceedings, March 1948.

48. Seventy-Fifth-Year Anniversary, Immanuel Baptist Church.

49. Sands, handwritten notes.

50. Proceedings, January 1947.

51. Proceedings, April 1945.

52. Deacon Minutes.

53. Proceedings, September 1946, ds.bgco.org/docushare/dsweb/Get/Document-9248/September%2026%2c%201946.pdf.

54. *86th Annual Sessions Report*, October 18, 2016, Pottawatomie-Lincoln Baptist Association.

55. Deacon Minutes.

56. Proceedings, 1945.

57. Proceedings, November 1949.

58. Proceedings, 1946, ds.bgco.org/docushare/dsweb/Get/Document-16450/1946.pdf.

59. Proceedings, 1947, ds.bgco.org/docushare/dsweb/Get/Document-16451/1947.pdf.

60. Proceedings, 1948, ds.bgco.org/docushare/dsweb/Get/Document-16452/1948.pdf.

61. Proceedings, November 1949.

62. Proceedings, 1952, ds.bgco.org/docushare/dsweb/Get/Document-16454/1952.pdf.

63. Proceedings, 1955, ds.bgco.org/docushare/dsweb/Get/Document-16370/1955.pdf.

64. Proceedings, June 1959, ds.bgco.org/docushare/dsweb/Get/Document-9897/June%2025%2c%201959.pdf.

65. www.bizapedia.com/people/OKLAHOMA/OKC/DEERING-CLAYBRON.html.

66. Proceedings, July 1963, ds.bgco.org/docushare/dsweb/Get/Document-10092/July%2011%2c%201963.pdf.

67. Proceedings, March 1971, ds.bgco.org/docushare/dsweb/Get/Document-10512/March%2018%2c%201971.pdf.

68. Proceedings, September 1972, ds.bgco.org/docushare/dsweb/Get/Document-10582/September%207%2c%201972.pdf.

69. Proceedings, November 1949.

70. "Muriel Hazel Robinson Deering," Find a Grave, last modified April 1, 2009, http:// findagrave.com/cgi-bin/fg.cgi?page=gr&GSln=Deering&GSiman=1&GScid=217127&GRid=35406703&.

Chapter 7: Steady Growth and Babyland

1. Seventy-Fifth-Year Anniversary, Immanuel Baptist Church.

2. Jennifer Rosenberg, "A Brief Timeline of the 1950s," ThoughtCo., last modified August 20, 2017, www.thoughtco.com/1950s-timeline-1779952.

3. "Trustee Elected," News OK, last modified November 19, 1981, newsok.com/article/1964348.

4. "Jackson, Missouri," Wikipedia, en.wikipedia.org/wiki/Jackson,_Missouri. ds.bgco.org/docushare/dsweb/Get/Document-9276/February%2010%2c%201949.pdf.

5. News OK.

6. "Leila Lake, Texas," Wikipedia, en.wikipedia.org/wiki/Lelia_Lake,_Texas.

7. tshaonline.org/handbook/online/articles/hna48.

8. Manoi Adair, undated and unaddressed website article, received April 25, 2017.

9. News OK.

10. Proceedings, March 1944.

11. Proceedings, 1944.

12. "Hollis, Oklahoma," Wikipedia, en.wikipedia.org/wiki/Hollis,Oklahoma.

13. "Greer County, Texas," Wikipedia, en.wikipedia.org/wiki/Greer_County,_Texas

14. Lori Hagans, e-mail to author, March 20, 2017.

15. "Lonnie Baugh Obituary," *The Oklahoman* Obituaries, published May 6, 2011,

16. legacy.newsok.com/obituaries/oklahoman/obituary.aspx?n=lonnie-baugh& pid=150822483.

17. Hagans, e-mail to author.

18. Proceedings, April 1945.

19. Proceedings, July 1945, ds.bgco.org/docushare/dsweb/Get/Document-9084/ July%2012%2c%201945.pdf.

20. Proceedings, August 1945, ds.bgco.org/docushare/dsweb/Get/Document-9053/ August%202%2c%201945.pdf.

21. Proceedings, September 1945, ds.bgco.org/docushare/dsweb/Get/Document-9142/ September%2027%2c%201945.pdf.

22. Proceedings, November 1945, ds.bgco.org/docushare/dsweb/Get/Document-9120/ November%201%2c%201945.pdf.

23. Proceedings, 1945.

24. Proceedings, March 1946.

25. Proceedings, September 1946.

26. Proceedings, September 1946.

27. Proceedings, 1946.

28. Proceedings, January 1947.

29. "Hobart, Oklahoma," Wikipedia, en.wikipedia.org/wiki/Hobart, Oklahoma.

30. Proceedings, March 1947, ds.bgco.org/docushare/dsweb/Get/Document-9206/March%2013%2c%201947.pdf.

31. Proceedings, April 1947, ds.bgco.org/docushare/dsweb/Get/Document-9147/ April%2010%2c%201947.pdf.

32. Proceedings, July 1947, ds.bgco.org/docushare/dsweb/Get/Document-9193/ July%2024%2c%201947.pdf.

33. Proceedings, September 1947, ds.bgco.org/docushare/dsweb/Get/Document-9247/September%2025%2c%201947.pdf.

34. Proceedings, October 1947, ds.bgco.org/docushare/dsweb/Get/Document-9242/October%209%2c%201947.pdf

35. Proceedings, March 1948.

36. "World Day of Prayer," Wikipedia, en.wikipedia.org/wiki/World_Day_of_Prayer.

37. Proceedings, March 1948.

38. Proceedings, 1948.

39. Proceedings, February 1949, ds.bgco.org/docushare/dsweb/Get/Document-9276/February%2010%2c%201949.pdf

40. Proceedings, February 1950, ds.bgco.org/docushare/dsweb/Get/Document-9384/February%2023%2c%201950.pdf.

41. Proceedings, 1949, ds.bgco.org/docushare/dsweb/Get/Document-16368/1949.pdf.

42. Proceedings, February 1950.

43. Deacon Minutes, 1950–1952.

44. Proceedings, July 1951, ds.bgco.org/docushare/dsweb/Get/Document-9397/July%2019%2c%201951.pdf.

45. Proceedings, February 1954, ds.bgco.org/docushare/dsweb/Get/Document-9594/February%204%2c%201954.pdf.

46. Deacon Minutes.

47. Proceedings, 1950, ds.bgco.org/docushare/dsweb/Get/Document-16369/1950.pdf.

48. Proceedings, 1951, ds.bgco.org/docushare/dsweb/Get/Document-16453/1951.pdf.

49. Proceedings, February 1951, ds.bgco.org/docushare/dsweb/Get/Document-9383/February%2022%2c%201951.pdf.

50. Deacon Minutes.

51. Proceedings, 1952.

52. Deacon Minutes, 1953–1954.

53. Sands, handwritten notes.

54. Deacon Minutes.

55. Proceedings, 1953, ds.bgco.org/docushare/dsweb/Get/Document-16455/1953.pdf

56. Proceedings, January 1955, ds.bgco.org/docushare/dsweb/Get/Document-9597/January%2020%2c%201955.pdf.

57. Deacon Minutes.

58. Proceedings, September 1953, ds.bgco.org/docushare/dsweb/Get/Document-9558/September%2024%2c%201953.pdf.

59. Deacon Minutes.

60. Proceedings, January 1955, ds.bgco.org/docushare/dsweb/Get/Document-9601/January%206%2c%201955.pdf.

61. Proceedings, September 1954, ds.bgco.org/docushare/dsweb/Get/Document-16456/1954.pdf.

62. Proceedings, March 1955, ds.bgco.org/docushare/dsweb/Get/Document-9623/March%2017%2c%201955.pdf.

63. Deacon Minutes, 1955–1956.

64. rootsweb.ancestry.com/~okbits/sh_star2006may.html.

65. Deacon Minutes.

66. Proceedings, August 1959, ds.bgco.org/docushare/dsweb/Get/Document-9876/August%2027%2c%201959.pdf.

67. Proceedings, 1955.

68. Minutes, 1956, Immanuel Baptist Church.

69. Proceedings, March 1956, ds.bgco.org/docushare/dsweb/Get/Document-9721/March%201%2c%201956.pdf.

70. Proceedings, April 1956, ds.bgco.org/docushare/dsweb/Get/Document-9666/April%2012%2c%201956.pdf.

71. Proceedings, July 1956, ds.bgco.org/docushare/dsweb/Get/Document-9712/July%205%2c%201956.pdf.

72. Adair, handwritten note.

73. Proceedings, September 1956, ds.bgco.org/docushare/dsweb/Get/Document-9759/September%2013%2c%201956.pdf.

74. Proceedings, October 1956, ds.bgco.org/docushare/dsweb/Get/Document-9754/October%2025%2c%201956.pdf.

75. Proceedings, November 1956, ds.bgco.org/docushare/dsweb/Get/Document-9748/November%208%2c%201956.pdf.

76. Proceedings, 1956, ds.bgco.org/docushare/dsweb/Get/Document-16371/1956.pdf.

77. Proceedings, November 1956.

78. Proceedings, January 1957, ds.bgco.org/docushare/dsweb/Get/Document-9701/January%203%2c%201957.pdf.

79. Proceedings, 1957, ds.bgco.org/docushare/dsweb/Get/Document-16372/1957.pdf.

80. Proceedings, January 1957.

81. Proceedings, February 1957, ds.bgco.org/docushare/dsweb/Get/Document-9687/February%2014%2c%201957.pdf.

82. Deacon Minutes, 1957.

83. Deacon Minutes, 1958–1959.

84. Proceedings, 1958, ds.bgco.org/docushare/dsweb/Get/Document-16373/1958.pdf.

85. Deacon Minutes, 1958–1959.

86. Proceedings, May 1959, ds.bgco.org/docushare/dsweb/Get/Document-9903/May%2014%2c%201959.pdf.

87. Sands, handwritten notes.

88. Jimmie L. Franklin, "Prohibition," *The Encyclopedia of Oklahoma History and Culture*, www.okhistory.org/publications/enc/entry.php?entry=PR018.

89. Proceedings, February 1959, ds.bgco.org/docushare/dsweb/Get/Document-9881/February%2012%2c%201959.pdf.

90. Franklin, "Prohibition."

91. Proceedings, April 1959, ds.bgco.org/docushare/dsweb/Get/Document-9871/April%2023%2c%201959.pdf.

92. Proceedings, June 1959, ds.bgco.org/docushare/dsweb/Get/Document-9898/June%204%2c%201959.pdf.

93. Proceedings, July 1959, ds.bgco.org/docushare/dsweb/Get/Document-9891/July%202%2c%201959.pdf.

94. Proceedings, May 1959.

95. Deacon Minutes.

96. Minutes, 1957–1959, Immanuel Baptist Church.

97. Proceedings, August 1959, ds.bgco.org/docushare/dsweb/Get/Document-9876/August%2027%2c%201959.pdf.

98. Proceedings, July 1960, ds.bgco.org/docushare/dsweb/Get/Document-9940/July%2014%2c%201960.pdf.

99. Proceedings, May 1962, ds.bgco.org/docushare/dsweb/Get/Document-10054/May%2017%2c%201962.pdf.

100. Ibid.

101. Proceedings, August 1962, ds.bgco.org/docushare/dsweb/Get/Document-10026/August%2023%2c%201962.pdf.

102. NewsOK.

103. "Christine Baugh Obituary," *The Oklahoman* Obituaries, published January 10, 2016, legacy.newsok.com/obituaries/oklahoman/obituary.aspx?page=lifestory&pid=177228803#sthash.y0kuy0Tl.dpuf.

104. Ibid.

105. Adair, undated and unaddressed website, April 25, 2017.

106. "Christine Baugh Obituary," *The Oklahoman* Obituaries.

Chapter 8: A Short Tenure

1. Seventy-Fifth-Year Anniversary, Immanuel Baptist Church.

2. "United States presidential election, 1960," Wikipedia, en.wikipedia.org/wiki/United_States_presidential_election, 1960#Debates.

3. Jennifer Rosenberg, "JFK, MLK, LBJ, Vietnam and the 1960s," ThoughtCo., modified August 28, 2017, www.thoughtco.com/1960s-timeline-1779953.

4. Robert L. Ross, *The Two Became One*, 1st ed. (TMD, 2005).

5. J. M. Gaskin, *A Profile of Joe Ingram*, (Historical Commission, Baptist General Convention of Oklahoma, 1987).

6. Ross, *The Two Became One*.

7. Gaskin, *A Profile of Joe Ingram*.

8. Proceedings, April 1951, ds.bgco.org/docushare/dsweb/Get/Document-9359/April%205%2c%201951.pdf.

9. Proceedings, August 1951, ds.bgco.org/docushare/dsweb/Get/Document-9364/August%202%2c%201951.pdf.

10. Proceedings, April 1952, ds.bgco.org/docushare/dsweb/Get/Document-9464/April%203%2c%201952.pdf.

11. Proceedings, 1953.

12. Proceedings, 1954, ds.bgco.org/docushare/dsweb/Get/Document-16456/1954.pdf.

13. Proceedings, February 1955, ds.bgco.org/docushare/dsweb/Get/Document-9587/February%2010%2c%201955.pdf.

14. Proceedings, 1955.

15. Proceedings, 1960, ds.bgco.org/docushare/dsweb/Get/Document-16458/1960.pdf.

16. Proceedings, May 1956, ds.bgco.org/docushare/dsweb/Get/Document-9730/May%2010%2c%201956.pdf.

17. Proceedings, January 1960, ds.bgco.org/docushare/dsweb/Get/Document-9938/January%2028%2c%201960.pdf.

18. Proceedings, January 1960, ds.bgco.org/docushare/dsweb/Get/Document-9936/January%2014%2c%201960.pdf.

19. Proceedings, February 1960, ds.bgco.org/docushare/dsweb/Get/Document-9932/February%2011%2c%201960.pdf.

20. Proceedings, June 1960, ds.bgco.org/docushare/dsweb/Get/Document-9947/June%2030%2c%201960.pdf.

21. Proceedings, July 1960, ds.bgco.org/docushare/dsweb/Get/Document-9941/July%2021%2c%201960.pdf.

22. Proceedings, December 1960, ds.bgco.org/docushare/dsweb/Get/Document-9928/December%201%2c%201960.pdf.

23. Proceedings, 1960.

24. Proceedings, November 1960, ds.bgco.org/docushare/dsweb/Get/Document-9960/November%2024%2c%201960.pdf.

25. "Baptist Jubilee Advance," Social Networks and Archival context, accessed September 11, 2017, socialarchive.iath.virginia.edu/ark:/99166/w6sz1fsp.

26. Proceedings, December 1960.

27. Proceedings, December 1960, ds.bgco.org/docushare/dsweb/Get/Document-9930/December%2022%2c%201960.pdf.

28. Proceedings, December 1960, ds.bgco.org/docushare/dsweb/Get/Document-9931/December%208%2c%201960.pdf.

29. Minutes and Financial Reports, January 1960–December 1960, Immanuel Baptist Church.

30. Minutes, October 18, 2016, Eighty-Sixth Annual Session of the Pottawatomie-Lincoln Baptist Association.

31. Proceedings, 1960.

32. Ross.

33. "Honorary Doctorates, Oklahoma Baptist University, accessed September 11, 2017, www.okbu.edu/alumni/honorary-doctorates.html.

34. Ross.

35. Gaskin.

Chapter 9: New Ideas and New Growth

1. Seventy-Fifth-Year Anniversary, Immanuel Baptist Church.

2. "Gwendolyn Griffitts Woodard Obituary," in Remembrance, accessed September 11, 2017, www.inremembrance.org/texas/graham/gwendolyn-griffitts-woodard/1386.

3. www.infoplease.com/year/1961.html#world.

4. www.infoplease.com/year/1963.html#world.

5. Dr. Alfred Woodard, letter to Dr. John Nichols, December 15, 2016.

6. 453 ., Charles G. Davis, "Fargo, TX," *Handbook of Texas Online*, accessed September 11, 2017, tshaonline.org/handbook/online/articles/hlf06.

7. Woodard, letter to Dr. John Nichols.

8. Woodard, letter to Dr. John Nichols, January 30, 2017.

9. Woodard, letter to Dr. John Nichols.

10. www.hsutx.edu/about/facts.

11. "Gwendolyn Griffitts Woodard Obituary," in Remembrance.

12. Laura F. McBeth Taxon, "Cowgirls, Then and Now – 1925–1974," Hardin-Simmons University, accessed September 11, 2017, connect.hsutx.edu/alumni-relations/ex-cowgirls-history.

13. Woodard, telephone interview with the author, December 14, 2016.

14. Woodard, letter to Dr. John Nichols.

15. Nancy Sue Ashmore, "Medicine Mound, Texas Ghost Town," TexasEscapes, published October 16, 2006, www.texasescapes.com/TexasTowns/Medicine-Mound-Texas.htm.

16. Woodard, letter to Dr. John Nichols.

17. "Gordon, Texas," Gordon, Texas, accessed September 11, 2017,

18. www.gordontexas.com/h_church.asp.

19. Woodard, letter to Dr. John Nichols.

20. Dr. Alfred Woodard, e-mail to Dr. John Nichols, January 31, 2017.

21. Proceedings, 1957.

22. Proceedings, 1958.

23. Proceedings, 1959, ds.bgco.org/docushare/dsweb/Get/Document-16457/1959.pdf.

24. Proceedings, 1960.

25. Minutes, 1963, Immanuel Baptist Church.

26. Deacon Minutes, January 1963–December 1963.

27. Minutes, Immanuel Baptist Church.

28. Proceedings, 1961, ds.bgco.org/docushare/dsweb/Get/Document-16459/1961.pdf.

29. Proceedings, 1962, ds.bgco.org/docushare/dsweb/Get/Document-16330/1962.pdf.

30. Proceedings, 1963, ds.bgco.org/docushare/dsweb/Get/Document-16464/1963.pdf.

31. Minutes, 1961–1962, Immanuel Baptist Church.

32. Minutes, 1963, Immanuel Baptist Church.

33. Doris Sager, class interview, Immanuel Baptist Church, January 29, 2017. ds.bgco.org/docushare/dsweb/Get/Document-16692/04182013.pdf.

34. Minutes, 1961–1962, Immanuel Baptist Church.

35. Woodard, telephone interview.

36. Seventy-Fifth-Year Anniversary, Immanuel Baptist Church.

37. 1975 Dedication Program.

38. Woodard, e-mail to Dr. John Nichols.

39. Sager, class interview.

40. Proceedings, August 1964, ds.bgco.org/docushare/dsweb/Get/Document-10128/August%2020%2c%201964.pdf.

41. Deacon Minutes, 1964.

42. Ross.

43. Woodard, telephone interview.

44. Woodard, letter to Dr. John Nichols.

45. "Southmayd, Texas," Wikipedia, en.wikipedia.org/wiki/Southmayd, Texas.

46. Woodard, letter to Dr. John Nichols.

47. Ibid., January 30, 2017.

Chapter 10: Stability, Growth, and Groundwork for the Family Life Center

1. Sands, handwritten notes.

2. Seventy-Fifth-Year Anniversary, Immanuel Baptist Church.

3. www.infoplease.com/year/1964.html#world.

4. www.infoplease.com/year/1965.html#world.

5. Rosenberg, "JFK, MLK, LBJ, Vietnam and the 1960s."

6. www.infoplease.com/year/1969.html#world.

7. www.thoughtco.com/1970s-timeline-1779954.

8. www.infoplease.com/year/1971.html#world.

9. Jennifer Rosenberg, "Vietnam, Watergate, Iran and the 1970s," ThoughtCo., accessed September 11, 2017, www.thoughtco.com/1970s-timeline-1779954.

10. www.infoplease.com/year/1974.html#world.

11. www.thoughtco.com/1960s-timeline-1779953.

12. www.infoplease.com/year/1964.html#world.

13. Rosenberg, "JFK, MLK, LBJ, Vietnam and the 1960s."

14. Ibid., "Vietnam, Watergate, Iran and the 1970s."

15. "Lawrence Reading Stewart," NewsOK, published May 26, 2006, accessed September 11, 2017, newsok.com/article/2945694.

16. "Britton, Oklahoma," Wikipedia, en.wikipedia.org/wiki/Britton, Oklahoma.

17. NewsOK.

18. *Yahnseh, 1950 Edition*, Oklahoma Baptist University.

19. Proceedings, October 1949, ds.bgco.org/docushare/dsweb/Get/Document-9334/October%2013%2c%201949.pdf.

20. Last Chance Baptist Church's Facebook page, accessed September 11, 2017, www.facebook.com/LastChanceBaptist.

21. Proceedings, October 1949.

22. Proceedings, January 1950, ds.bgco.org/docushare/dsweb/Get/Document-9392/January%2026%2c%201950.pdf.

23. Proceedings, 1948.

24. Proceedings, 1949.

25. Proceedings, 1950.

26. Proceedings, April 1954, ds.bgco.org/docushare/dsweb/Get/Document-9567/April%2022%2c%201954.pdf.

27. Proceedings, 1954.

28. Proceedings, April 1955, ds.bgco.org/docushare/dsweb/Get/Document-9566/April%2021%2c%201955.pdf.

29. Proceedings, March 1955.

30. Proceedings, May 1955, ds.bgco.org/docushare/dsweb/Get/Document-9630/May%2012%2c%201955.pdf.

31. Proceedings, April 1958, ds.bgco.org/docushare/dsweb/Get/Document-9772/April%2024%2c%201958.pdf.

32. Proceedings, April 1956, ds.bgco.org/docushare/dsweb/Get/Document-9666/April%2012%2c%201956.pdf.

33. Proceedings, May 1956, ds.bgco.org/docushare/dsweb/Get/Document-9730/May%2010%2c%201956.pdf.

34. Proceedings, April 1958.

35. Proceedings, October 1958, ds.bgco.org/docushare/dsweb/Get/Document-9855/October%2023%2c%201958.pdf.

36. Proceedings, May 1959.

37. Proceedings, September 1959.

38. Proceedings, October 1959, ds.bgco.org/docushare/dsweb/Get/Document-9914/October%2029%2c%201959.pdf.

39. Adair, handwritten note.

40. Proceedings, 1959.

41. Proceedings, April 1960, ds.bgco.org/docushare/dsweb/Get/Document-9923/April%2028%2c%201960.pdf.

42. Proceedings, September 1960, ds.bgco.org/docushare/dsweb/Get/Document-9968/September%2022%2c%201960.pdf.

43. Proceedings, December 1960, ds.bgco.org/docushare/dsweb/Get/Document-9929/December%2015%2c%201960.pdf

44. Proceedings, November 1960, ds.bgco.org/docushare/dsweb/Get/Document-9959/November%2017%2c%201960.pdf.

45. Proceedings, April 1964, ds.bgco.org/docushare/dsweb/Get/Document-10125/April%2030%2c%201964.pdf.

46. Proceedings, September 1964, ds.bgco.org/docushare/dsweb/Get/Document-10171/September%2024%2c%201964.pdf.

47. Proceedings, November 1964, ds.bgco.org/docushare/dsweb/Get/Document-10163/November%205%2c%201964.pdf.

48. Deacon Minutes, 1964.

49. Proceedings, November 1964.

50. Pat Coker, telephone conversation with author, March 8, 2017.

51. Manoi Adair, hallway conversation with author, April 9, 2017.

52. Proceedings, July 1965, ds.bgco.org/docushare/dsweb/Get/Document-10194/July%2015%2c%201965.pdf.

53. Proceedings, 1965, ds.bgco.org/docushare/dsweb/Get/Document-16466/1965.pdf.

54. Proceedings, December 1965, ds.bgco.org/docushare/dsweb/Get/Document-10183/December%2023%2c%201965.pdf

55. Proceedings, April 1966, ds.bgco.org/docushare/dsweb/Get/Document-10225/April%2021%2c%201966.pdf.

56. Proceedings, September 1966, ds.bgco.org/docushare/dsweb/Get/Document-10269/September%201%2c%201966.pdf.

57. Minutes, 1966, Immanuel Baptist Church.

58. Minutes, 1968, Immanuel Baptist Church.

59. Minutes, 1969, Immanuel Baptist Church.

60. Proceedings, January 1970, ds.bgco.org/docushare/dsweb/Get/Document-10445/January%201%2c%201970.pdf.

61. Minutes, Immanuel Baptist Church.

62. Proceedings, January 1970.

63. Proceedings, December 1971, ds.bgco.org/docushare/dsweb/Get/Document-10526/October%207%2c%201971.pdf.

64. Proceedings, March 1967, ds.bgco.org/docushare/dsweb/Get/Document-10303/March%2016%2c%201967.pdf.

65. Janice Maynard, e-mail to author, April 27, 2017.

66. *86th Annual Sessions Report*, October 18, 2016, Pottawatomie-Lincoln Baptist Association.

67. Deacon Minutes, 1972.

68. Minutes, 1973, Immanuel Baptist Church.

69. "History," First Baptist Church of Sedalia, accessed September 12, 2011, www.fbcsedalia.org/get-to-know-us/history/

70. Proceedings, June 1974, ds.bgco.org/docushare/dsweb/Get/Document-10661/June%2027%2c%201974.pdf.

71. Proceedings, April 1990, ds.bgco.org/docushare/dsweb/Get/Document-11451/April%2019%2c%201990.pdf.

72. Proceedings, May 1990, ds.bgco.org/docushare/dsweb/Get/Document-11483/May%2017%2c%201990.pdf.

73. Proceedings, September 1995, ds.bgco.org/docushare/dsweb/Get/Document-11755/September%2014%2c%201995.pdf.

74. NewsOK.

75. Adair, handwritten note.

Chapter 11: The Renovation of Amazing Immanuel

1. Dr. Larry and Mrs. Edwine Adams, lunch interview, September 23, 2016, Outback Restaurant, Oklahoma City, OK.

2. www.infoplease.com/year/1974.html#world.

3. www.infoplease.com/year/1975.html#world.

4. www.infoplease.com/year/1976.html#world.

5. www.infoplease.com/year/1978.html#world.

6. www.infoplease.com/year/1979.html#world.

7. www.infoplease.com/year/1981.html#world.

8. www.infoplease.com/year/1982.html#world.

9. www.infoplease.com/year/1974.html#world.

10. www.infoplease.com/year/1976.html#world.

11. www.infoplease.com/year/1977.html#world.

12. www.infoplease.com/year/1978.html#world.

13. www.infoplease.com/year/1979.html#world.

14. www.infoplease.com/year/1981.html#world.

15. www.infoplease.com/year/1982.html#world.

16. Adams, interview.

17. Ibid.

18. Ibid.
19. Ibid.
20. Sager, class interview.
21. Adams, interview.
22. 1975 Dedication Program.
23. Dr. Larry and Mrs. Edwine Adams, Outback Restaurant, Oklahoma City, OK, September 23, 2016.
24. Sager, class interview.
25. Manoi Adair, note sent to author, June 15, 2017.
26. Adams, interview.
27. Sager, class interview.
28. Adams, interview.
29. Ibid.
30. Minutes, 1982, Immanuel Baptist Church.
31. Deacon Minutes, January 1978–November 1984.
32. Minutes, 1982, Immanuel Baptist Church.
33. Adams, interview.
34. Baptist Retirement Center Press Release, February 12, 2012.
35. Adams, interview.

Chapter 12: Steady Growth and Service

1. Eightieth-Year Anniversary, Immanuel Baptist Church.
2. www.infoplease.com/year/1982#world.
3. www.infoplease.com/year/1984#world.
4. www.infoplease.com/year/1985#world.
5. www.infoplease.com/year/1983#world.
6. Jennifer Rosenberg, "Go Back in Time with This 1980s History Timeline," ThoughtCo., modified August 20, 2017, accessed September 12, 2017, www.thoughtco.com/1980s-timeline-1779955
7. Ibid.
8. "Little Rock, Arkansas," Wikipedia, en.wikipedia.org/wiki/Little_Rock,_Arkansas.
9. "Steve M. Boehning Sr. Obituary," *Houston Chronicle* Obituary, published December 5, 2004, www.legacy.com/obituaries/houstonchronicle/obituary.aspx?pid=2888116.
10. Proceedings, December 1973, ds.bgco.org/docushare/dsweb/Get/Document-10593/December%2020%2c%201973.pdf.

11. "Steve M. Boehning Sr. Obituary."

12. Proceedings, 1977, ds.bgco.org/docushare/dsweb/Get/Document-16341/1977. pdf.

13. Proceedings, 1978, ds.bgco.org/docushare/dsweb/Get/Document-16342/1978. pdf.

14. Proceedings, 1979, ds.bgco.org/docushare/dsweb/Get/Document-16343/1979. pdf.

15. Proceedings, 1980, ds.bgco.org/docushare/dsweb/Get/Document-16344/1980. pdf.

16. Proceedings, January 1980, ds.bgco.org/docushare/dsweb/Get/Document-10958/ January%2024%2c%201980.pdf.

17. Proceedings, May 1980, ds.bgco.org/docushare/dsweb/Get/Document-10976/ May%2022%2c%201980.pdf.

18. Proceedings, 1981, ds.bgco.org/docushare/dsweb/Get/Document-16345/1981. pdf.

19. Proceedings, August 1981, ds.bgco.org/docushare/dsweb/Get/Document-11000/ August%2027%2c%201981.pdf.

20. Proceedings, 1981, ds.bgco.org/docushare/dsweb/Get/Document-16345/1981. pdf.

21. Proceedings, January 1982, ds.bgco.org/docushare/dsweb/Get/Document-11060/ January%2014%2c%201982.pdf.

22. Proceedings, April 1982, ds.bgco.org/docushare/dsweb/Get/Document-11046/ April%2015%2c%201982.pdf.

23. Proceedings, July 1982, ds.bgco.org/docushare/dsweb/Get/Document-11068/ July%208%2c%201982.pdf.

24. Minutes, 1982, Immanuel Baptist Church.

25. Proceedings, October 1982, ds.bgco.org/docushare/dsweb/Get/Document-11085/ October%2014%2c%201982.pdf.

26. Deacon Minutes, January 1978–November 1984.

27. Proceedings, 1982, ds.bgco.org/docushare/dsweb/Get/Document-16346/1982. pdf.

28. Minutes, 1982, Immanuel Baptist Church.

29. Minutes, 1983, Immanuel Baptist Church.

30. Proceedings, April 1983, ds.bgco.org/docushare/dsweb/Get/Document-11095/ April%2014%2c%201983.pdf.

31. Minutes, 1983, Immanuel Baptist Church.

32. Proceedings, 1983, ds.bgco.org/docushare/dsweb/Get/Document-16347/1983.pdf.

33. Proceedings, October 1983, ds.bgco.org/docushare/dsweb/Get/Document-11136/October%2020%2c%201983.pdf.

34. Minutes, 1984, Immanuel Baptist Church.

35. Proceedings, March 1984, ds.bgco.org/docushare/dsweb/Get/Document-11173/March%2022%2c%201984.pdf.

36. Deacon Minutes.

37. Proceedings, 1984, ds.bgco.org/docushare/dsweb/Get/Document-16348/1984.pdf.

38. Minutes, 1985, Immanuel Baptist Church.

39. Proceedings, May 1985, ds.bgco.org/docushare/dsweb/Get/Document-11226/May%2016%2c%201985.pdf.

40. Proceedings, 1985, ds.bgco.org/docushare/dsweb/Get/Document-16349/1985.pdf.

41. Minutes, 1986, Immanuel Baptist Church.

42. "Steve M. Boehning Sr. Obituary."

Chapter 13: A Biblical Scholar with a Heart for Evangelism

1. Eightieth-Year Anniversary History, Immanuel Baptist Church.

2. www.infoplease.com/year/1987.html#world.

3. www.infoplease.com/year/1988.html#world.

4. www.infoplease.com/year/1989.html#world.

5. www.infoplease.com/year/1990.html#world.

6. www.infoplease.com/year/1991.html#world.

7. www.infoplease.com/year/1992.html#world.

8. www.infoplease.com/year/1988.html#world.

9. www.infoplease.com/year/1989.html#world.

10. www.infoplease.com/year/1991.html#world.

11. www.infoplease.com/year/1992.html#world.

12. Dr. Mike Taylor, lunch interview with author, October 19, 2016, Paul's Place, Shawnee, OK.

13. Sutton, Jerry; *The Baptist Reformation*, Broadman & Holman Publisher, 2000, pp. 174, 398, 419.

14. "State Baptist Meeting Set," *The Oklahoman*, NewsOk, published November 4, 1995, www.newsok.com/article/2519414

15. Taylor, interview.
16. Ibid.
17. Ibid.
18. Seventy-Fifth-Year Anniversary, Immanuel Baptist Church
19. Taylor, interview.
20. Ibid.
21. Ibid.
22. Ibid.
23. Ibid.
24. Ibid.

Chapter 14: The First Relocation Attempt

1. Eightieth-Year Anniversary History, Immanuel Baptist Church, September 14, 1997.
2. www.infoplease.com/year/1993.html#world.
3. www.infoplease.com/year/1994.html#world.
4. www.infoplease.com/year/1995.html#world.
5. www.infoplease.com/year/1993.html#world.
6. www.infoplease.com/year/1994.html#world.
7. www.infoplease.com/year/1995.html#world.
8. Dr. Joe Dan Fowler, telephone interview with author, December 15, 2016.
9. 9. Ibid.
10. Ibid.
11. Ibid.
12. "Gober Baptist Church," Fannin County Historical Commission," accessed September 12, 2017, www.fannincountyhistory.org/gober-baptist-church.html.
13. Ibid.
14. "George Washington Truett," Southern Baptist Historical Library and Archives, accessed September 12, 2017, www.sbhla.org/bio_gtruett.htm.
15. Ibid.
16. Ibid.
17. Eightieth-Year Anniversary History , Immanuel Baptist Church.
18. Fowler, telephone interview.
19. Adair, handwritten note.

20. Eightieth-Year Anniversary History, Immanuel Baptist Church, September 14, 1997.
21. Fowler, telephone interview.
22. Ibid.

Chapter 15: Land Purchased for a New Home

1. Dr. Jeff and Sharla Moore, interview with the author, The Plaza Restaurant, October 8, 2016, Altus, OK.
2. www.infoplease.com/year/1996.html#world.
3. www.infoplease.com/year/1997.html#world.
4. www.infoplease.com/year/1998.html#world.
5. www.infoplease.com/year/1999.html#world.
6. www.infoplease.com/year/2000.html#world.
7. www.infoplease.com/year/2001html#world.
8. www.infoplease.com/year/2002.html#world.
9. www.infoplease.com/year/1996.html#world.
10. www.infoplease.com/year/1997.html#world.
11. www.infoplease.com/year/1998.html#world.
12. www.infoplease.com/year/1999.html#world.
13. www.infoplease.com/year/2000.html#world.
14. www.infoplease.com/year/2001.html#world.
15. www.infoplease.com/year/2002.html#world.
16. Moore, interview.
17. Eightieth-Year Anniversary History, Immanuel Baptist Church.
18. Moore, interview.
19. www.lifeway.com/n/Product-Family/FAITH-Evangelism.
20. Moore, interview.
21. Dr. Todd Fisher, office interview with author, January 9, 2017, Immanuel Baptist Church, Shawnee, OK.
22. Moore, interview.
23. Ibid,
24. www.fbcaltus.org,
25. Moore, interview.

Chapter 16: The Final Days on Main Street

1. Dr. Todd Fisher, interview, December 13, 2016, Immanuel Baptist Church, Shawnee, OK.
2. www.infoplease.com/year/2003.html#world.
3. www.infoplease.com/year/2005.html#world.
4. www.infoplease.com/year/2004.html#world.
5. www.infoplease.com/year/2006.html#world.
6. www.infoplease.com/year/2008.html#world.
7. www.infoplease.com/year/2003.html#world.
8. www.infoplease.com/year/2004.html#world.
9. www.infoplease.com/year/2005.html#world.
10. www.infoplease.com/year/2007.html#world.
11. www.infoplease.com/year/2008.html#world.
12. Fisher, interview.
13. Ibid.
14. Ibid.
15. Ibid.
16. Ibid.
17. Ibid.
18. Ibid.
19. Ibid.
20. Rev. Scott Schooler, office interview with the author, January 12, 2016, Immanuel Baptist Church, Shawnee, OK.
21. Fisher, interview.
22. Rev. Mark Wright, office interview with the author, January 12, 2017, Immanuel Baptist Church, Shawnee, OK.
23. Fisher, interview.
24. Ibid.
25. Ibid.
26. Ibid.

Chapter 17: The Forty-Fourth Street Years

1. Fisher, interview, January 9, 2017.
2. www.infoplease.com/year/2008.html#world.
3. www.infoplease.com/year/2009.html#world.
4. www.infoplease.com/year/2010.html#world.

5. www.infoplease.com/year/2011.html#world.

6. www.infoplease.com/year/2012.html#world.

7. www.infoplease.com/year/2013.html#world.

8. www.infoplease.com/year/2014.html#world.

9. "The Biggest News Events of 2015," *Newsweek*, accessed September 12, 2017, www.newsweek.com/front-page-news-2015-402024.

10. www.infoplease.com/year/2008.html#world.

11. www.infoplease.com/year/2009.html#world.

12. www.infoplease.com/year/2010.html#world.

13. www.infoplease.com/year/2011.html#world.

14. www.infoplease.com/year/2012.html#world.

15. www.infoplease.com/year/2013.html#world.

16. www.infoplease.com/year/2014.html#world.

17. "The Biggest News Events of 2015," *Newsweek*.

18. Fisher, interview.

19. Ibid.

20. Schooler, interview.

21. Wright, interview.

22. Dr. Russell Cook, telephone interview with the author, January 23, 2017.

23. Fisher, interview.

24. Schooler, interview.

25. Fisher, interview.

26. Ibid., January 9, 2017.

27. Resources page of Immanuel Baptist Church, accessed September 12, 2017, ibcshawnee.org/resources.

CPSIA information can be obtained
at www.ICGtesting.com
Printed in the USA
FFOW05n0259291117